APPLICATIONS OF GROUP ANALYSIS FOR THE TWENTY-FIRST CENTURY

NEW INTERNATIONAL LIBRARY OF GROUP ANALYSIS

Series Editor: Earl Hopper

Other titles in the Series

Difficult Topics in Group Psychotherapy: My Journey from Shame to Courage
Jerome S. Gans

Resistance, Rebellion and Refusal in Groups: The 3 Rs
Richard M. Billow

The Social Unconscious in Persons, Groups, and Societies: Volume 1: Mainly Theory
edited by Earl Hopper and Haim Weinberg

The Social Nature of Persons: One Person is No Person
A. P. Tom Ormay

Trauma and Organizations
edited by Earl Hopper

Small, Large, and Median Groups: The Work of Patrick de Maré
edited by Rachel Lenn and Karen Stefano

The Dialogues In and Of the Group: Lacanian Perspectives on the Psychoanalytic Group
Macario Giraldo

From Psychoanalysis to Group Analysis: The Pioneering Work of Trigant Burrow
edited by Edi Gatti Pertegato and Giorgio Orghe Pertegato

The One and the Many: Relational Psychoanalysis and Group Analysis
Juan Tubert-Oklander

Listening with the Fourth Ear: Unconscious Dynamics in Analytic Group Psychotherapy
Leonard Horwitz

Forensic Group Psychotherapy: The Portman Clinic Approach
edited by John Woods and Andrew Williams
(joint publication with The Portman Papers)

Nationalism and the Body Politic: Psychoanalysis and the Rise of Ethnocentrism and Xenophobia
edited by Lene Auestad

The Paradox of Internet Groups: Alone in the Presence of Virtual Others
Haim Weinberg

The Art of Group Analysis in Organisations: The Use of Intuitive and Experiential Knowledge
Gerhard Wilke

The World within the Group: Developing Theory for Group Analysis
Martin Weegman

Developing Nuclear Ideas: Relational Group Psychotherapy
Richard M. Billow

The Courage of Simplicity: Essential Ideas in the Work of W.R. Bion
Hanni Biran

Foundations of Group Analysis for the Twenty-First Century
edited by Jason Maratos

The Social Unconscious in Persons, Groups, and Societies: Volume 2: Mainly Foundation Matrices
edited by Earl Hopper and Haim Weinberg

APPLICATIONS OF GROUP ANALYSIS FOR THE TWENTY-FIRST CENTURY

Edited by
Jason Maratos

Routledge
Taylor & Francis Group
LONDON AND NEW YORK

First published 2016 by Karnac Books Ltd.

Published 2019 by Routledge
2 Park Square, Milton Park, Abingdon, Oxon OX14 4RN
52 Vanderbilt Avenue, New York, NY 10017

First issued in hardback 2019

Routledge is an imprint of the Taylor & Francis Group, an informa business

British Library Cataloguing in Publication Data

A C.I.P. for this book is available from the British Library

ISBN 13: 978-0-367-10262-3 (hbk)
ISBN 13: 978-1-78220-113-7 (pbk)

Typeset by Medlar Publishing Solutions Pvt Ltd, India

CONTENTS

PART VIII: RESEARCH

PART IX: ADDICTIONS

PERMISSIONS

Chapter One

Welldon, E. V. (1997). Let the treatment fit the crime: Forensic group psychotherapy, 20th S. H. Foulkes Annual Lecture. *Group Analysis, 30*: 5–26.

This paper was previously published by *Group Analysis* in 1997 and is reprinted with kind permission of Sage Publications.

Chapter Two

Behr, H. L. (1994). Families and Group Analysis. In: D. Brown & L. Zinkin (Eds.), *The Psyche and the Social World,* London: Routledge.

This chapter was previously published by Routledge in 1994 and is reprinted with kind permission of the publisher.

Chapter Three

Marrone, M. (1994). Attachment theory and group analysis. In: D. Brown & L. Zinkin (Eds.), *The Psyche and the Social World.* London: Routledge.

This chapter was previously published by Routledge in 1994 and is reprinted with kind permission of the publisher.

Chapter Four

Behr, H. (1988). Group analysis with early adolescents: Some clinical issues. *Group Analysis, 21*: 119–131.

This paper was previously published by *Group Analysis* in 1988 and is reprinted with kind permission of Sage Publications.

Chapter Five

Wilke, G. (2014). Group analysis in organisations: What it takes. In: *The Art of Group Analysis in Organisations: The Use of Intuitive and Experiential Knowledge* (pp. 3–38). London: Karnac.

This chapter was previously published by Karnac in 2014 and is reprinted with kind permission of the publisher.

Chapter Six

Burman, E. (2004). Organising for change? Group-analytic perspectives on a feminist action research project. *Group Analysis, 37*: 91–108.

This paper was previously published by *Group Analysis* in 2004 and is reprinted with kind permission of Sage Publications.

Chapter Seven

Behr, H. (1995). The integration of theory and practice. In: M. Sharpe (Ed.), *The Third Eye: Supervision of Analytic Groups* (pp. 4–17). Routledge: London.

This chapter was previously published by Routledge in 1995 and is reprinted with kind permission of the publisher.

Chapter Eight

Abercrombie, M. L. J. (1981). Beyond the unconscious: Group-analysis applied. *Group Analysis, XIV*: 2–14.

This paper was previously published by *Group Analysis* in 1981 and is reprinted with kind permission of Sage Publications.

Chapter Nine

Maratos, J. (2000). Combined therapies—a group analytic perspective. In: S. Brooks & P. Hodson (Eds.), *The Invisible Matrix* (pp. 128–148). London: Rebus Press.

This chapter was previously published by Rebus Press in 2000 and is reprinted with kind permission of the publisher.

Chapter Ten
Dick, B. M. (1975). A ten-year study of out-patient analytic group therapy. *The British Journal of Psychiatry, 127*: 365–375.

This paper was previously published by *The British Journal of Psychiatry* in 1975 and is reprinted with kind permission of the Royal College of Psychiatrists.

Chapter Eleven
Maratos, J., & Kennedy, M. (1974). Evaluation of ward group meetings in a psychiatric unit of a General Hospital. *The British Journal of Psychiatry, 125*: 479–482.

This paper was previously published by *The British Journal of Psychiatry* in 1974 and is reprinted with kind permission of the Royal College of Psychiatrists.

Chapter Twelve
Mace, C. (2006). Special section: Setting the world on wheels: Some clinical challenges of evidence-based practice. *Group Analysis, 39*: 304–320.

This paper was previously published by *Group Analysis* in 2006 and is reprinted with kind permission of Sage Publications.

Chapter Thirteen
Weegman, M., & English, C. (2010). Beyond the shadow of drugs: groups with substance misusers. *Group Analysis, 43*(1): 1–21.

This paper (now revised and expanded) was previously published by *Group Analysis* in 2010 and is reprinted with kind permission of Sage Publications.

ABOUT THE EDITOR AND CONTRIBUTORS

Jane Abercrombie was a zoologist who taught and published extensively. Her *New Biology* and the *Dictionary of Biology* (published by Penguin Books) reached numerous editions. She first became a member of one of Dr Foulkes's groups and then joined him as a co-therapist. Jane Abercrombie was interested in the dynamics of learning and applied her insights to the teaching of medical students in Cambridge. She was a founder member of the Group-Analytic Society (now GASi) and later its President. She died on 25th November 1984 aged 75.

Dr Harold L. Behr, DPM, FRCPsych, was born in Johannesburg, South Africa. After qualifying in Medicine and Psychiatry he emigrated to the United Kingdom in 1971, where he trained in Child Psychiatry and Family Therapy at the Maudsley, University College and the Royal Free Hospitals. He held a post as Consultant Child Psychiatrist at Central Middlesex Hospital until his retirement from the Health Service in 1996. He continued to practise as an independent psychotherapist until his retirement in 2013. He is a Training Group Analyst for the Institute of Group Analysis and former editor of the journal *Group Analysis*. His special interests include the teaching of group analysis, group work with adolescents, integration of family therapy with group analysis and the application of psychological thinking to history. He is co-author of a book, *Group-Analytic Psychotherapy: A Meeting of Minds*, published in 2005. In 1997 he was awarded honorary membership of the Norwegian Institute of Group Analysis for his work as a Trainer and Convenor of the IGA (UK) Course which led to the establishment of the Norwegian IGA.

Erica Burman is Professor of Education in the Manchester Institute of Education, School of Environment, Education and Development, University of Manchester, UK. She co-founded (with Ian Parker) the Discourse Unit, a transdisciplinary and transinstitutional network of researchers concerned with the transformation of language and subjectivity. She is a recent past Chair of the Psychology of Women Section of the British Psychological Society (2009–2011), and is known for connecting feminist analyses to challenge oppressive consequences of psychological theories, methods and practices–across developmental and educational psychology and health and social care settings. She has been involved in various feminist antiracist research projects on the intersections of state and interpersonal violence, as well the relations between culture, marginalisation and distress. She is a UKCP registered Group Analyst (carrying Full Membership of the Institute of Group Analysis) and a qualified Iyengar Yoga teacher (member of the Iyengar Yoga Association).

Barbara M. Dick (1914–1997) was a psychiatrist who had been trained in Jungian Analysis who applied her knowledge and experience not only in her clinical practice but also in training and supervising members of what was then the Marriage Guidance Council (later Relate). Dr Dick was a pioneer in the development of psychotherapy in Manchester and the founder of the first group-based psychotherapy service (initially known as the Wilton Unit, later as The Red House Psychotherapy Service). Group Analysis North recognised her as one of its founders and established the annual lecture which bears her name. The research included in this volume combines her scientific and psychoanalytical (group-analytical) mind at a time when the discipline was in its infancy.

Margaret J. Kennedy was a Canadian clinical psychologist at Hackney Hospital. She was interested in research and contributed to the introduction and study of group work in the acute psychiatric unit of that hospital.

Christopher John (Chris) Mace (1956–2010) was a Psychiatrist who worked as a Consultant Psychotherapist/Group Analyst for twenty years in the NHS. He channelled his energies not only in treating patients but also in developing services, locally and Nationally (he was a founder member of the New Savoy Partnership). He served as Chair of Psychotherapy Faculty of the Royal College of Psychiatrists (2006–2010). In his positions as Associate Professor Department of Psychology of the University of Warwick and member of the Society of Psychotherapy Research he was active in the teaching of psychotherapy and in promoting research. He published widely; his books included *Heart and Soul: The Therapeutic Face of Philosophy* (2003) and *Mindfulness and Mental Health: Therapy, Theory and Science* (2007). He died very prematurely, at the peak of his creativity.

Dr Jason Maratos is a Training Group-Analyst and a Fellow of the Royal College of Psychiatrists. He is a Consultant in Child and Adolescent Psychiatry and works clinically and as an Expert Witness appearing in the High Court and County Courts in family matters and trauma. In a recent publication, he explored ways in which the legal process can be less traumatic and potentially therapeutic. He is the Medical Director of PPCS and a Responsible Officer. Dr Maratos has published chapters in books and papers in peer-reviewed journals in English, Italian, Greek and Czech and has lectured/taught in various courses in the UK, Italy, Greece, Brazil and Hong Kong. His publications reflect his interest in research, Self Psychology, Attachment Theory and Psychoanalysis. He has challenged the notion of the Death Instinct ("Thanatos; Does it Exist?") and expanded on the Oedipus Complex ("The Laius Complex") by exploring the psycho-pathology of the father and its impact on the emotional and cognitive development of a child. He edited a collection of papers by the late Dennis Brown (*Resonance and Reciprocity*).

Dr Mario Marrone was formerly an NHS psychiatrist, and is a group analyst and psychoanalyst. He has published several books in several languages and has lectured internationally on attachment theory, psychopathology and group analysis.

Martin Weegmann is a Consultant Clinical Psychologist and Group Analyst, with 30 years NHS experience. He has specialised in substance misuse and personality disorders and is a well-known trainer, delivering workshops and lectures throughout the UK. Martin has edited two influential books, *Psychodynamics of Addiction* (2002, Wiley) and *Group Psychotherapy and Addiction* (2004, Wiley), and published many book chapters and papers, in a range of journals. *The World within the Group: Developing Theory for Group Analysis* (Karnac, 2014) is a major contribution to group analysis and currently he is writing *Permission to Narrate: Explorations with Group Analysis* (Karnac, forthcoming 2016).

Estela V. Welldon is a psychoanalytical psychotherapist who worked for three decades at the Portman Clinic, and in private practice. She is the founder of the International Association for Forensic Psychotherapy, a Fellow of the Royal College of Psychiatrists, an Honorary Consultant Psychiatrist in Psychotherapy at Tavistock-Portman Portman NHS Clinics, a Senior Member of the British Association for Psychotherapy, a member of the American Group Analysis, of the British Psychoanalytic Council, of the International Association of Group Psychotherapy and of the Confederation of British Psychotherapists. She is an honorary member of the Institute of Group Analysis and of the Society of Couple Psychoanalytic Psychotherapists, Tavistock Clinic. She is a teaching staff member of the IGA. She has written extensively about group analytical psychotherapy as the essential tool in Forensic Psychotherapy. In 1996 she delivered the Foulkes lecture under the title: "Let the treatment fit the Crime." She is most famous for her book *Mother, Madonna, Whore: The Idealization and Denigration of Motherhood* (1988) which quashed the myth that "perversion" was largely a male preserve and opened up a whole new field of therapeutic enquiry. In 1997 Oxford Brookes University awarded Dr. Welldon an Honorary Doctorate of Science (D.Sc.) for her contribution in the field of forensic psychotherapy, and in 2013, she was invited to become an honorary member of the American Psychoanalytic Association. She is principal editor of *A Practical Guide to Forensic Psychotherapy* (1997) and author of *Sadomasochism* (2002). Her latest publication is *Playing with Dynamite: A Personal Approach to the Understanding of Perversions, Violence and Criminality* (Karnac, 2011).

Gerhard Wilke MA, Dip. FHE, Honorary Member I.A.G.P., IGA London, is an organisational and leadership development consultant and group analyst who has spent the last fifteen years working with the leaders, groups, departments and whole systems on how to adapt more successfully to a permanently changing organisational landscape.

Gerhard is an Associate of Ashridge Business School and co-authored the very successful book *Living Leadership: A Practical Guide for Ordinary Heroes*, FT Prentice Hall, 2012. During the last two decades Gerhard also worked at all levels of the NHS and published *How to be a Good Enough GP: Surviving and Thriving in the New Primary Care Organisations* in 2000. Gerhard is the group analyst on the leadership development programme of the Nation Institute of Health Research. In 2007, Gerhard gave the Foulkes memorial lecture in London and he has published and researched since 1975.

INTRODUCTION

Group Analysis (Foulkes, 1946) (Bridger, 1946) developed in parallel to the movement of therapeutic communities (Jones, 1956; Main, 1946), and with a further version of group therapy adopted by the Tavistock Clinic (Bion, 1946). Group Analysis has stimulated developments in numerous other fields and various forms of therapies, some of which have developed well beyond its origins. The present volume aims to introduce the reader to the wide breadth of such developments. The order of publication does not indicate any hierarchy of values.

One of the early pioneers in the application of Group Analysis in the field of Forensic Psychotherapy is Dr Estela Welldon. In her Foulkes lecture (Welldon, 1997) she brings into relief the practice of Group Analysis in this exciting but very difficult field. Dr Welldon explores the wide spectrum of issues but also delves deeply into the unconscious of very troubled people and does so with appropriate therapeutic concern when lesser able professionals are tempted to adopt a moralistic or even a punitive stance.

Family Therapy was first taught in the UK by the Introductory Course of the Institute of Group Analysis before the main teachers of that course founded the Institute of Family Therapy (IFT). One of the founders of IFT was Robin Skynner whose paper (Skynner, 1979) was the basis of a burgeoning of research and a wide range of publications. One of Dr Skynner's closest colleagues, Dr Behr (Behr, 1994) built on the foundations set by Dr Skynner and his paper covers a wide range of issues which connect Group Analysis and family therapy.

Group Analysis was built on and has developed through the integration of diverse theories. In the same way that group members are enriched through the interaction with others, group-analytic theory has developed through interaction and selective integration of elements of other theories. Group-analytic principles have, in turn, enriched other branches of science and philosophy. Marrone's (Marrone, 1994) article on Attachment Theory has been included because it demonstrates this beneficial integration of two important theoretical perspectives.

One of the early applications of Group Analysis has been in the field of adolescent psychotherapy. Adolescence is a time when the peer group acquires significance in a child's development and this natural developmental phenomenon presents and opportunity to be used therapeutically. Behr, a pioneer in this field, presents in Chapter Four of this volume some important early ideas on how it could be practiced, and explores the dynamics within and beyond the group. The author (Behr, 1988) refers to adolescence as a period of crisis but I wish to point out that, although the changes that take place in young people at this time of their life are significant, they are not universally accepted as "a crisis"(Coleman, 1980), or at least no more than the transition from home to school, from school (or generally education) to work, from single-state to engaging in a committed relationship, from that to having a family, from work to retirement and finally to negotiating old age and the final stages of life.

One of the prominent contributors in the field of group-analytic organisational consultancy is Gerhard Wilke (Wilke, 2014). In Chapter Five he elucidates how Group Analysis informs one's understanding of organisational pathology and he gives examples of how the group-analytic perspective offers an effective means of improving organisational dynamics and effectiveness. True to the group-analytic tradition, Wilke integrates contributions from various disciplines such as anthropology, sociology and psychoanalysis.

Group Analysis has contributed to the anti-discrimination movements and has been enriched by them; I refer to movements such as feminism and anti-racism. The article by E. Burman (Burman, 2004) contributes a wealth of ideas arising from and shaping an action research programme in the context of violence and offer of a refuge to women who were members of minority (minoritised as the author refers to them) groups and were victims of domestic violence.

Supervision of trainees has been an integral part of the group-analytic training right from its inception. Over years of practice, this has developed and has given rise to a separate training course which leads to a qualification. H. Behr, initially with Lisbeth Hearst, developed such a course and Meg Sharpe (Sharpe, 1995) edited a landmark volume in which supervision was explored from diverse aspects. The chapter, contributed by Behr contains the principles and original thoughts on the subject and forms an invaluable stimulus for thought and enriches the overall theory of Group Analysis.

One of the special pleasures of compiling this volume was that it gave me the opportunity of including and bringing to the readers' attention "forgotten treasures". Such is the Foulkes Lecture given by Jane Abercrombie (Abercrombie, 1981) which advocates and demonstrates the application of Group Analysis in higher (and by extension to all) education and learning. This is a unique and extremely useful application, which could also be taken advantage of by the readers of this volume from the moment they turn this page! Unfortunately, the illustrations of Dr. Abercrombie could not be included but the editor believes that the loss did not lessen the meaning of the paper significantly. It is significant that Dr. Abercrombie introduced her method well before the student "revolutions" of the sixties. Dr. Abercrombie introduced in a systematic way not only the making conscious the unconscious dynamics of the relationships between students and teachers but also between students and their chosen subject of study.

Considering how prevalent combined therapies are it is surprising that so very little is written about this practice. Individuals in therapy may also receive marital or family therapy or group members may also need individual work (at least for a period of time) which they may receive from their group therapist or another therapist of similar or diverse training. The field is as full of dangers as it is often necessary and potentially useful. The chapter on combined therapies (Maratos, 2000) aims to highlight some of the important issues so that the practitioner can avoid dangers and convert potential disasters to therapeutic interventions.

At present, when the demand for evidence-based practice becomes more pressing, research (both as a method and as a collection of reliable and valid findings) becomes an important instrument. Research in itself will not be adequate in changing attitudes towards therapies (and the current search for quick fixes) but can play a significant part in this effort. To the usual challenge "You claim it is useful but have you got any evidence to support your claim?" we can respond, "Yes, there is a growing body of evidence." The three chapters of this part (Part VIII Research) describe an impressive study with a ten-year follow-up (Dick, 1975), an objective comparison of two acute psychiatric wards with and without a group intervention (Maratos & Kennedy, 1974) and an original and thorough view of the recent demands for Evidence-Based Practice by (the so prematurely lost) Chris Mace (Mace, 2006).

This volume is concluded with an excellent contribution by Weegmann and English. The authors demonstrate a deep understanding of the theory of psychotherapy of addictions and of group-analysis and use profound insights derived from scientific and non-scientific literature (such as that of famous alcoholics, as Eugene O'Neil) and introduce new concepts as that of "freedom of non-using." Their approach is faithful to the group-analytic philosophy of integrating diverse views instead of generating further "pseudo-problems."

Finally, I would like to conclude with a personal note. Compiling this work has taught me a lot and I am convinced that it offers the opportunity for similar gains to any open-minded reader.

References

Abercrombie, M. L. J. (1981). Beyond the unconscious: Group-analysis applied. *Group Analysis, 16*(2 Supplement): 2–14.

Behr, H. (1988). Group analysis with early dolescents: Some clinical issues. *Group Analysis, 21*(2): 119–131.

Behr, H. (1994). Families and group analysis. In: D. G. Brown & L. M. Zinkin (Eds.), *The Psyche and the Social World.* London: Routledge.

Bion, W. R. (1946). The leaderless group project. *Bulletin of the Menninger Clinic, 10*: 77–81.

Bridger, H. (1946). The Northfield experiment. *Bulletin of the Menninger Clinic, 10*: 71–76.

Burman, E. (2004). Organising for change? Group-analytic perspectives on a Feminist Action Research Project. *Group Analysis, 37*(1): 91–108. Available at: http://gaq.sagepub.com/content/37/1/91.abstract

Coleman, J. C. (1980). *The Nature of Adolescence.* London: Methuen.

Dick, B. M. (1975). A ten-year study of out-patient analytic group therapy. *British Journal of Psychiatry, 127*: 365–375.

Foulkes, S. H. (1946). Principles and practice of group-therapy. *Bulletin of the Menninger Clinic, 10*: 85–89.

Jones, M. (1956). The concept of a therapeutic community. *The American Journal of Psychiatry*.

Mace, C. (2006). Special section: Setting the world on wheels: Some clinical challenges of evidence-based practice. *Group Analysis, 39*(3): 304–320. Available at: http://gaq.sagepub.com/content/39/3/304.abstract

Main, T. F. (1946). The hospital as a therapeutic institution. *Bulletin of the Menninger Clinic, 10*: 66–70.

Maratos, J. (2000). Combined therapies—A Group Analytic Perspective. In: S. A. H. P. Brooks (Ed.), *The Invisible Matrix* (pp. 128–148). London: Rebus Press.

Maratos, J. & M. Kennedy (1974). Evaluation of ward group meetings in a psychiatric unit of a general hospital. *British Journal of Psychiatry, 125*: 479–482.

Marrone, M. (1994). Attachment theory and group analysis. In: D. Brown & L. Zinkin (Eds.), *The Psyche and the Social World* (pp. 146–162). London: Routledge.

Sharpe, M. (1995). *The Third Eye: Supervision of Analytic Groups*. London: Routledge.

Skynner, A. C. R. (1979). Reflections on the family therapist as family scapegoat. *Journal of Family Therapy, I*: 7–22.

Welldon, E. V. (1997). Let the treatment fit the crime: Forensic group psychotherapy, 20th S. H. Foulkes Annual Lecture. *Group Analysis, 30*(1): 5–26.

Wilke, G. (2014). Group analysis in organisations: What it takes. In: *The Art of Group Analysis in Organisations: The Use if Intuitive and Experiential Knowledge* (pp. 3–38). London: Karnac.

PART I

FORENSIC PSYCHOTHERAPY

CHAPTER ONE

Let the treatment fit the crime: forensic group psychotherapy*

Estela V. Welldon

I'm deeply indebted to the Group-Analytic Society for inviting me to be this year's Foulkes Lecturer. It is a great honour, and it acknowledges my work with groups. I am first and foremost a clinician. For over thirty years I have spent my professional career trying to find a treatment that fits the problems of patients in the field of forensic psychotherapy. In preparation for this lecture, I read again some of Foulkes's work and his autobiographical notes and I recognised some of my own sense of discovery and excitement in my efforts to apply group analysis to patients with social and sexual disturbances. For example, Foulkes wrote:

> I forged my method and technique through trial and error, but above all by thinking about my experiences, as I still do. The practice of group analytic psychotherapy (in the change of human altogether) is the experimental situation in which theories are continuously

*This chapter was previously published as: Welldon, E. V. (1997). Let the treatment fit the crime: Forensic group psychotherapy, 20th S. H. Foulkes Annual Lecture. *Group Analysis, 30*: 5–26.

> put to the test of observation and are reformulated and revised (1969, p. 204).

Indeed, my own failures slowly began to emerge as successes when I was able to allow my patients to become my teachers and my colleagues my fellow students in dealing with difficult predicaments involving serious risks to others and themselves. Foulkes developed further his group-analytic experience in responding to the need to work at Northfield with a heterogeneous group of men who had become psychologically unable to continue with warfare, which society required of them during the Second World War. In talking about this experience he said:

> Thus for me what could have been a frustrating time of trying to cure partly unwilling people in much too short a time and under altogether not very favourable conditions, became a fascinating and arresting period (1969, p. 204).

Thus, from the very beginning, group analysis was both art and science and it was applied in a social context. And it is this mixture of theory born from a pragmatic approach that has inspired my long journey in applying group analysis to those patients who present with social and sexual deviancy. Early in my career I was personally influenced by the teaching of Karl Menninger who believed that punishment neither helps the criminal nor protects society. As early as 1930 Menninger wrote that "the great joke" is that in every prison "the considerable majority of all prisoners are there for the second, third, sixth, or 20th time". Nor does punishment deter others: it is an old story that in the crowds gathered to watch the hanging of pickpockets in England many had their pockets picked while they watched. Menninger said that regardless of its futility and expense, punishing criminals gratifies, comforts, and even delights the general public: "sadistic attacks in the name of righteousness" deal with the public's unconscious guilt. I was fortunate to train at the Henderson Hospital which gave me a renewed sense of trust that a therapeutic place can exist for the benefit of the patients and not the staff. Stuart Whiteley of the Group-Analytic Society was Medical Director during the latter part of my time there.

In this Foulkes Lecture, I shall be talking about the application of group analysis in forensic psychotherapy, which is a new discipline aimed at the psychodynamic comprehension of the offender and his or her consequent treatment. It involves the understanding of the unconscious as well as conscious motivations for particular offending behaviour. I do not seek to condone the crime or to excuse the criminal. On the contrary, I wish to help the offender acknowledge responsibility in order to save both the offender and society from the perpetration of further crimes.

Resistance attached to the "real" understanding of the forensic patient is deeply ingrained. I believe that this illustrates our unconscious need to punish. For example, during the process of publicising this lecture, even its title underwent a significant change in one batch of the "fliers"; my title "Let the Treatment Fit the Crime" was altered to "Let the Punishment Fit the Crime." Similarly, in their daily coverage of perverse or criminal acts, our tabloid newspapers gratify the need of their readers to feel reassured of their own "goodness."

Many years ago I decided that my work in therapeutic groups should be carried out exclusively with forensic patients within the National Health Service. In 1971, I joined the staff of the Portman Clinic where analytical psychotherapy is used exclusively with patients who engage in acts of delinquency or criminal behaviour or who suffer from sexual perversions. Now we have had more than twenty years' experience of treating sexually and socially deviant patients together in group therapy in an out-patient setting. Before describing how we work with such patients in analytical group psychotherapy, it may be helpful to discuss several important aspects of these very difficult patients.

Most of the Portman's patients have deeply disturbed backgrounds. Some have criminal records and a very low sense of self-esteem, which is often covered by a facade of cockiness and arrogance; their impulse control is minimal and they are suspicious and full of hate towards people in authority. Some rebellious and violent ex-convicts have long histories of crimes against property and persons. Others, who feel insecure, inadequate and ashamed, tend to be self-referrals. They enact their pathological sexual deviancy, such as exhibitionism, paedophilia or voyeurism, in a very secretive manner, so that only their victims know about their behaviour.

The person suffering from "perversion" is unable to think before the perverse act because he or she is not mentally equipped to make the necessary links. The affect pervades the whole personality: the thinking process is not functioning in his or her particular area of perversity. At times the patient's tendency to make sadistic attacks on his or her own capacity for thought and reflection is also directed against the therapist's capacity to think and reflect, and it is then that the therapist feels confused, numbed and unable to make any useful interpretations. The failure of therapists' treatment is for such patients a bitter triumph. It carries the inevitable axiom that the patients are untreatable, just as they felt as infants, unwanted, unlovable and unworthy of any consistent caring-therapeutic effort. Through their self-destructiveness they perpetuate the emotional pain inflicted by their parents. These adult patients have experienced—as infants—a sense of having been messed about in crucial circumstances in which both psychological and biological survival were at stake. In other words they were *actually*—in *reality,* not only in fantasy—at the mercy of others. These traumatic and inconsistent attitudes towards them have effectively interfered with the process of individuation and separation. There is a basic lack of trust towards the significant carer, which accompanies them all through their lives.

We have found that group-analytical therapy may often be the best treatment for severely disturbed patients suffering from sexual perversions. We have reached this conclusion after much careful thought and research. Our own initial sense of frustration, disillusionment, hopelessness has led us gradually into changes regarding selection criteria, preparation, composition of the groups and leadership techniques. I have felt the need to challenge both my own previous selection criteria and those of others, the most familiar and obvious criteria being those of Irvin Yalom, in which he advocates group treatment for those Young, Attractive, Verbal, Intelligent, and Successful—also called YAVIS—people. As a matter of fact, I believe that often the opposite holds true. Those who are thought to be old, ugly, illiterate, unverbal, dull, and failures can do extremely well in group therapy. I have found it most rewarding to watch a metamorphosis taking place and these people become attractive, intelligent, verbal, and successful!

Similarly, whereas I once thought that extreme secretiveness was in itself a contra-indication, clinical evidence has proved that group analysis can be the treatment of choice in incest, in which victims and perpetrators share, by nature of their predicament, a history of an engulfing, intense, inappropriate, distorted, physical and sexual relationship of a highly secretive type within the family situation. Assessments of these patients can easily trigger off emotional responses in the professionals which may interfere with clear and unbiased treatment recommendations.

Fiona, aged forty, had a history of prostitution, the outcome of having been a victim of paternal incest. On previous occasions she had tried to obtain help because of a suffocating attitude, which included sexual approaches, towards her daughter aged nine. Her requests had never been taken seriously; on the contrary, she had been told not to worry, this was "only due to her maternal instinct." She was so determined to give her daughter better mothering than she ever had, that she began to work as a prostitute at night when her daughter was asleep.

Incidentally, Fiona was one of the women who initially alerted me of the existence of maternal incestuous feelings and acts which led me to further my research on female perversion, later published in my book *Mother, Madonna, Whore: The Idealization and Denigration of Motherhood* (1988).

Treatment programmes may fail because of inappropriate professional interactions. For example, the victims could succeed in making the therapist feel not only protective but also possessive about them, which in turn could lead to patients feeling favoured and unique in individual treatment. Alternatively, the therapist might feel either like the consenting child or the seductive parent in the incest situation. On the other hand, when dealing with the perpetrators, the therapist may feel cornered or blackmailed by confidentiality issues which may provoke feelings of collusion. Such patients present great difficulties for group-analytic psychotherapy, yet they present a worthwhile challenge, when the potential benefits of a group experience for such "antisocial" and "asocial" people are considered. It was often claimed that these patients either did not respond to group therapy or that it could be effective only if one such patient were integrated into a "neurotic" group. However, such claims do not derive from experience. It could just as easily be claimed that individual therapy deprives these patients of the benefit of being able to interact with the social microcosm provided by group therapy and which can afford them a much better understanding of their problems since they are so deeply related to antisocial actions.

I have observed that the group, by facilitating solidarity and open rivalry among its members, effectively stops the offer or "pushing" of a gift, a frequent occurrence in individual therapy which at times may render the therapist a receiver of stolen goods.

Some exclusion criteria are also born from clinical experience. For example, voyeurism and chronic schizoid forms of paedophilia have clinically proved to be contra-indications for this treatment. Group sessions are used by voyeurs as a captive audience for the concrete acting-out for their perversion without the intricacies of inner changes associated with the acting-in during the sessions. They become in reality "peeping Toms" who are very inquisitive and appear superficially to be "insightful" in their questioning of female patients' sexual lives. Their inclusion in these groups has deleterious effects on the other members and hinders the development of trust and cohesiveness in the group process.

I believe that basically, family influence is crucial, and, therefore patients who have been subjected to an intense, suffocating relationship with one parent are particularly suitable candidates for group therapy. Groups provide them with a much warmer and less threatening atmosphere than they could usually find in one-to-one therapy, in which their experience of authority is so intense. Also, most violent patients are unable to tolerate closeness and intimacy, feeling uncontained in a one-to-one relationship. They experience intense, fearful vulnerability at any separation, which is immediately felt to be traumatic because they do not believe that the therapy will last, and they are convinced that they will be let down by the therapist. This, too, tends to stimulate aggressive and violent impulses and to increase the likelihood of an attack on the therapist. Such patients function better in groups with their peers, in which they experience their violence to be much better contained and understood. Serious criminal patterns are not reasons in themselves for exclusion, providing the delinquency does not preclude the personal disclosures required for therapeutic progress. This could become rather complicated with patients whose daily life depends on their close associates' delinquent actions, which could be disclosed or "leaked" in the sessions.

We are aware that our patients are very much in need of three structures: fellow patients, therapist and institution. All are deeply related in their mental representations which constitute a process of healthy triangulation. Because of their fears of intimacy in a one-to-one situation these patients form a strong transference to the Clinic as an institution. The setting is of utmost importance for both therapist and patients whose problems involve acts against society and this is better served within the National Health Service. The therapists' inner knowledge that the state is paying for their professional services becomes invaluable while working with this patient population. It reinforces both parties in the contractual agreement on which the therapy is based. The therapists are protected from blackmail and the patients feel neither exploited nor able to exploit about money matters.

Preparation techniques

Many patients used to drop out after the first few sessions of group therapy. I decided that this might be related, at least in part, to the length of time that had elapsed between initial selection and the inception of treatment. Therefore, now, from the first diagnostic consultation when patients have been thought to be suitable for group treatment, I offer them irregular, brief sessions so that they can discuss their fears and feelings related to starting the group. The point of being irregular and brief is not to become involved in actual therapy but much more to give some nurturing in a series of holding sessions. I warn them that whereas at the start they might feel tempted to drop out it is worthwhile to persevere and to sustain the effort of continuing attendance, for in a short time they will develop a sense of belonging to the group and they will feel more at ease about it.

In these individual sessions they are told of the rules and regulations, such as the necessity for a serious commitment to group treatment, which will take years as opposed to weeks or months; the importance of being punctual; and if attendance at a session is impossible, prior notification of absence. Also all communication becomes the property of the group and the therapist is not available for any individual communications. Messages about absenteeism or lateness will be given to the group, who are expected to take action, for example, in writing letters to absent members via the Clinic. In the case of requests for information, such as court reports or reports to other pertinent professional bodies, all group members have to voice their views and suggestions. They are also advised that to see the other members outside of group sessions might jeopardise then-treatment. I believe that giving rules is not entirely helpful, but on balance I consider that they are essential, because they create a sense of belonging and a sense of responsibility for the development of the group.

Patients are told that the process of termination is of vital importance in consolidating the improvements and changes achieved. A general consensus should be reached among members and therapist about the date for leaving and this should be agreed at least three months prior to the actual termination. This will give some time to deal with the anticipation of missing therapy for those who are to leave and also for those who are to stay to voice feelings about missing them. In this way, they become aware both of previous unacknowledged grief and mourning for many losses in their lives and they start to value what they are about to offer of themselves to others.

There are a few practicalities which are expected from patients, such as ticking their own names with a pen of their own on the weekly attendance sheet. Chairs are not pre-arranged but group members are expected to set out a number of chairs to sit on. If a decision is reached to write a letter, they get the stationery from the receptionist, write and sign it themselves (never expecting me to sign the letters). However, it is my responsibility to take the letter and have it posted, as they have no access to anybody's address.

Leadership, authority and power

At the start of a group both authority and power reside within the therapist and institution. From the preparation time patients become aware of their own participation as essential for the group's survival and development. If there are no patients, there is no group. The patients' anti-authority feelings are so *deceitfully present* and their vulnerability so *apparently absent* that for them it is excruciatingly difficult to be aware of their own sense of power, in which they experience the group as theirs and not the therapist's. It is only when power is located in the patients' membership and authority in the therapist that gaining of insight and real changes can take place.

This provides the right balance for them to exercise their power in attending or not, in being late, in producing havoc during group sessions and in challenging the therapist's authority. The group therapist has to use his authority in offering the necessary ingredients for patients to feel contained and able to express their anger, which facilitates the relocation of power in patients. The therapist will also offer links which will make it possible for patients to learn about thinking.

Each and every member experiences a powerful sense of belonging to the group. Throughout treatment patients gain a capacity for self-assertion, emotional growth, independence, and individuation. They see themselves and others developing into respected individuals with self-esteem which is acknowledged by others and by themselves. They are not only allowed but encouraged openly to express anger and frustration which has been kept hidden for lengthy periods. This encouragement comes especially from "old" members who have gone through similar predicaments and who are now ready to leave.

What type of group therapy and why?

Group analysis offers a strict sense of boundaries with awareness of links between acts and unconscious motivations. The interpretation of "vertical" transference of the group in relation to the therapist, usually with regressive elements, facilitates independence. "Horizontal" interpretations to do with mixed feelings about sibling figures provide the needed capacity to empathise with "others," who actually represent parts of themselves. These are multiple transference processes, which are effectively used for the working through. These are not to be thought of as diluted, since they lead to heightened degrees of awareness.

Modified heterogeneity, in the sense of mixing social and sexual deviances, allows for a more comprehensive understanding of all dynamic processes involved, especially those related to their inability to think and their identification with the aggressor, actually present in their early lives. Patients become aware of the reasons for their lack of trust and their intense need to be in control of all situations.

A *slow-open* group offers different developmental stages from dependency to self-assertion, giving opportunities for "senior" members to take more caring roles confronting "junior" members in therapeutic ways. It also provides evidence of the emotional growing, which is acknowledged by other members and by the therapist, facilitating individuation/separation never allowed by uncaring, neglectful parents and never observed in individual therapy. I cannot stress enough the importance of this approach, especially in our present political times when economic priorities have become the main consideration. For example, the emphasis has been placed on "short, sharp and shock" treatment but in relying on this we are doomed to fail since *time* is the key to open areas of the most primitive defence mechanisms.

A single therapist

I have always worked with these patients on my own, without a co-therapist. Two therapists recreate the primal scene in its most concrete terms, which is potential dynamite for our patients who often experience the parental coupling associated with extreme sado-masochistic behaviour. Given the nature of our patients' early deprivation and broken homes, the response to co-therapists would be one of provocation and humiliation. These patients have more skills in breaking up "parental bonding" than co-therapists have in containing their primitive anxieties, intense envy, and destructive impulses within the group.

Our groups are composed mostly of people who see themselves as victims, experiencing the world as divided into the "haves" and the "have nots". Although the therapist holds the authority, working alone the therapist is seen as unsupported, almost a "have not", and has to trust the group. Members have intense oral needs and want the therapist to be available at all times. They find it very difficult to adjust to the "weekly feed" and cling to it in a very infantile manner. Holidays are always determined by the therapist and are very much resented by patients who tend at the beginning of treatment to relapse into a lot of acting out, sometimes in relation to their own previous offences which are perhaps recurring after a long period of time. They fantasise about the therapist's wonderful holidays involving great sex and are outraged at missing the group because of the therapist's perfect family lifestyle.

Leadership techniques

Democratic leadership is experienced as seductive; authoritarian leadership reinforces persecutory anxieties in these patients. Both styles deprive patients of a necessary sense of boundary and recreate disturbing familial patterns.

A reflective, attentive therapist acts as a model to encourage patients to think, rather than to act. Nevertheless, the therapist needs to be capable of firm and rigorous action at times, allowing active confrontation not only amongst members but also between group members and the therapist, when firm leadership is needed to relieve their anxieties about uncaring, ineffectual parental figures. At times therapeutic interventions involving a very active response from the therapist are needed, rather than a well-prepared interpretation. I think of them as therapeutic because they derive from experience only acquired by treating this patient population. For example, a therapist vigorously tells a patient: "Shut up" at exactly the right time, when the patient has provoked a great sense of fear and insecurity in the whole group (including the patient). The fact that the whole group feels contained, including the member who was threatening the cohesiveness of the group, provides us with the evidence that this intervention has been effective. Not only has it provided containment but it has also stopped a process of escalation to enormous acting-out, including both the inner and outer worlds. Hence this could never be termed as the therapist's "acting-in" or "acting-out."

Of interest is that my style of conducting would change. Group members made perceptive remarks about this; to the effect that, if they were expected to change, why shouldn't the therapist change too? They noticed my adaptation to their needs, rather than clinging to a technique which might provide me with a sense of security but would have left them feeling insecure and anonymous. I began to blend different techniques, according to the needs of each patient and what I thought was best for all.

Individual as opposed to group interpretations

A technique which provides patients only with group interpretations seems to reinforce feelings of dehumanisation and alienation, increasing their insecurity and lowering their self-esteem even further. I realised that it would be more efficacious after giving a group interpretation to link this with individual patient psychopathology. I have also learnt that it is important not only to make from the start interpretations of the negative transference but also to acknowledge their "good bits," which are often concealed with a tremendous sense of embarrassment. All interpretations should rightly acknowledge the patients' and not their therapist's achievements.

All patients in our groups suffer from perversions and/or are engaged in violent or criminal activities. During the last 25 years at the Portman Clinic I have worked with a variety of offenders, including rapists, arsonists, exhibitionists, shoplifters, burglars, murderers and other violent offenders. In order to illustrate more clearly these dynamics I shall concentrate on one particular group, which is for the treatment of victims *and* perpetrators of incest. Lip-service is often paid to the idea that victims may sometimes become victimisers, but I believe that the full clinical import of this concepts poorly understood. I have chosen to offer clinical material from a forensic psychotherapy group for both victims and perpetrators, shocking though it may seem, because in this context, we can see more clearly the victimised aspects of the abusers, and the potentially abusing and murderous aspects of the victims.

Group treatment of the victims and perpetrators of incest together 3Ut not related offers unexpected qualities of containment and insight which are virtually impossible in a one-to-one situation. Perpetrators become deeply aware of the extensive long-term consequences of their actions. When confronted by other members mirroring the predicaments of the perpetrators' victims they are able to reflect and see how unable they are to see themselves as separate human beings, but only as denigrated parts of their parental figures.

From now on I shall be offering clinical vignettes, introducing three patients and their evolution in different phases of the group processes, as a way to familiarise you with this specific work. I hope this will illustrate some of the theoretical ideas I am proposing in regard to the treatment not only of victims and perpetrators of incest but also of other offenders in group-analytical therapy.

Keith was referred for treatment after the disclosure of his incestuous relationship with his stepdaughter. I saw him for several diagnostic interviews. These were beset with complications as all the different agencies involved demanded information about his activities. However Keith demanded complete confidentiality. I began to feel cornered and blackmailed into giving him treatment in the utmost confidentiality, which actually in this particular case meant "secrecy" with dirty undertones. I became deeply aware of the transference-countertransference issues involved in "incest with a consenting child." These were very powerful feelings. At times I would feel like the child keeping quiet about it all; at other times, I would feel like the controlling and exploitative parental figure. After a great deal of careful thought I decided to offer him group therapy, a suggestion which first surprised and then enraged him. I gave him time to think about it, and tried to explain to him clearly why this would be the most suitable therapy for him: secrecy between parent and child is a key pathological trait in incest, which in group therapy becomes no longer available. Everything is open to everyone. A few weeks later it was my turn to be surprised when he accepted my recommendation.

Keith joined the group two years after its inception. When he was admitted to the group Fiona reacted with the most anger to his admission of incest. She had many rows with him because she saw a mirror image of herself in Keith, in her own engulfing relationship with her daughter and previously with her father. Keith confronted her with the inconsistency between her alleged wish to change jobs and her feeble attempts to do so; by now it was obvious that she was still a practising prostitute. Keith himself was a conscientious worker, had kept his job and been promoted several times. Fiona, on the other hand, confronted Keith with his erotic feelings towards his stepdaughter, which he admitted with much pain, since they were truthful.

Patricia was a victim of incest which had taken place from the age of 11 to 21. She joined the group at the age of 36 after referral from her general practitioner when, for the first time in her life, she admitted first to herself and then to him her repressed or "forgotten" history of incest. Though her GP was an experienced doctor, he had for 15 years felt puzzled at not being able to understand the causes for her extensive and serious psychosomatic complaints. During the assessment I felt protective of her and had the idea that the only person capable of fully understanding her was myself. At that point, I became aware of alarm bells ringing, which indicated that my initial response was in itself a contra-indication for offering individual therapy. When I offered her group therapy, she was terrified at the prospect of having to confront and be confronted by so many strangers about "her secret" but was able to understand the reasons for this recommendation. Patricia joined the same group 18 months after Keith.

It is not uncommon to observe that female patients with a history of early incest may behave from the very start in the group as "ideal assistants" to the therapist. Even those who have never been familiar with unconscious processes seem to discover immediately "appropriate" ways to "help" the therapist-mother-father keep the group-family together. Fellow patients often react with surprise and bewilderment at this show of "maturity." Later on this is replaced with competitiveness. When interpretations are made to the effect that the newcomer is only repeating a pathological pattern learnt early in life, other fellow patients seem relieved by this understanding but it is then the turn of the "helper" to be filled with rage at this interpretation. After all, she is "doing her best"; why is she being so "harshly criticised"? This is exactly what happened as soon as Patricia joined the group. Patricia fulfilled perfectly the ro1e of the incest victim who tries to "keep the family together." This produced much aggravation amongst most members but especially in Fiona, who in her adult life, as you may remember, had "chosen" the "prostitution solution" as opposed to the psychosomatic one "chosen" by Patricia. In a subsequent session, there was a very active confrontation between the two of them in which both were "assessed" by other members who thought Patricia to be by far the more mature of the two, despite her recent admission. All sorts of interpretations on my part about Patricia's re-enactment of her early behaviour seemed to be of no avail. Fiona felt hurt and humiliated by the others "misunderstanding" her maternal role; she failed to attend and wrote several letters threatening to leave the group. Eventually, and on subsequent occasions, she returned to the group. (Incidentally after five years of group treatment she left in a healthy way, after she had obtained a very good professional position and her daughter was continuing treatment for her own problems.)

Eroticisation as a defence against the therapeutic alliance

During the middle phases of these groups a common theme that emerges is that of the "erotisation of the group process". A traumatic situation, usually linked with separation anxieties, triggers off the erotisation which represents a resistance to the therapeutic process. Patients who have been rather quiet and secretive about their actions in the initial phases start talking in an erotic way about sexually perverse material. This apparent freedom in talking so openly about actions of which they had previously felt so ashamed should make the therapist suspicious. It soon becomes obvious that patients are using the therapeutic situation, the group session itself, as the partner to the perversion. In other words, by describing in such detail his or her criminal and sexual offences, the patient is trying to seduce and excite the other members, thereby getting an enormous amount of sexual gratification. On these occasions a climate of high excitement is created by disclosing fulsomely descriptive material to which the rest of the group reacts by being immobilised. The time and the place for therapy has now become the time and place for the perversion itself. This creates the situation of fear mixed with excitement, which makes our patients feel so vulnerable.

Initially, Fiona showed much reluctance in talking about her prostitution. A few months after the conflicts between Patricia and herself eased up, just before the Easter holidays, she began to show bits of herself in a provocative and seductive manner. She talked of her difficulties in having a one-to-one relationship, her contempt of men not being as competent or capable as she was expecting them to be, her fears of commitment, her close association with her daughter aged nine, her sense of boredom, her skill in mastering men, and eventually, in a most histrionic manner, the way she seduced men for financial profit. By then the group was behaving like a dirty old man, unable to question or to confront her but only too willing to give her all the attention and whatever she wanted out of the situation.

Eroticisation facilitates the process of acting-in and this easily leads to acting-out. One of the group members feels in open rivalry and competition with the therapist's authority. They see the therapist as ineffectual, uncaring, deserting and passive and this makes them operate in a very active and seductive manner. In this case Fiona was acting-in her envy towards me and was attempting to become the alternative radical therapist, making her feel powerful, but weak.

Mirroring processes

Eventually, Fiona started a series of clerical jobs in which she usually got into conflict with women in authority. All this had to do with her idealisation/denigration of me. Group members were confronted with great expectations of and dependency on the mother figure, but simultaneously with fears that I would be inadequate in dealing with all their demands, as had happened with their real mothers. This was interpreted in transferential terms which involved the whole group, since this experience was shared by all.

In one session, Fiona caused much alarm when she mentioned how much she had regressed in her relationship with her daughter, to such an extent indeed that in accordance with the group members' suggestion I took the unprecedented action of suggesting a referral of her daughter for treatment to a Child Guidance Clinic. The draft of this referral letter was left on the table, in the centre of the group, where all communications about patients and outside agents are shown. Fiona was at first distressed by this, but quite soon she was able to come to terms with it as being the best solution. The other patients appeared to be contained and held by this action, with which they had all agreed. From then on Fiona began to appear more reassured, far less resistant and more insightful. She had experienced me and the group as caring and supportive in her feelings of inadequacy in dealing with her functioning as a mother. In so doing, she had used projective identification with me as an omnipotent mother, who was supposed to deal with all problems within the group, even the outside ones.

Everyone in the group had some lesson to learn from my lack of resources to deal with everyone's problems solely by treatment within the group. This was acknowledged by my requesting help from outside, which was promptly implemented. I was not aware that this experience had been so deeply felt until we eventually learnt that Keith had followed suit and had himself referred his stepdaughter to the same place for treatment. We got to know about these two years later when Keith confronted Fiona over her folly in wanting to stop her daughter's therapy. He told her that he knew all the processes; since he had thought it such a good idea that he had taken his stepdaughter for treatment. Obviously there was a degree of identification and role-modelling in operation which could never have occurred in individual treatment.

Months after Patricia was admitted to the group many members still clung to the belief that she was the most assured member and quite healthy, such was their wish for a "healthy incest" which could have no damaging effects on the victims. However, at a later session Patricia appeared distraught. She told us how the evening before she had been "prevented" from watching a TV programme on incest, because of her father's telephone call at exactly the time of this programme, which ended after the programme was over. Now it was Keith's turn to become aware of the deep implications that incest had for Patricia when he confronted her with her inability to stop her father and with her lack of assertiveness in not being able even to ask him to "phone her an hour later."

A few weeks later she was in tears telling us of her extreme humiliation in her recent visit to her parents, who knew of her decision to be a vegetarian. She had already told her mother clearly about this and had reaffirmed it before spending the weekend with them. So she was flabbergasted when confronted on Saturday morning with an enormous breakfast of sausages and bacon, cooked "especially" by her father, which she reluctantly but acquiescently ate. These two incidents gave a strong indication of her "consenting" attitude. However, it looked as if father had "read" some inner changes on her part, because later on he angrily "questioned her about being in some sort of nonsense or therapy."

Whereas previously Keith and Patricia had been unable to make any connection, even refusing eye contact, they were now in open confrontation with one another. Keith indignantly questioned her inability to assert herself and her compulsion to give in to her father's requests. Suddenly and quite unexpectedly a complete understanding of their own respective roles and of the implications was available to us all. We all became aware that incest is much larger than life, that its power is not only physical, sexual or erotic. This secret union provides both partners with a "uniqueness" which it is almost impossible to describe. It gives as much as it takes away. No one was able to resist the realisation of Patricia's suffering despite her maturity, helpfulness and "insight." Fiona now learnt about Patricia's real predicament, and became caring and helpful to her in a realistic manner and was able to see the chronic disabilities that incest had inflicted on Patricia. She had consistently been compliant with any wish of her father's and of her mother's too. In the group treatment she began to assert herself slowly and in a determined fashion, but only after an initial period of being extremely compliant to the therapist in order to keep the "family" together. Eventually, she began to express anger, when she was able to scream at another group member and tell him to "sod off." She and everyone else were extremely surprised at this and we all experienced a sense of achievement at her newly gained ability to express anger.

Our reaction was completely different when a few months later we saw her looking extremely elated, radiating a sense of triumph. Although everyone was aware of her mood as soon as she entered the room, nobody felt at ease with this feeling and somebody asked the reason for her feeling so triumphant. Her answer was: "The bastard got what he deserved." At that point everybody knew who she was talking about but nobody knew what she was referring to. Then she said; "The bloody bastard just got to know that his testicles will be removed because of cancer. Isn't that wonderful?" A few members attempted a smile but most people felt extremely worried about her. I offered her an interpretation dealing with her inability to separate herself from her father in her strong need for revenge.

We all know that the expression of anger is therapeutic and a healthy sign, but the wish for revenge is an unhealthy trait which poisons the person who suffers from it and everybody around the person too.

This situation revealed how much the victims cling to the perpetrators like a necessary enemy.

Termination issues

Many incidents took place in the seven years that Keith remained in the group for treatment, and they offered many unexpected insights. For example, the crucial unconscious link between acting-out and denial of mourning became vital when Keith could remember some repressed feelings he had when his firstborn son died of cot death.

This occurred after a violent fight he had with his wife when he suddenly left home, only to return a few days later when his wife contacted him to tell him about this death. He failed to react in any way except for apathy and lethargy. In contrast his wife was overwhelmed by grief to the point of becoming emotionally unavailable. A few months later he approached his stepdaughter sexually and the incest began. I'd like to concentrate here on some of the powerful dynamic changes which it is possible to achieve through group analysis and which are elicited and evidenced in our powerful counter-transference responses to equally strong transference processes in our patients.

When Keith announced that the following week would be his last session, which had been decided within the group a long time before, I felt a need to work through my own countertransference, including a deep sense of bereavement about his departure from the group. By then he was the most senior member and the most experienced one. Members found it very difficult to express any feelings about his departure since his input was of great importance; in a way he had taken up the "co-therapist" role most effectively.

This is a very important feature in the life of the patients which only emerges in a single therapist group as opposed to a co-therapist group. I questioned myself: shall I need to perform the co-therapist duties? On reflection I considered that what I should miss the most about him was the element of hope he provided us all with, especially in myself. After all, the first time I met him eight years earlier I disliked him immensely and thought he had no chances for improvement. (This is rather unusual since I am known to be naively optimistic about the most intractable cases.) I offered him a place in a group with a near conviction of his refusal to accept it. He was resistant in so many ways: pedantic, pompous, superior, arrogant, full of complaints about other colleagues. But now I experienced him as one of the most rewarding patients. I also realised that I must facilitate his exit, to let him go, and to acknowledge in this way the important degree of his changes. I am also aware that with our patient population envy runs high and sometimes fellow patients make it difficult for others to depart, especially because of their difficulties in acknowledging someone else's improvement.

In the next session the other members did not want to know about his leaving; there was much denial and they were unable to deal with any idea of being faced with mourning processes. Keith talked of his enormous changes and that on the whole he felt grown-up enough now to stand on his own two feet and to leave. It is a duty he has to perform. He confronted the group and told us how he came here for one problem, the incest, but by now he has learnt so much more about everything in his life. He has got an awareness and wisdom he never envisaged before. Eventually he was also able to say how much and how deeply he has got to know himself. Reluctantly, then, he admitted to being grateful to me for having "shaken him up a few times." While saying this he looked at me with Labrador-dog eyes.

I felt very moved and quite unable to make an interpretation which would accurately convey all those years of seeing him interacting very little with others to start with and later on challenging others with their "consenting" behaviour and his own way of interacting and making others aware of their collusiveness and lack of insight. These also included his own reactions of initial rage and his later response to confrontations, admitting consequences of his own actions and his increasing development into maturity.

How to convey all this? I just said: "This is a time for loss, mourning and hope; he has learnt so much and his changes are so apparent that everyone is experiencing great difficulty in letting him go, because they fear they are letting the hope go." Keith then asked Patricia how she felt about now being the senior person of the group. She recognised this was a very difficult step for her, since she would miss him a lot.

The group is still going on, and there are still members from that time. After Keith left there was much grieving for him, but later on we became ready, with trepidation and anticipation, to welcome a new batch of members to join us four months later. Such is the magnitude of the learning processes we go through in group therapy and its intricacies, which involve most feelings but especially those to do with hope and its inherent inner changes.

I very much hope I have been able to convey accurately not only the difficulties but also the great rewards found in applying group analysis to this challenging group of patients. I am most grateful for being provided with this opportunity to share my experiences with you all.

References

Foulkes, S. H. (1969). Some autobiographical notes. Part II. *Group Analysis, 1*(3): 202–205.

Welldon, Estela V. (1988). *Mother, Madonna, Whore: The Idealization and Denigration of Motherhood.* London: Free Association Books.

PART II

FAMILY DYNAMICS

CHAPTER TWO

Families and group analysis*

Harold L. Behr

The family is a group, subject to group dynamics in much the same way as a typically constituted therapy group, but complicated by other powerful interpersonal factors which are intrinsic to family life. Family therapy is in fact a form of small-group therapy. As such, it falls technically within the purview of group analysis. Yet it is not easy to discern a distinctive group-analytic approach to family therapy which could stand comparison with other significant models of family therapy, notably those derived from the systems theory.

S. H. Foulkes on families

S. H. Foulkes remarked only briefly on family therapy in his writings. He recognised the family as a "life group", a naturally occurring network, or "plexus", as he called it, in which the members were "vitally interrelated" and interdependent, but having no single occupation

---

*This chapter was previously published in 2000 as: Behr, H. L., Families and Group Analysis. Chapter 11 in: D. Brown & L. Zinkin (Eds.), *The Psyche and the Social World.* London: Routledge.

as a group. Although speaking positively of family therapy, Foulkes acknowledged that his own experience in the field was limited. "I myself have treated families only off and on," he wrote (Foulkes, 1975), "sometimes with considerable success and in a very short time, relatively speaking". But we are left in the dark about his technique. He makes the point, however, that although the family is a group, it does not follow that we should address and treat it all the time as a whole. "On the contrary", he states, "here as at any time we treat the individuals composing this group in the context of the group" (p. 14).

Having given family therapy his blessing, Foulkes retired from the fray. He was more enthusiastic about the "psycho-diagnostic" value of family interviews. The nuclear family, "with its intimate, inter-linked system of interaction and transactions", provided him with a special opportunity to study transpersonal processes and to discover patterns of interaction in their chronological sequence, passed down from one generation to the next. But such study had to await the individual's emergence from childhood.

> As far as I can see, this primary family is best studied at a later stage when the children are more or less adolescent, or even adult. One can then get a clear picture as to the way in which they have been moulded and forced into shape by the conditions prevailing in the family into which they were born, and of which they form a part. (1975, p. 16)

There is little else specific to families that can be gleaned from Foulkes' writings. However, he does make one essential point: the family group is the exact opposite of the standard group-analytic group in terms of the ideal criteria for classic group analysis.

Group analysis: the dialectic between psychoanalysis and systems theory

Several factors have militated against the emergence of a specific group-analytic school of family therapy. The contrast between a family presenting itself for therapy and a therapy group made up of individuals who have never previously met (a so-called "stranger" group) is so great that it is not surprising that entirely different techniques have evolved in each case. In family therapy, approaches generally reflect the need to engage the already established family group as quickly as possible. In stranger-group therapy, issues of change are addressed within a gradually unfolding context. The stranger group, carefully assembled by a therapist and unencumbered by a shared past, is immediately a well-functioning group. Such disturbance as there is, is initially contained within the individual members and only later shared within the group-as-a-whole. The pace of engagement can therefore be much slower, governed in the early stages by all group members' mutual ignorance of one another, and the need to reduce the anxiety of unfamiliarity (actually, the anxiety of not being in one's own family).

The core of the group-analytic training experience lies with the stranger group. Although Foulkes could be regarded as having adumbrated a systems approach to groups, his model of small-group psychotherapy derives largely from the psychoanalytic perspective which has had little impact on mainstream family therapy approaches. On the other hand, systems thinking, a relatively undeveloped strand of thought in group analysis, has had a profound influence on the family therapy world, leading to the development of highly specialised interventions, techniques, and schools of practice built around the notion of the family as the prototype of an open system (see, for example, Haley, 1976; Minuchin & Fishman, 1981; Hoffman, 1981; Haley, 1976; Minuchin & Fishman, 1981; Palazzoli, Cecchin, Pratao, & Boscolo, et al. 1978). Richly developed models of structural, systemic, and strategic family therapy hold sway, and have created a climate of practice in family therapy which has made it difficult for psychoanalytically orientated family therapists to assert their position.

The systems, or structural, approaches to family therapy primarily emphasise the current, interactional, interpersonal structure of the family. Issues of power and control, boundary maintenance and the achievement of separation are addressed within a here-and-now context. Psychoanalytic family therapists tend to focus on historical aspects of the family such as unresolved mourning, obsolete intergenerational attitudes based on family myths, and failure to negotiate crucial transitions in the family life cycle. The literature contains plausible efforts to reconcile psychoanalysis with systems theory (Dare, 1979; Cooklin, 1979; Dare, 1979). A. C. R. Skynner, a group analyst who worked closely with Foulkes, has openly embraced systems theory, and has extensively developed an integrated model of family therapy which adheres closely to the Foulkesian spirit of group analysis (see, for example, Skynner, 1981, 1987).

The family group and the stranger group

If it can be postulated that the nature of the group determines the style and technique of the therapy, it will be apparent that the family, as an already established group, will require more vigorous interventions to bring about change than those generally associated with classical group analysis. The traditionally reflective, non-prescriptive, non-directive posture of the group-analytic conductor, appropriate for the slowly unfolding therapeutic context of the stranger group, is a formula for therapeutic failure in the face of the family, a group consisting of individuals with a deep mutual investment in one another which has grown organically over a long period of time prior to entry into therapy. In addition, family members have vastly different levels of maturation and development, and usually bring with them divergent attitudes towards the therapeutic process. Thus considerable technical problems would be set any group analyst determined to pursue, without modification, techniques applicable to the carefully composed, well-prepared group of *individuals* meeting together in an attitude of analytic contemplation. While the untempered analytic attitude is inappropriate for family work, it is perhaps true that some of the mechanistic techniques inspired by systems thinking can be leavened by exposure to group-analytic ways of thinking and working.

In essence, group analysts who intend to work with families have to adjust to a foreshortened time scale for the therapy. They have to be prepared to intervene in highly structured, directive ways without feeling that they are doing injury to the group-analytic ethos.

The family: a group with children and adults

The group analyst working with families is faced with the complication posed by the coexistence of children and adults in the same therapeutic setting. Family therapists need to have in mind a model of therapeutic communication which takes account of the different developmental stages of children, adolescents, and adults communicating within a fraught, often crisis-ridden context. This introduces yet another dimension of specialised practice involving an understanding of childhood language and logic, play and activity, and the ability to interpret and translate developmentally governed modes of communication into meaningful signals both within the family and to and from the therapist. The fact that group-analytic training is based almost entirely on experience with adults puts the onus on those whose primary training is as group analysts to acquire their skills in communicating with children along a different professional pathway.

The group analyst's capacity for using metaphor and symbolic language finds considerable application in a family therapy interview where small children interact through the medium of drawing, play, and the obligatory logic of childhood cognition.

The loneliness of the family therapist

The Foulkesian tenet that the conductor can for the most part entrust the task of therapy to the group-as-a-whole, does not apply to families. As Foulkes observed, the family, by its very nature, fails dismally to meet the criteria for selection which would apply to the composition of a well-balanced stranger group. Its organic growth over a period of years, fuelled by primitive affinities, could not provide a more striking contrast with the stranger group created "at a stroke" and whose individual members are carefully chosen and matched for complementary personality traits and a diversity of symptoms. Roles, which are relatively fixed in a family, have yet to be negotiated in a stranger group. The language and patterns of communication within the family accommodate to members at vastly different levels of maturation, while the language and patterns of communication within a stranger group confer on all the ability to give and take in equal measure, to analyse and be analysed, each to contribute his idiosyncratic style towards the enrichment of the group-as-a-whole.

With the stranger group providing its own social microcosm, the therapist can afford to be relatively unobtrusive. In the case of family therapy, the therapist, faced with a dysfunctional group, shoulders the responsibility of becoming the agent of social reality. Single-handedly, the therapist may hold up a mirror to the family, turning it this way and that, to reveal to the family their collective and individual identities. The therapist may of course make use of a therapeutic team to conduct a carefully planned programme of interventions designed to tilt or unbalance the family system. But the principle of a therapeutic sub-group consisting of professional or professionals, engaging with a family group which is essentially dysfunctional, underlines the point that it is the family therapist alone (or in consultation with the team) who in the first instance has to perform all the numerous tasks designed to achieve therapeutic change.

The "outsider" dynamic

An interesting perspective on the contrasting techniques of family and group therapy is obtained by looking at the group which is formed when the family is joined by a therapist. This new group, which might be called the "family therapy group" ("the therapeutic system", in systems parlance) provides a striking contrast with the stranger group, which is also strictly speaking a group of individuals who have been joined by a therapist. With this tilt of the lens it becomes apparent that the therapist within the family therapy group is much more conspicuously the outsider than the therapist joining the stranger group. Therefore, whether intuitively or by training, the family therapist mobilises techniques designed to counteract a group dynamic by which the group copes with an outsider. The stranger-group therapist grapples with the problem of retaining outsiders, retrieving potential drop-outs, and averting scapegoating situations. From the outset the stranger-group therapist works to create a climate in which outsider characteristics are minimised.

Group techniques for dealing with outsider dynamics

In a stranger group, all are in one sense outsiders. The therapist is one among several, and although he or she is somewhat distinguished by virtue of a known professional role, can afford to be far more leisurely in moving towards the other members of the group, since all are moving cautiously towards one another in their efforts to communicate. The therapist has also to be careful to avoid introducing to the group anyone who will conspicuously assume the role of an outsider, or group deviant. Such a person, who deviates from the rest of the group in any single characteristic, is at risk of dropping out or being excluded from the group, or becoming the group scapegoat.

The group analyst works constantly to discourage a scapegoating climate by encouraging the circulation and redistribution of "outsider" characteristics. That which is alien to the self is ultimately owned, contained, and shared by the group. The group analyst therefore works to instil an affirmative, supportive mode of communication in the group as a background against which more painful feelings and phantasies can be allowed to surface. Because of the extreme suggestibility of the stranger group, who look towards the therapist for cues on the shaping of the group culture, this task is relatively easy to achieve in a stranger group.

The therapist as "outsider" in the family therapy group

Engagement of whole families is more likely to occur when the outsider dynamic is constantly borne in mind. Techniques for dealing with the outsider dynamic are implicit in many family therapy approaches. They consist of either deliberately accentuating the role of the outsider, drawing a sharp divide between the "self" and "other" of the family therapy grouping, or rapidly diminishing the distance between the outsider and the rest of group (namely, the family itself). They often involve highly active strategies aimed at exchanging information between family members and the therapist, "joining" the family, overcoming mutual ignorance between family and therapist, and redefining problems in interpersonal language which includes the therapist.

The family therapist is at a disadvantage not only by virtue of the outsider status conferred on him by the group, but because of the timing and circumstances of his entry into the group. It is quite likely that the therapist will be encountering the group at a moment in its life when great stress, possibly crisis, is impinging on the group. In addition, the therapist is not only entering the group but also attempting to influence it significantly, to change its culture even, or to restructure it in a radical fashion. Looked at in stranger-group terms, the therapist is also asking that the group assemble at a time and venue of the therapist's choosing. The therapist is, moreover, the only member of the group who does not continue to participate in the life of the group between the therapeutic sessions.

In effect, the therapist is only too well placed at the outset to become the group scapegoat, and to suffer the fate of expulsion from the group, which of course in practice means that the family fails to engage or drops out of therapy.

Groups under stress tend also to adopt another solution to the problem of the outsider. They may invest them with tremendous power, lavish them with magical expectations, and adopt a correspondingly dependent, helpless, and compliant posture in relation to the outsider. The family therapist therefore sometimes finds himself coping with feelings of exceptional power within the family therapy group. The success of the therapeutic encounter largely depends on how the therapist divests himself of this power and uses it to imbue the family with its own power for change. All too often the family group swings from exaggerated attributions of power to a scapegoating mode.

The family therapist, unlike the stranger-group therapist, therefore finds himself buffeted by strong group pressures early on in the life of the therapeutic group. The techniques of family therapy can be regarded as having the implicit and explicit recognition of the need to compensate for these pressures. This is expressed, for example, in Minuchin's ideas on "joining" and "accommodation" (Minuchin, 1974; Minuchin & Fishman, 1981). The techniques of stranger-group therapy have evolved around the need to wait, in calmer waters, for the emergence of the inner world and its reflection in the group.

Group-analytic engagement of families

Bearing in mind the outsider dynamic, the race against time, the crisis atmosphere of many families presenting for therapy, and the complex arena of different developmental and motivational attitudes, the group analyst wishing to work with families is faced with a group where the usual techniques of stranger-group therapy are likely to be of little use. It is possible, nevertheless, to retain the group-analytic framework while accepting the need for a vastly modified set of techniques. In effect, the therapist has to reframe the therapeutic situation as an anxiety-laden group consisting of two sub-groups; the family itself and the therapist, or therapeutic sub-group.

Symptom formation in families

The unifying principle of group-analytic technique, regardless of the group, lies in the promotion of a network of communication to counteract the effects of isolation. In Foulkes' terms, isolation is synonymous with symptom formation. The one cannot occur without the other, and communication is the antidote to both. Group analysis rests on the belief that man is a social being. Disturbances which have arisen in social groupings such as the family, can be re-experienced in the therapeutic group and corrected through the process of communication. Through this participation in the group the individual is slowly helped to yield up his isolation. The symptomatic, incommunicable parts of the self are translated into communicable language, a process which in stranger groups may run to months and years.

Language is the key which unlocks the individual from his isolation. Each individual in the group, by talking and listening, contributes uniquely to the network of communication which springs up instantly at the beginning of the group. Each member helps to diminish the isolation of the others, yet each protects their own area of isolation, surrounding them with highly charged affective barriers. With the passage of time the areas of isolation are thrown into greater relief. The individual experiences an insistent pressure to find words with which to express their isolation.

Where isolation persists, a focus of irritation develops within the social group network. The therapeutic group is a contrivance to coax the individual into dialogue with the group about his isolation. Translated into families, the collective response of the family has been to nominate its own symptomatic area which may be lodged in an individual such as the child, or within a dysfunctional dyadic or multiperson relationship. It is as if the family is functioning with one mind, like an individual, while the therapist, paradoxically, has to function as if he were an entire group.

Since the family generally presents itself with its disturbance crystallised into a symptom located within one member, who is nominated by the family as the patient, the therapist is obliged to address the symptomatic area head-on without the luxury of a gradual development of the non-symptomatic context which characterises stranger-group therapy.

Families often hold a shared view of the whole child as the symptom, or they may see the symptom as residing within the child, such as a psychosomatic problem which renders the whole family dysfunctional. For example, the family may believe that a wetting or soiling problem-reflects a disturbance of bladder or bowel in isolation from any other aspect of the individual or his network. Families functioning at a more integrated level of communication may locate the problem within a relationship. An example of this might be a family which recognises that difficulties in the relationship between the parents are affecting the children and creating disturbance in other parts of the network. Some families are even able to acknowledge at the outset that the disturbance is located within the family network as a whole, and they are prepared to let the therapist join the network and to communicate with him as the person who can help the family to change their own pattern of relationship. Yet other families come into therapy with disturbance located within the family's relationship to the outside world. The boundary between the family and the wider network may be the focus of disturbance, and effective therapy may need to involve, as part of the minimum sufficient network, individuals or agencies (for example, a school) over whom the disturbance is dispersed (Skynner, 1971).

Unable to bypass the symptom, and remembering that each family is unique, the therapist attempts to identify the interpersonal ramifications of the symptom as quickly as possible. Without any group to assist him, and without a great deal of time before the "outsider" dynamic begins to drive him towards the periphery of the group and possibly exclude him, he has to identify the symptom and immediately begin the process of translating it into interpersonal language. Again, he does not have the support of the group here. At the same time he has to make himself known to the family so that before the end of the first session, the family's anxieties in relation to the therapeutic situation will have been reduced to a point where the family will return or at least accept the therapist's recommendation for alternative ways of helping them. The therapist functions as the host to the family, and observes social courtesies which serve to close the gap between himself and the family, reduce anxiety, and create a climate in which the family story can be told.

Successful engagement is likely if the therapist responds promptly to the multiplicity of cues which the family will be offering him through both verbal and non-verbal communications. Questions are readily answered and readily asked, exchange of information takes place at a rapid rate, and the therapist works swiftly to contain anxiety, and especially anxiety-driven activity on the part of children, by structuring the interview with words and objects. Silence in early family sessions, however empathically intended, is likely to be construed in a negative light, raising rather than lowering anxiety.

Family disturbance generally declares itself quite conspicuously at an early stage, and the therapist may need to provide a counterbalancing influence by drawing the family's attention to his awareness of their strengths and assets, as well as their obvious shortcomings.

Family members who have come reluctantly, without seeing themselves as involved in the disturbance, have to be acknowledged as important participants and helped towards an awareness of their own part in the family network. They may need to be helped to verbalise their resistance to coming, and to be shown that their own perception of events and relationships is valued. The therapist will have taken account of each family member's role within the family and will have attempted to engage each member individually before the end of the first session.

After exploring the symptom with its interpersonal ramifications, the therapist traces communication from the symptom to the emotionally charged interactions which generated it. This is a to-and-fro exercise which may lead periodically back to the symptom, but may, if the family is amenable, open up the way to a deeper understanding of the problem in a way which renders the symptom redundant. The group-analytic family therapist is comfortable exploring the past, using metaphor and analogy, interacting playfully with the family but at the same time being prepared to apply specialised strategies such as task setting, derived from systemic practice.

Adopting the symptom

By listening to the group, the therapist discovers that the symptom drifts towards him. In the first place, information about the symptom is automatically directed towards him. Whether in a chorus or a cacophony, the family demonstrates the symptom to the therapist. But the process goes beyond this. The therapist attracts not only the symptom but the feelings attached to it. He begins to experience, in the counter-transference, the missing dimension of the group which has led to symptom formation. To a greater or lesser extent the therapist may even take on the symptom, perhaps intentionally cultivating it in order to facilitate the process of change within the family. Skynner has drawn attention to the important therapeutic dynamic whereby the therapist intentionally becomes the group scapegoat, relieving the nominated scapegoat within the family of that role, and by virtue of the therapist's articulate authority and nurturing capacity, being able to reflect back to the family the meaning of their choice of scapegoat. Projections onto the therapist are thus redistributed onto the group-as-a-whole (Skynner, 1979).

Taking on the role of the scapegoat is only one way in which the family therapist adopts or absorbs the dysfunctional, symptomatic element of the family. Usually within a short space of time, the therapist accumulates a charge, so to speak, which until that moment has clustered around the symptomatic part of the family. He comes to acquire the symptom in a shared relationship with the symptomatic member or members of the family. By feeling the pressure to which the symptomatic member is subjected, the therapist forms a subtle alliance with that member and allows himself to be manoeuvred into the symptomatic relationship. The therapist may, for example, come to feel a sense of sadness in the midst of a lively discussion in which jokey denial is operating to keep depression at bay. As another example, the therapist may experience a sense of mischievous playfulness in a sombre, intense, or depressed family atmosphere. Often the therapist comes to experience himself as the container of anxiety, or the longed-for agent of control in an otherwise uncontained family system. Another frequent experience for the group-analytic family therapist is an ill-defined urge to "mother" or "father" the family or individuals within it. Feelings of perplexity, apathy, or anger may also gather in an aura around the therapist, who, by opening himself up to these feelings, completes the new therapeutic group and sets the stage for the process of translating the symptom out of its isolated state.

Mirroring and resonance as therapeutic instruments

An important therapeutic element in stranger groups is the mirroring function provided by the group (Pines, 1982). Individuals become aware of hidden aspects of themselves which they see reflected in other members. The group-as-a-whole may reflect back to the individual aspects of himself of which he was previously unaware. A sense of shared identity and commonality emerges with the passage of time. The family can be a grotesquely distorting mirror, reflecting ugly images, freezing images in time, imposing the features of the dead on those of the living, turning the young into the old, the old into the young, or, like a vampire, failing to reflect an image at all. The family may be collectively blind to many aspects of its own identity.

The therapist is, in a manner of speaking, the mirror to the family. For some families, particularly the isolated, emotionally blind family, the mirroring role is specially significant. The therapist may simply describe what he sees at first, deepening the communication later to reflect the deeper, hidden layers of meaning within the family communication network.

Resonance calls for the therapist to fall in with prevailing patterns of communication within the family in order to become accepted by the family. In stranger groups, each communication resonates at some level with the group matrix, opening up further opportunities to communicate at any of the levels (Roberts, 1984). In families, resonance occurs when the therapist mingles with the family in its style of language and expression, making it easier for any member of the family to express a hitherto unexpressed thought or feeling. The therapist sounds a note, as it were, which echoes through the family and triggers off other notes. Mirroring and resonance may have to be introduced quickly into the family as techniques of engagement, while in stranger groups they evolve slowly over many weeks and months, affecting all group members simultaneously.

From symptom to story

For many families the act of telling their story to a stranger is in itself therapeutic. Families often remark with gratitude on the unexpected benefits of talking for the first time about issues which have been harboured silently within the family, or displaced into symptom formation. The authority of the stranger who assembles the family and (in a manner of speaking) forces them to talk openly provides a significant impetus for change. Whether fluent or halting, strung out over weeks or months, or poured out in bursts over a short period of time, the tale of each family member unfolds in a climate of acceptance. Each story is listened to and responded to, perhaps with silence, but more often helped along by questions and reflections. Working with children and relatively inarticulate adults, the therapist frequently has to find words to put to the family which can be accepted or repudiated. Sometimes the therapist offers a tentative challenge, speaking first for one family member then for another, moving deftly between question and statement. The struggle to find words for the family's story is a therapeutic task in itself.

The family story is presented in many guises. For some it begins with the current relationship. With the help of the group a picture is built up, examined and turned around for the story-teller to reflect upon.

For others, the first chapter of the story lies in the past, a traumatic event, perhaps, or a phase of life. Again the therapist painstakingly assembles the picture, analyses it, and returns it to the family.

The therapeutic situation forces family members to listen to one another, perhaps for the first time. Parents listen in surprise to their children as they discover the unknown self of the child they thought they knew. Not uncommonly, parents are astonished to hear their child's piping voice announce fears and wishes previously unexpressed, reveal memories of events previously unacknowledged, display affections previously unrecognised, or confess to grievances previously unimagined by the rest of the family. Conversely, parents are sometimes able to tell each other, and their children, stories about themselves previously untold.

The therapist listens to the stories and occasionally translates them to other members of the family. The rendering of private thoughts into public communications is often accompanied by anxiety and painful feelings of grief. The therapist has to work sensitively with these feelings, sometimes speaking for the person, drawing comparable experiences from other members of the family, underlining the shared nature of the feelings evoked, and occasionally helping the speaker to remain silent, to contain the thoughts and feelings, or to express them in different language.

For some families the story-telling forum is enough for them to undergo considerable relief. These are families with relatively low levels of intrafamilial conflict, attempting to come to terms with traumatic events in the past, or attempting to integrate new members (for example, a step-parent or adopted child). In group-analytic terms these families may be regarded as having a well-developed group matrix, and a sensitive capacity to resonate to one another and mirror one another. The therapist merely provides the containing environment and gives permission to talk with appropriate affect.

Families in conflict

In a stranger group, conflict between group members occasionally flares up and gains expression through violent language in both form and content. The anxiety attached to these confrontations often discourages the group from talking openly, and although at the time there may be a sense of excitement or vicarious satisfaction from such exchanges, in the long run they tend to be counter-therapeutic unless immediately addressed as a problem for the whole group. Powerful expressions of affect erupting into the group have to be contained and moderated by the therapist. The group has to be assisted back into a working mode in order to examine the meaning of the conflict for the group-as-a-whole. The isolation of the protagonists is thereby diminished and the cohesion of the group protected.

In many families, conflict is uncontained and frequently discharged into action. The group-analytic family therapist envisages the therapeutic setting as a container, discouraging high anxiety states which drive family members impulsively towards either escape from the situation or attacking behaviour (so-called "fight-flight"* action). The therapist works to translate conflict behaviour into communicable language. He finds himself reformulating communications in more temperate language, identifying first with one, then another protagonist in the conflict, drawing the conflict towards himself. Sometimes he breaks up the family into therapeutic sub-groups, to work piecemeal with family members as a prelude to reuniting them.

Enmeshed families

The boundary around a group sometimes becomes so impermeable that very little communication flows between the group and the outside world. The sense of cohesiveness within the group gives way to an oppressively close, mutually interdependent network of relationships in which individual boundaries weaken and dissolve. The inner self is breached inappropriately, communication becomes highly charged with strong affects binding individuals to one another and limiting the capacity to think. The entire group becomes symptomatic, and in that sense, isolated. Primitive, repetitive patterns of communication prevail, devoid of mental imagery, and the task of the therapist is impeded by the deceptively facile use of language as a means of warding off incursions from the world outside the group.

In group-analytic terms, the therapist has to increase the flow of communication from the outside world into the group, and the reverse. For the time being he is the representative of the outside world and as such comes to experience the projections from the family of unwanted elements which are thought to threaten the integrity of the family. In practice, this means that the therapist is perceived as thoroughly alien, and powerful in a destructive way. To join with such a family the therapist has to introduce a modicum *of* structure into the communication system.

He may, for instance, adhere scrupulously to a model of addressing each member of the family in turn, thereby creating some degree of interpersonal distance between the family members. Interventions are likely to be presented as clearly understood or concrete tasks relating to the presenting problems and delivered with all the authority with which the family have imbued the therapist. Sooner or later individuals within the enmeshed family may have to be diverted into alternative therapeutic situations, such as individual or stranger-group therapy, to facilitate the process of separation and individuation.

Families with secrets

The deliberate withholding of information within a group, for fear of the destructive consequences of its disclosure, creates an area of isolation in the group which disturbs the network of communication. The isolated, or symptomatic, area becomes walled off by a barrier of tension across which thoughts and phantasies are projected. Individuals in a stranger group harbour secrets until the levels of tension accompanying them have dropped to a point where they feel safe enough to disclose the secrets. Again, this may take many months, or even years, during which time the individual becomes known and accepted in other aspects of himself. The disclosure of a secret and the attendant feelings of shame or guilt are compensated for by the understanding that all—communication in the group is shared. One member's shame or guilt becomes the whole group's shame or guilt.

In families, the pressure to disclose secrets is often more marked, with a greater sense of urgency. The price of disclosure is often greater, and the therapist may be faced with a silent, hostile, vigilant group of family members, prepared to resort to guile, subterfuge, and frank aggression to keep the secret from the therapist.

Under these circumstances the therapist becomes an unwanted member of the family therapy group. His best prospect for bringing about change lies in the formation of a bond with a sub-group within the family which lies outside the secret area. From this position he may be able to acknowledge to the family the fact that a secret exists. Subsequently, the family may be able to talk about the social repercussions of their secret, their fears of what disclosure would entail, and the imagined benefits of retaining secrecy. Once again, the therapist might have to aid the process by speaking for the family.

Families in crisis

Occasionally, a stranger group enters a crisis, but this is rare. The setting of a stranger group is scrupulously constructed in order to minimise the development of a crisis atmosphere. Sessions are carefully spaced at regular frequencies, with an open-ended time perspective, or a precisely determined end-point in mind. Individuals may from time to time be in crisis, but the group-as-a-whole, with its predictability and its capacity to absorb anxiety, usually manages to contain the crisis and slow down the interpersonal transactions which generated the crisis. Everything about a group-analytic stranger group militates against the kind of rapid change that makes up the substance of a crisis.

The family therapist, is, however, often faced with a family group in crisis. Entering the group and completing the missing dynamic, he experiences strong anxiety which impels him to act. He often has to expand the group, to bring in more members, other professionals from other agencies, for instance, to contain the anxiety and reduce it to a level where interpersonal communication can be expressed in words. Crisis work demands attention to the here-and-now of the group. Panic is reduced by putting words to the immediately present feelings. Only later can the group move into the past tense, or focus on the world outside the group.

Group-analytic family therapy: the nature of the beast

In group-analytic terms, both stranger-group therapy and family therapy take the individual on a journey from isolation to communication, from telling the story of the symptom to telling the story of its meanings. In both types of group the individual members listen to one another, helped along by the therapist and the setting. In both types of group the symptom and its affects are ultimately shared by the whole group, translated into communicable language and dispersed into the group matrix.

However, the strange paradox of the therapist of the family having to act as if he were a group, to perform the manifold tasks which in a stranger group he could leave to the group itself, imposes on the family therapist a pace and style which rests uncomfortably with the therapist schooled in stranger-group therapy. Family therapists can retain a group-analytic perspective alongside techniques derived from systems theory. This means that the therapist can step mentally in and out of the family and move between foreground and background of the group which the therapist has created, and of which he is potentially the most powerful and most vulnerable member.

It is perhaps premature to postulate a distinctive group-analytic section of family therapy. In so far as technique is concerned, group-analytic thinking, elaborated largely in stranger groups and larger social groups, is not sufficiently specialised to provide a specific repertoire of interventions in family therapy. Group-analytic family therapists must look for technical inspiration to those schools of family therapy informed by systems thinking. Conversely, the systemic therapies may have become too focused on technique at the expense of a broader perspective, and could be enriched by an infusion of the more analogical, analytic, and group-dynamic way of thinking which colours group-analytic theory and practice.

References

Cooklin, A. (1979). Psychoanalytic framework for a systemic approach. *Journal of Family Therapy, 1*: 153–165.

Dare, C. (1979). Psychoanalysis and systems in family therapy. *Journal of Family therapy, 1*: 137–152.

Foulkes, S. H. (1975). *Group-Analytic Psychotherapy—Methods and Principles.* London: Interface, Gordon & Breach; [reprinted Karnac, 1986].

Haley, J. (1976). *Problem-Solving Therapy.* San Francisco: Jossey-Bass.

Hoffman, L. (1981). *Foundations of Family Therapy.* New York: Basic Books.

Minuchin, S. (1974). *Families and Family Therapy.* London: Tavistock Publications.

Minuchin, S., & Fishman, C. (1981). *Family Therapy Techniques.* Cambridge, MA: Harvard University Press.

Palazzoli, M. S., Cecchin, G., Pratao, G., & Boscolo, L. (1978). *Paradox and Ccounter-Paradox.* New York: Jason Aronson.

Skynner, A. C. R. (1981). An open-systems, group-analytic approach to family therapy. In: A. S. Gurman & D. P. Kniskern (Eds.), *Handbook of Family Therapy.* New York: Brunner/Mazel.

Skynner, A. C. R. (1987). *Explorations with families: Group analysis and family therapy.* J. R. Schlapobersky (Ed.). London: Methuen.

CHAPTER THREE

Attachment theory and group analysis*

Mario Marrone

An outline of attachment theory

Attachment theory was first proposed to explain observations made in the course of research on maternal deprivation, but its subject of study has now widened considerably to include other issues in the fields of psychoanalysis, developmental and cognitive psychology, social psychology, psychopathology, and psychotherapy.

Attachment theory emerged in the context of psychoanalytic ideas and particularly of object relations theory. It was formulated by John Bowlby (Bowlby, 1969; Bowlby, 1973; Bowlby, 1980) (1907–1990), a British psychoanalyst. Attachment theory is the result of the convergence of psychoanalytic formulations with several important trends in the biological, psychological, and social sciences. It might be best described as "programmatic" and open-ended in the sense that it does not intend to be a tight system of propositions but a new paradigm. The aim of this paradigm is to create new areas of scientific insight within

*This chapter was previously published as: Marrone, M. (1994). Attachment theory and group analysis. In: *The Psyche and the Social World.*, (eds. D. Brown & L. Zinkin), pp. 146–162. Routledge: London.

a conceptual system rather than to replace the system completely. This new paradigm (attachment theory) expects to be assimilated into an old and wider theoretical system (psychoanalysis) on the assumption that the old system is capable of assimilating the new paradigm.

This new paradigm has six areas of application: (1) psychoanalytic meta-psychology; (2) psychoanalytic epistemology; (3) methodology of research in early social development; (4) psychopathology; (5) therapy; and (6) prophylaxis.

1. *In terms of psychoanalytic theory, it formulates a new meta-psychology.* Following Rapaport and Gill (1959), who have classified Freud's theory of drive, instinct, and motivation into five viewpoints (structural, genetic, adaptive, dynamic, and economic), Bowlby (1969) endorsed the first three viewpoints but replaced the dynamic and economic by a cybernetic model which contains new propositions about instinctive behaviour. Once the dynamic and economic viewpoints—together with traditional instinct theory—are abandoned, the use of terms and concepts rooted in them become redundant.
2. *In terms of psychoanalytic epistemology, this paradigm concerns itself with issues such as the object of psychoanalytic study and the nature and scientific status of psychoanalysis.* Bowlby proposed four fundamental ideas:

   (a) That any science is defined by its object of study and not by any particular ideology, theory, or method; therefore what defines psychoanalysis is its object of study and not any school of thought or any particular and exclusive method of collecting data;
   (b) That the objects of study of psychoanalysis as a science are the unconscious mental processes of the individual in a developmental and social context. In other words, the individual's system of unconscious processes that has been called "the inner world" *together with the interactions between the inner world and the environment (or social context)* are the object of study of psychoanalysis.
   (c) That, in psychoanalysis as in any other science, there can be various ways of acquiring information, not only that of treating a patient psychoanalytically. However productive any method may be, it is bound to have its limitations, while there is always a prospect that some other method may compensate for them. Therefore, there is no reason to exclude complementary methods of obtaining data, such as baby observation, observation of families as well as others derived from neighbouring disciplines

such as social psychology, ethology, developmental psychology, and so on. The object of psychoanalytic study can be regarded as a complex non-linear system. The analysis of this system may require multiple approaches and may not be expressed canonically. This is so because even the simplest of non-linear systems can behave in a complex dynamic way at any given time and the study of this behaviour cannot be effectively done with only one method.

(d) The epistemological problems of psychoanalysis can only be productively approached if the discipline is regarded as a natural science as opposed to a hermeneutics. Because Freud drew so much of his scientific inspiration from late-nineteenth-century biological thought, Bowlby felt justified in trying to find inspiration in contemporary biology and ethology. In 1980 he wrote:

> To accept that psychoanalysis should abandon its aim of becoming a natural science and instead should regard itself as a hermeneutic discipline has seemed to me to be not only a result of obsolete ideas about science but also a counsel of despair; because, in a hermeneutic discipline, there are no criteria by the application of which it is ever possible to resolve disagreement.

3. In terms of methodology of research in early social development, an enormous amount of work has been accomplished. Bowlby's work has generated an ever-expanding field of study. The list of contributors is too long to be mentioned here, although the name of Mary Ainsworth (Ainsworth, 1978) has a place as one of the most creative pioneers. Research guided by attachment theory is branching out in exciting new directions, including attachment issues across the life span, across generations, and across cultures. The central point here is the development of a set of methodological tools to investigate and assess how relationships are internalised and how these internalisations predict future outcomes.

In addition to the notion that attachment behaviour represents an independent, biologically based system that does not derive from sexuality or other sources, there are three important propositions which have been validated by empirical research:

(a) That the quality of primary attachment relationships depends on the degree of empathy and responsiveness of the caregiver (or parental figure) as it is subjectively experienced by the growing individual;

(b) That the quality of primary attachment relationships strongly influences early personality organisation, especially the child's concept of self and others (normally known as self and object representations or *internal working models*);

(c) The organisation of social behaviour is an ongoing process that depends on the interaction between the person's self and object representations and the individual's adaptive reactions to their interpersonal environment. Early experience is of basic importance because each successive adaptation is a product of the new situation and of development to that point (Sroufe, 1986).

4. *In terms of psychopathology, a variety of evidence also attests to the significance of attachment relationships.* Prospective studies inspired by Bowlby's original ideas suggest fundamental links between insecurity of early attachments, anxiety, and later psychopathology.
5. *In terms of therapy, the main task of the analytic process is seen as that of eliciting, integrating, and modifying internal working models of oneself and others.* This is an issue that we shall explore later.
6. *In terms of prophylaxis, accumulated knowledge about the trauma resulting from separation, insecurity, and lack of empathic responsiveness will help to prevent such ill effects.* Bowlby's 1951 report for the World Health Organisation, *Maternal Care and Mental Health*, served as a guideline for the organisation of paediatric in-patient care, social services policies, and educational systems in a good number of countries and institutions. Appreciation of the fact that optimal personality development depends on the continuity, nature, and quality of child care should make us aware that the improvement of these conditions (even if they may be difficult to achieve) have expectable positive outcomes.

John Bowlby

Bowlby began his psychoanalytic training when he was still a medical student. He had analysis with Joan Riviere and qualified in medicine in 1933. He worked for two years at the Maudsley Hospital and moved later to the London Child Guidance Clinic where he worked as a child psychiatrist until the outbreak of war. On the basis of case material that he saw in this clinic he wrote his paper "The influence of early environment in the development of neurosis and neurotic character" (1940).

He found that mothers of neurotic children tend to displace hostility originally related to their own parents onto their own children, and that these mothers may also attempt to satisfy previously unmet affectional needs by making inordinate and inappropriate demands on their own children. In this early chapter, Bowlby showed his concern with family interaction and intergenerational phenomena. Whereas in this chapter, Bowlby referred to the pathology of a mother–child relationship, in later chapters he showed increasing concern about the ill effects of early separation, loss, and deprivation of maternal care.

In 1944 he published his paper "Forty-four juvenile thieves", in which he suggested that the "affectionless character" was rooted in early deprivation. In this way, he offered a systematic alternative to the ideas of those analysts who, having been so intensively preoccupied with the individual's intra-psychic life and his world of unconscious phantasies, have shown little interest and belief in the patient's account of his real-past experiences.

Between 1946 and 1956 Bowlby dedicated a great deal of his time and energy to build the Department for Children and Parents of the Tavistock Clinic. His clinical experience confirmed his idea that continuity of maternal care is essential for the psychological well-being of young children. Research done by his associates Joyce and James Robertson supported this view.

Until the mid-fifties only one view of the nature and origin of affectional bonds was prevalent among psychoanalysts: the attachment between child and mother—it was said—develops because the child discovers that in order to reduce instinctual tension (for example his hunger), a maternal figure is necessary. According to this view, the child needs to be fed and gratified orally, but the specificity of his relationship with a single maternal figure was not sufficiently taken into account, let alone explained.

The work of some British object relations theorists, like Bion, recognised that the child's first contacts with his mother and other persons of his immediate environment have a special quality that has profound importance for his later development. But often too much emphasis was put on orality, and the relationship of the child not with mother as a whole human being (capable of all sorts of responses) but with her breast. This could be seen as an important meta-psychological problem.

At this point, Bowlby, through discussions with Robert Hinde and Julian Huxley, became interested in the contribution that ethological studies could make to resolve this theoretical problem. Studies on imprinting—and particularly filial imprinting—and its biological function (protection and survival) were relevant. Consequently, Bowlby thought that some parts of psychoanalytic theory could be rewritten in the light of ethological principles. He concluded that the child's tendency to form a strong and fundamental bond with a maternal figure is part of an archaic heritage whose function is species survival (protection from predators in the environment of evolutionary adaptedness) and that this tendency is independent from libidinal or sexual urges.

In 1958 Bowlby sketched the outline of a theory of attachment and introduced the term in his paper "The nature of the child's tie to his mother". In 1956 he began working on what was going to be his seminal work, *Attachment and Loss*, which appeared in three volumes in 1969, 1973, and 1980.

Throughout the 1960s Bowlby repeatedly convened the Tavistock Mother–Infant Interaction multidisciplinary seminars, whose participants included Mary Ainsworth, Robert Hinde, and many others, a group quite diverse in background and theoretical orientation. The first pieces of attachment-orientated research were engendered by these seminars and included Ainsworth's Baltimore study. In the 1970s research in mother-infant attachment began to accelerate, particularly in the United States, and many insights gained from these studies were incorporated into the general body of attachment theory.

Meanwhile, Bowlby continued to have a dialogue with clinicians and to think about the possible application of attachment theory to clinical work. Emanuel Peterfreund, an eminent psychoanalyst from New York, became very sympathetic to his ideas and was one of his good friends and interlocutors.

Although Bowlby was not a group analyst, he became interested in the theory and practice of group analysis through conversations with Liza Glenn and myself. In the early 1980s, I convened yearly series of seminars on the clinical applications of attachment theory and its position in the context of contemporary psychoanalytic thinking, which were held at the Institute of Group Analysis (London). Bowlby attended these seminars as main speaker or discussant of other people's presentations. These group discussions generated a great deal of interest and enthusiasm. Since then, attachment theory has been included in the curriculum of the Institute's Qualifying Course in Group Analysis.

Bowlby died quite suddenly of a stroke in September 1990, shortly after he published his last book *Charles Darwin: A Biography*, at a time in which, in spite of his advanced age, he was still working a few hours a week at the Tavistock Clinic and maintaining a high level of intellectual productivity.

Some key issues in attachment theory

One of the major features of attachment theory is the concept of a behavioural system. It assumes that there are several mental systems which lead to certain kinds of behaviour. Each one of these systems is designed to serve a particular biological function and has a particular set-goal. Feeding, sexual, affiliative, exploratory, and care-giving functions are served by respective behavioural systems. Any one of these systems can be activated in the presence of certain conditions. When the attachment system is activated, the individual needs to gain proximity or contact with a preferred individual, who is usually conceived as stronger, wiser, and/or better able to cope with life. The individual has formed with that preferred individual "an attachment", which is specific to that person and durable. Each individual has attachments with different persons but only in accordance with a scale of priorities (some persons are more important than others). Activating conditions of attachment are strangeness, hunger, fatigue, and anything frightening. We must make the distinction between "attachment behaviour"—which is an organised set of emotional, cognitive, and behavioural responses—and "attachment" itself, attachment as a bond.

Attachment behaviour interplays with exploratory behaviour: the first is related with seeking proximity to the person one is attached to, the second is related with trying to gain distance from that person in order to explore other areas of interest.

Sexual behaviour can be complementary to attachment behaviour but they are not the same thing. In maturity, a person may establish a specific relationship with somebody who is also the primordial object of sexual interest, yet, sexuality and attachment should be distinguished one from the other instead of being put together under the term "libidinal".

Attachment theorists assume that individuals, from infancy on, are capable of experiencing reality at a subjective, cognitive, and emotional level. Their experience suffers no distortion by virtue of wishes, phantasies, or defences, but only those made inevitable by immaturity. This contrasts with a predominant view in psychoanalysis that the most relevant subjective experiences of the infant are reality-distorting phantasies. However, attachment theorists do allow for the fact that reality is interpreted from a subjective perspective, but they understand this experience as the result of an interactional process whereby interpersonal communications can be misconstrued in its semantic meaning.

Developmental pathways

Early experiences of loss and deprivation on the one hand, a whole range of pathological patterns of relatedness and communication in the intact family on the other, can produce a deviation of psychological development from an optimal pathway in childhood and adolescence. The concept of developmental pathway was proposed by the biologist, C. H. Waddington (1957). Within this framework, human personality is conceived as a structure that develops along one or another of an array of possible pathways during all the years of immaturity from infancy to late adolescence. An important variable that determines the pathway an individual is taking at any given time of his development is the way his parental figures treat him. According to this view, pathology is not explained as the result of "fixation" or "regression" but as the outcome of the individual having taken a deviant pathway at some early stage.

Internal working models of self and others

A central point in attachment theory is the concept of *internal working model*, formulated by Bowlby (1969) and Peterfreund (1983). This is a concept that developed from two main sources: (1) the psychoanalytic notion of self and object representation, particularly as it was defined by Hartmann (1950) and Jacobson (1964) and (2) Piaget's (1954) theory of representation. Indeed, the concepts of internal working model and self and object representation are almost identical, although—in my view, as I shall explain below—the latter is a special type of the former. However, it seems that Bowlby formulated the concept of internal working model while being inspired by a book by Craik (1943), in which mental representations of external reality are seen as the base on which a repertoire of possible and quick adaptive reactions is organised. As Bretherton says,

> As a conceptual metaphor, the term "internal working model" has several advantages. First, the adjective "working" draws attention to the dynamic aspects of representation. By operating on mental models, an individual can generate interpretations of the present and evaluate alternative courses of future action. Second, the word "model" implies constructions, and hence development, with later, more complex working models coming to replace earlier and simpler versions.
>
> (Bretherton & Waters, 1985, pp. 74–79)

Working models are cognitive maps, representations, schemes, or scripts that an individual has about himself (as an unique bodily and psychic entity) and his environment. Such maps can be of all degrees of sophistication from elementary constructs to complex ones. A working model is a selected representation of whatever is mapped: aspects of a person, aspects of the world (anything that may be the object of knowledge or psychic representation). There is a complex set of notions or "concepts" about oneself, other people, and any other object of knowledge that the individual builds, stores, ascribes meaning to, and uses at various levels of consciousness or unconsciousness.[1] This set of notions acts as reference framework to organise responses to the world (that is to say, to organise adaptive behaviour).

Initial working models of something that was experienced in the past may mismatch what one is confronting in the current reality. In other circumstances, working models can be corrected or updated by experience. If a pre-existing model is to be used in a novel situation, and if this model does not fit with the reality of the new situation, one of two things may happen: (1) the new situation is perceived with distortions created by the pre-existing model, or (2) the new situation is perceived correctly and the pre-existing model is modified or "Fine-tuned" by experience (that is to say, by means of error-correcting feedback).

As Peter Freund (1983) puts it, from childhood to adulthood we understand the world through our constantly changing working models. We each interpret existing information in our own way, selecting and processing it to arrive at our particular view of the world, our individual "reality".

It is through those interpretations that information attains meaning. Our working models enable us to rearrange the world we know, imagine new contributions and possibilities, imagine how things would appear in different circumstances, predict the possible consequences of action to be taken. If this model is to be successfully used in novel situations, it must be extended imaginatively to cover potential realities as well as experienced ones. Thus, working models provide a platform to test and evaluate.

Internal working models are emotionally charged. In other words, there is an emotional component to the cognitive system. And this emotional charge is more marked in self and object representations, which are highly specific forms of working models.

The possibility of updating, correcting, integrating, and synthesising working models depends on the availability of these models to consciousness. Only if we are aware of their existence can we modify them. Representational models may remain unconscious for a variety of reasons, but one of these is the need to set defences against painful or unpleasant emotions associated with them.

When multiple models of a single attachment figure are operative, they are likely to differ in regard to their origin, their dominance, and the extent to which the subject is aware of them. A person may be in a particular mental state under the influence of a particular working model—whose influential position has been re-activated by a particular environmental trigger—without being aware of the existence of this working model and its dominance and without identifying the trigger that has reactivated it.

In terms of Bowlby's theory of defensive processes, incompatible models of attachment figures are understood as the product of incompatible interpretations of experience that may become defensively dissociated. Such dissociations are more likely to occur when the child cannot cope with viewing rejecting parents in an unfavourable light or when parents try to persuade the child that their rejecting behaviour is legitimate and justified (often inducing guilt if the child reacts) or even a particular form of loving. Defensive exclusion from consciousness of negative representations of parents may provide emotional relief but creates two sets of problems: (1) the person has to work with an inadequate model of reality, leading to inappropriate, perhaps even pathological, behaviour; and (2) because the model is defensively excluded from consciousness, it cannot be reconstructed or updated as a serviceable model should be.

Depending on the organisation, integration, and quality of self and object representations, the individual develops to a lesser or greater degree his capacities to form and sustain discriminatory attachments, to manifest warmth, concern, and empathy, to experience, contain, and tolerate ambivalence, to maintain a certain degree of emotional stability despite stresses in everyday life, to be able to be creative, resourceful, self-confident, and thoughtful in coping with and mastering the environment. Seen under this light, transference is one direct manifestation of self and object representations.

Group analysis and attachment theory

Group analysis and attachment theory share some essential principles. Foulkes, founder of group analysis in Britain, believed that the proper study of the individual is within his natural groups, particularly his family. He saw group analysis not only as a method of treatment but also as an ever-evolving theoretical body based on the confluence of psychoanalysis with sociology and other disciplines. The main concern of this theoretical body is the location of psychic functioning in a developmental and social context.

Group analysis makes use of psychoanalytic insights without being applied psychoanalysis. Group analysts have tried to integrate into their theoretical body ideas taken from different schools of psychoanalytic thought. If we examine the extensive literature on group analysis we realise that this discipline has never cut its umbilical cord from psychoanalysis. In other words, even if group analysis is a theoretical body with an identity of its own, still, its theoretical foundations depend to a large degree on psychoanalytic thinking. If we accept this fact, then our task is: (1) to incorporate meta-psychological and developmental concepts drawn from psychoanalysis, which are compatible with basic group-analytical principles; and (2) to apply to our work a way of clinical understanding that emanates from such a theoretical approach.

Group analysis and integration of working models

Once a small group of people gather together and begin to communicate and meet on a regular basis, one of the dominant phenomena that occur is that a new micro-social system is established. This new system is a place in which, inevitably, individuals' existing working models are used and brought to play. In this way, each group member presents different notions and ideas, different perceptions and ways of understanding the world. These are manifested implicitly or explicitly. These notions, ideas, and so on can refer to a wide range of themes, subjects, ideologies, and areas of knowledge.

The fact that these working models are brought for analysis in a group context can be very productive because the group provides richness of experience and, at the same time, many minds to think. For instance, as has been done in Argentina (Adamson et al., 1985), a group of architects can do this type of work in order to elicit the working models they use in their profession, working models related with styles, symbolisms, conceptions about structures and functions, and so forth. Consequently, the analysis of working models can facilitate the movement from hypothesis to thesis, from thesis to antithesis, from antithesis to synthesis.

In therapy (and more specifically, in terms of attachment theory), the main tasks of the group are to elicit and explore one type of working model: models of oneself and significant others (self and object representations). Since transference is a direct manifestation of self and object representations, a good part of the group analytic process consists of analysing transference as it occurs in the group context (Marrone, 1984).

A group analyst orientated by attachment theory has four main tasks to accomplish:

> *Task 1.* To increase (through analytic means) cohesiveness and a sense of affiliation in the group so that the group can become a secure base from which it is possible to explore the members' inner worlds.

In my experience, the sense of closeness and togetherness that makes the group feel like a secure base is most effectively achieved when the group members can relinquish their false self and get in contact with one another through their true self. I use here the metaphor formulated by Winnicott (1960) and adopted by Bowlby (1980) as a key point of attachment theory, which refers to the false self as a defensive armour that the individual builds in compliance with parents' expectations, which covers and denies access to the true self: the needy, authentic, and emotionally ridden core of oneself.

Task 2. To assist the group members in exploring their present circumstances: what situations they find themselves in, what role they play in creating these situations, how they choose people they form relationships with, how they respond to them, and what the consequences of their behaviour are. These explorations usually involve making correlations between the patient's possible behaviour outside the group and their behaviour as it can be seen in the group.

Task 3. To assist the group members in finding out how they interpret one another's behaviour (including the group analyst's behaviour) and explore their expectations about the quality of responses they expect to get.

Task 4. To assist the group members in making links between past and present and to consider how the internal working models they built in the past influence the way they behave, react, interpret responses, and forecast outcomes in the present, both in the group and outside it.

In order to do this the attachment theory-orientated group analyst used a technical device which Bowlby called "informed inquiry." The group analyst, being acquainted with the possible repertoire of pathogenic situations in childhood and adolescence, construes a set of hypotheses on which to guide his enquiries. Following the patient's own associative path, he may take certain opportunities given by the group and by each individual patient and ask certain questions about past events. In this way, he also offers a model that group members can use to mutually facilitate reliving and reviving experiences in the recent and remote past, focusing on a process leading to discovery and insight.

Placing the analytic work in a historical context is advantageous for two reasons: (1) it increases areas of awareness in terms of eliciting information about one's personal history which would be lost if the analytic interventions were otherwise only confined to the "here and now"; (2) it helps to provide a corrective emotional experience because when a patient talks about past events (particularly if they were painful and the patient can talk about them with emotion) the group tends to respond in an empathic, friendly, and supportive manner.

These questions are aimed at eliciting memories of attachment events and evaluations of experience in two contrasting forms: overall evaluation of experience, and specific biographical episodes. This is based on a piece of scientific knowledge. Bowlby (1980), using data provided by cognitive psychologists (Tulving, 1972), makes the distinction between "episodic storage" (storing information according to personal experiences, autobiographically), and "semantic storage" (storing it according to its meaning, its global appreciation, its contribution to personal knowledge).

Bowlby says:

> My reason for calling attention to the different types of storage and the consequent opportunities for cognitive and emotional conflict is that during therapeutic work it is not uncommon to uncover gross inconsistencies between the generalisations a patient makes about his parents and what is implied by some of the episodes he recalls of how they actually behaved and what they said on particular occasions.

After explaining this point in greater detail, Bowlby says that, similarly, it is not unusual to uncover gross inconsistencies between the generalised judgements a patient makes about himself and the picture we build up of how he commonly thinks, feels, and behaves on particular occasions. He adds:

> For these reasons it is often helpful for a patient to be encouraged to recall actual events in as much detail as he can, so that he can appraise afresh, with all the appropriate feeling, both what his own desires, feeling and behaviour may have been on each particular occasion and also what his parents' behaviour may have been. In so doing he has an opportunity to correct or modify images in semantic store that are found to be out of keeping with the evidence, historical and current.
>
> (Bowlby, 1980, pp. 61–63)

I have tested the effectiveness of this technical approach, in my own clinical experience as a group analyst and also in experiential workshops for trained psychotherapists who wish to gain a clearer understanding of attachment theory and its clinical applications. In these workshops, I initially ask the participants to pair off and apply to each other a version of the Adult Attachment Interview. This is the scheme of a moderately structured interview which includes features of both the high structured "questionnaire" and a much more open model of a This scheme was devised by Carol George, Nancy Kaplan, and Mary Main (March, 1985) of the Department of Psychology of California University in Berkeley, as an instrument of research about the organisation and origins of internal working models in cross-sections of the adult population. The interview contains questions which are asked in a set order. Specific probes are used when questions are not answered. The interviewing technique creates space for free association. In other words, the interviewer follows the associative path that is more evocative in reviving past experiences and in discovering unique and personal meaning.

In summary, the first questions concern issues such as the subject's early family situation and interpersonal network, deaths in the family, early separations and losses, and so on. There are also questions aimed at (1) eliciting the subject's overall evaluation of their relationships with parental figures and important others during all the years of immaturity and; (2) visualising the subject's conception of each individual parent's availability and responsiveness to care-eliciting communications. Next, there are questions regarding the subject's perception of changes in their relationship with their parents over the years, from childhood to the present. This may lead to considerations regarding changes across the life cycle, adolescent rebelliousness, reparation, and forgiveness. Finally, there is a set of questions about the subject's own children, their feelings and long-term expectations about them and their capacity to learn from experience—and use this learning for the benefit of the relationship with the child.

My own version of the Adult Attachment Interview is adapted to: (1) making it more congenial with a clinical interview; (2) applying it to teaching rather than research.

In my workshops, once each pair of participants has interviewed each other, we all come together as a group and have an unstructured group discussion to share, evaluate, and integrate the material that emerged in the first part of the session.

In these workshops, participants seem to be able to understand in both a cognitive and emotional level the following points:

1. One's whole attachment history, from birth to the present time (not just earliest events), is relevant to understand internal working models.

2. Some pathogenic patterns of interaction between parents and children tend to extend from early times throughout the whole duration of the relationship.
3. One's appraisal of one's attachment history is often organised according to a clear split between a "semantic" view of important relationships and "episodic" recollection of past events.
4. The episodic recollection of past events tends to evoke associated emotions in a way that semantic recollection does not.
5. Internal working models are formed in the course of episodes or scenes of one's life and can only be modified if these episodes and their related emotions are revived and relived.

Of course, what can be gained with trained psychotherapists in one intensive workshop is very different from what can be gained through years of psychotherapeutic work in an ongoing group. Any significant modification and integration of internal working models is part of an unfolding process which, in optimal conditions, takes place over several years in the context of a stable group.

Clinical implications

The group analyst who is informed by attachment theory still places their work in the general context of compatible ideas taken from group analysis and psychoanalysis. In their interventions they are inspired by a number of concepts and experiences which constitute a wide spectrum of working models which, it is hoped, they may have been able to integrate to an optimal degree. The group analyst focuses on a process leading to discovery through free-floating communication, following the associative path that is most evocative at any given moment. Yet, they use some opportunities, offered by the group, to investigate the attachment history of each group member and to offer a model of enquiry that members can apply to one another. This involves relating present experiences with past events, eliciting and comparing semantic and episodic memories, discovering unique and personal meanings, scanning for significant transference phenomena which are then placed in a historical developmental context, making links between cognitive findings and emotional contents.

Often a group session is initiated by a story that a patient gives, which normally consists of an account of their recent or present circumstances, perhaps an episode of every-day life that is charged with anxiety. This anxiety is a manifestation of conflict. As the group session develops, other patients react to this story in many different ways. This interaction becomes a scene of the group life that necessarily involves transference phenomena. Members unconsciously take one another, the conductor, and the group-as-a-whole as transference figures.

The group analyst pays attention to the story the patient is telling the group and its possible significance for understanding the patient's representational models, ways of relating, and conflicts. He may detect anxiety and/or defences against it (which may take the form of denial, projection, and so on). He may try to elicit transference phenomena. He may also try to define the present group scene as a manifestation of a "latent scene", a scene that belongs to the realm of memory and hence belongs to the past. In making this sort of scrutiny, the group analyst can indeed formulate a hypothesis regarding the nature of the anxiety that those patients who are actively involved in communication in the group may be manifesting; the transference situation that reactivates this anxiety and the pattern of parent-child relationship that may have given rise to this type of transference reaction.

If the group analyst believes that the timing of his intervention is appropriate, he proceeds as follows: first, he assists the patient to recognise the presence of excessive anxiety (or anxiety-ridden feelings) and—if pertinent—the operation of defence mechanisms. Second, he draws the patient's attention to the fact that the present situation that the patient is describing, or is involved in, does not warrant such an amount of anxiety. Third, he explains that, in fact, the present or recent situation only reactivates an anxiety that—because of its intensity—is likely to belong to the past. From that, the group analyst may suggest that this anxiety may have been induced by a particular type of early parent–child interaction and can help the patient to reconstruct pieces of their attachment history.

Often, once the anxiety or anxiety-ridden feeling has been recognised in the here-and-now, the analyst needs do no more than ask, "Is this feeling familiar to you? Have you experienced it before?" in order to elicit a relevant response. If the patient is open to further explorations, the group analyst may try to bring to the surface episodic memories and their associated affects.

While all this is going on, other group members may help the group analyst or even take the lead to advance the analytic process. When a group member is able to recall painful episodes of his life together with the emotions linked to them, other group members—by way of a mechanism that Foulkes called "resonance"—recapture similar experiences of their own lives and/or develop insight into the nature of their anxieties and defences. When pain and tears are shown and shared, one can say that group members, instead of relating with one another through their "false selves" are now relating through their "true selves".

They are discovering and acknowledging their pain, their despair, their neediness, their sense of vulnerability. They discover that they can fruitfully use one another and the group experience. Consequently, a sense of cohesiveness develops. Attachments between group members consolidate, and members are more prepared to extend their membership over a long period of time, as long as necessary, in order to reorganise their internal working models to a more satisfactory degree.

Note

1. Pichon Riviere (1977), in Argentina, quite independently, formulated a very similar concept, ECRO, which in Spanish stands for "conceptual, referential and operative scheme". This concept is well known in the Spanish-speaking world and has been applied to group therapy and learning in groups.

References

Adamson, G., Martinez, B. C., & Sarquis, J. A. (1985). Creatividad en Arquitectura desde el Psicoanalisis, Buenos Aires, Paidos.

Ainsworth, M. (1978). *Patterns of Attachment: A Psychological Study of the Strange Situation* Hillsdale, NJ: Erlbaum.

Bowlby, J. (1940). The influence of early environment in the development of neurosis and neurotic character. *International Journal of Psycho-analysis, 21*: 154–78.

Bowlby, J. (1951). *Maternal care and mental health,* Geneva, World Health Organisation.

Bowlby, J. (1969). *Attachment and Loss. Volume 1: Attachment.* Harmondsworth, Penguin Books (1971).

Bowlby, J. (1973). *Attachment and Loss. Volume 2: Separation: Anxiety and Anger.* Harmondsworth: Penguin Books (1975).

Bowlby, J. (1980). *Attachment and Loss. Volume 3: Loss: Sadness and Depression.* Harmondsworth: Penguin Books (1981).

Bowlby, J. (1990). *Charles Darwin: A Biography*, London, Hutchinson.

Bretherton, I., & Waters, E. (1985). Growing Points in Attachment Theory and Research, Chicago, Monographs of the Society for Research in Child Development, Serial Number 209, Vol. 50, Nos 1–2.

Craik, K. (1943). *The Nature of Explanation*, Cambridge, Cambridge University Press.

Geroge, C., Kaplan, N., & Main, M. (1985). *The Adult Attachment Interview*. Manuscript from the authors given by Dr Bowlby.

Jacobson, E. (1964). *The Self and the Object World*. New York. International University Press.

Hartman, H. (1958). Comments on the Psychoanalytic theory of the ego; psychoanalytic Study of the Child. 5; 74–96.

Peterfreund, E. (1983). *The Process of Psychoanalytic Therapy*. Hillsdale, NJ. The Analytic Press.

Piaget, J. (1954). *The Construcction of Reality in the Child*. New York: Basic Books.

Rapaport, D., & Gill, M. M. (1959). The points of view and assumptions of metapsychology. *International Journal of Psycho-Analysis, 40*: 153–162.

Sroufe, L. A. (1986). Appraisal: Bowlby's contribution to psychoanalytic theory and developmental psychology; Attachment: Separation: Loss. *Journal of Child Psychology and Psychiatry, 27*(6): 841–849.

Tulving, E. (1972). Episodic and Semantic Memory in E. Tulving and W. Donaldson (eds.) *Organisation of Memory*, New York, Academic Press.

Waddington, C. H. (1957). The Strategy of the Genes, London, Allen and Unwin.

Winnicott, D. W. (1960). Ego distortions in terms of true and false self, reprinted in D. W. Winnicott (1965), *The Maturational Process and the Facilitating Environment*, London, Hogarth Press, pp. 140–154.

CHAPTER FOUR

Group analysis with early adolescents: some clinical issues*

Harold L. Behr

Adolescence is a developmental crisis during which a rapid, dramatic and sometimes convulsive transformation of the self occurs. The adolescent is buffeted by change both from within and without. To compensate for this, like a person walking in a high wind, he takes up exaggerated postures to prevent his newly emergent self from being blown away. Adolescence may be thought of as the Age of Extremism, of extreme identifications, massive denial, polarised thinking, and testing of boundaries. By the same token it is also a period of great fragility, sensitivity to stress and hyperactivity. The Latin "adolescere" means "to blossom" or "bud." The metaphor, therefore, of a delicate plant opening its leaves to the elements, is useful when considering psychotherapy for the adolescent. The emphasis should be on creating a climate within which the adolescent's tentative excursions into the surroundings can be encouraged, and his swift recoils accepted as part of the process of growth and exploration.

In group-analytic psychotherapy, the conductor of an adolescent group exercises a dual function, just as he does with an adult group. First, he

*This chapter was previously published as: Behr, H. (1988). Group analysis with early adolescents: Some clinical issues. *Group Analysis*, *21*: 119–131.

becomes the dynamic administrator for the group, taking responsibility for everything to do with the provision and maintenance of the therapeutic setting, providing the props, both in time and space, as the dynamic template around which the group matrix organises itself and monitoring the flow of communication into and out of the group. Second, he is the group analyst, working within the sessions themselves like any other group member, but with a special, trained awareness of the group as a whole and the activity around the boundary of the group.

The main differences between an adolescent group-analytic group and an adult one can be stated as follows: dynamic administration plays a much more prominent part in adolescent groups, boundary activities (or boundary incidents) impinge more strongly on the group process, and the style and pace of communication reflect that of the adolescent membership, namely rapidly changing themes, volatile moods, evanescent thinking and a tendency towards action.

The boundary in an adolescent group

The whole of adolescence may be characterised as a boundary state which demarcates childhood from young adulthood. Consequently all the phenomena associated with boundary formation and dissolution can be expected to replicate themselves in adolescent groups: projection across rigid boundaries; splitting; denial; testing of limits; anxiety over loss of identity; confusion; and bewildering changes in presentation of the self-reflecting changes in self-image and in the body's own physical boundaries. The adolescent has to let go of the family and cross the boundary which separates him from the outside world. The image of the idealised parent is dismantled and new objects of identification are incorporated from the outside world. This process may at best be gradual, through oscillation across the family boundary, or it may be sudden, massive and violent, leaving the devastated adolescent to form powerful attachments to alternative parent figures in the guise of other adults, peer groups or partners. When adolescents gather in groups the group boundary comes under immediate scrutiny and assault, and this is particularly apparent in therapeutic groups for young adolescents, groups which are likely to have been convened in an alien environment chosen by the adult-authority-figure therapist and at a particular moment in the adolescent's life of great stress, namely during the formation of a symptom within the system of which the adolescent is a part.

Concern with the group boundary shows itself in a number of ways:

(a) "Dropping-In" and "Dropping-Out". It is not unusual for sessions to be interrupted by passage in and out of the room by one or more group members exercising the well-known childhood prerogative of visiting the toilet, retrieving a schoolbag from the waiting room, or exiting for a drink or a "smoke." This crossing and recrossing of the room boundary during the actual session can generally be curtailed quite easily by a simple injunction, bearing in mind that the anxiety which prompts such activity has to be addressed in due course.

A variation on this theme is the tendency to interfere with the time boundaries of the group. For example, late-coming and early departure for a host of plausible reasons are much more in evidence than in adult groups. The very early arrival for the group is also quite common. In passing it may be noted that adolescents, when they have invested the group with their emotional energy (which they do very quickly if it is to happen at all), tend to invest the whole building and agency with similar energy, so that a proprietorial air is assumed and the waiting-room and other public parts of the building are annexed to the group room. Therefore early arrivals for the group and tardy departures from it carry the hazard of providing opportunities for acting out what should rightfully be expressed in the group. Not only the territory within the agency but familiar members of staff may be inveigled into this process. I generally keep a watchful eye on early arrivals and late departures, stretching the boundary of the group to the point where I escort the departing gaggle off the premises.

"Stuttering" attendance is another boundary phenomenon characteristic of early adolescent groups. Unexplained absence for one or more sessions is unexpectedly followed by sudden reappearance in the group. The therapist has to work quite energetically to counteract these drop-in and drop-out patterns by striving to make the group safe enough and attractive enough to provide the incentive for regular participation.

Repeated experience of having the time boundaries of the group tampered with by the young adolescent members has led me towards the model of running closed groups rather than slow-open groups. The model I have evolved is of running blocks of eight to ten weekly sessions three times a year, corresponding roughly with the school terms. Towards the end of each block, in the process of working through the ending, I make it clear that there will be a place in the next block for anyone in the current group who wishes to commit himself or herself to a further block of sessions. This gives those leaving the group a chance to do so properly, with a sense of completion and success, while it affords those who need continuing group therapy an opportunity to make a further decision about renewal and further commitment, to a "new" group. The incentive to regular attendance is therefore much greater because of the limited timespan, and this is also an important factor in working with the crisis mentality which adolescence by its very nature imposes on the young person.

I have also, over the years, reduced the timespan of the sessions from one-and-a-half hours to one hour for groups of very young, immature adolescents with strong acting-out proclivities. Groups of older adolescents can sustain one-and-a-quarter to one-and-a-half hour sessions, of course keeping the time constant for any particular block.

(b) Bringing Parts of the Outside World into the Group. Of the many vexing boundary problems posed by adolescent groups, I find that the one calling for the most skilful technical acrobatics is the tendency which adolescents have to react fervently with objects (both animate and inanimate) to which they form an intense attachment, as if part of themselves, however fleeting in time this attachment may be. This phenomenon can also be seen as an attempt to introduce structure and stability into an otherwise unpredictable and chaotic world. Nevertheless it presents a number of difficulties to the group conductor, who has to make decisions as to whether a particular appendage or part-object is likely, through its presence in the group, to hinder or help the therapeutic process.

A few examples are apposite: It is quite common for a group member, having sniffed out the group as a congenial place to be, to arrive at a subsequent session with his or her best friend in tow, eager for that young person to join the group as well, forthwith and without any of the preliminaries that graced the legitimate group member's entry into the group. I have, in the past, with slow-open groups, conceded with the group's consent that the visitor could sit in for one session, but would thereafter have to go through the process of referral, family assessment and parental consent if he or she were to join the group on a regular basis. The benefits are sometimes to be seen in the way in which the group member and his or her "auxiliary ego" together help the group member to become more integrated into the group. Difficulties arise, however, in relation to confidentiality issues, disturbance of a prevailing culture of trust and intimacy and the complication of seeing a young person in a therapeutic context without parental consent. Self-selected peer group therapy is a distinctive approach to adolescent group work, but falls outside the scope of discussion of the carefully composed and balanced "stranger" groups referred to here.

A less problematic instance of bringing another familiar person into the therapy group is that of an adolescent, usually timid, phobic, or withdrawn, who will not enter the group unless accompanied to the clinic by his or her mother, or who balks at the notion of facing the group alone. An invitation to the mother to be present at the first group session provides sufficient impetus for the boy or girl to attend. I have been interested to observe how a delighted mother will enter into the group interaction with zest, clearly gaining vicarious satisfaction from her short-lived membership, and incidentally, of course, surveying the group and the therapist in an over-protective fashion before relinquishing her hold on the youngster and passing him or her over to the group. Adolescents can be wonderfully accepting in the sheltered atmosphere of the group, and the parent-member is greeted with respect and understanding. Such grafts onto the group of children with marked separation-anxiety generally take well. As discussed later, the parent has to be worked with in parallel, in a different therapeutic context, if change is to be sustained.

By far the majority of transitional objects brought into the group from the outside are, however, of the inanimate variety. Group members frequently stagger in with school cases, carrier bags and assorted containers from which food, drink, books, magazines, cassettes, radios and the paraphernalia of school may appear to be used in a multiplicity of ways to impede and facilitate communication within the group. A shy girl hides behind a comic; a boy boastfully brandishes a flick-knife; another boy offers around a packet of sweets which he has "nicked"; another boy slowly and surreptitiously turns up the volume of his transistor radio; girls examine each other's bracelets, unfolding newly bought clothes, and so on. On one occasion an incontinent, out-of-control puppy dominated the session, providing a source of rich associations for the group, especially for its shy, over-controlled owner.

The dilemma for the therapist lies in how far to sanction these objects as a means of broadening and deepening communication within the group for members who may need such concrete manifestations of their inner world in order to express themselves, or to restrict their usage as defensive and an interference in the group process.

(c) The Boundary between Talking and Action. The constant swing between childish, regressed modes of behaviour and startlingly adult communications taxes the therapist's versatility to the full. The problem is how to provide a structure which is at once containing and limit-setting. What one group member may experience as persecuting in its restriction, another group member may experience as alarmingly permissive. As part of the preparation for joining the group I enunciate quite explicitly a number of "rules": there can be no hitting, punching, kicking or similar violations of body space; it is expected that they will all remain in their chairs for the duration of the session, and there must be no interference with any of the property in the room; smoking is not allowed.

The degree to which these negative injunctions are emphasised depends largely upon the young person's known patterns of disturbance. Timid, phobic youngsters are often relieved to hear these prohibitions spelt out and realise that a climate of disruption is unlikely to exist in the group. Preparation also includes positive injunctions to the effect that anything may be talked about and that one of the purposes of the group is to be able to talk about matters which cannot easily be talked about elsewhere.

Confidentiality is emphasised too, especially as two or three members of the group, perhaps even the whole group, are likely to come from the same neighbourhood and there may even be group members attending the same school. In a service with a restricted catchment area it is a counsel of perfection to advise selection which avoids these problems. In my experience respectful confidentiality is earnestly granted by the group members. Less easy to achieve is the constraint on extra-group socialisation. The hyper-reactive nature of adolescents leads to clustering before and after the group. Part of the work of the therapy is to bring these pre- and post-group encounters into the sessions themselves.

Despite injunctions to respect one another's individual boundaries, the impetus towards minor activity is great, especially when anxiety is running high. Objects are frequently thrown, snatched and bandied about. Fellow group members are sometimes playfully hit, pinched, stroked, embraced, or displaced from their chairs. Here the group conductor has to intervene in a way that is seldom called for in adult groups: he has to say "No!", "Stop!", or issue similar mutative remarks designed to restore the group to a working mode. At the back of his mind is an attempt to understand the underlying anxiety and steer the group swiftly towards a discussion of it.

(d) Testing the Therapist's Boundaries. The therapist of an adolescent group is probed by forays not only against the group's boundary but against his own individual boundary in a manner which unlike most adult groups can be blatant, crude and disconcerting. It is usual for the group members to throw searching personal questions at the therapist. The therapist may, for instance, have to face an interrogation about his marital and parental status, sex life, childhood, attitudes towards various social and political issues of the day, professional motivation and so on. The way in which these emotionally charged enquiries are dealt with by the therapist will be an important determinant of the therapeutic culture. My own inclination is to veer towards being more self-disclosing than in an adult group but never to transgress the bounds of personal comfort. I assume that the group-analytic process is enhanced by the modelling factor of the therapist as a self-disclosing person and by the need to reduce the distance between a sub-group of twelve- to fifteen-year-olds on the one hand and an adult on the other. Naturally the questions, whether answered or not, are reflected back to the group at some point in the search for meaning which is as much a part of an adolescent group as it is of an adult group.

(e) Teasing as a Boundary Phenomenon. Teasing is a common, I would say almost invariable, feature of adolescent groups and the degree to which it exists is an important indicator of the group's anxieties about its own boundary. By its very nature teasing is an exquisitely ambivalent communication. The teaser is beckoning the one who is teased to come closer and at the same time to keep away. In its most benign manifestation, teasing can be affectionate, gentle and playful, a means of coaxing someone who is slightly outside the group to become more involved. Teasing can however assume an aggressive, sadistic quality in which the one who is teased becomes a victim and may be driven out of the group.

Once again, the therapist walks a tightrope between allowing some teasing to take place through playful interaction and discouraging the brand of teasing which passes over into tormenting, bullying, sado-masochistic types of interaction. A group in a teasing mode is also incapable of experiencing sadness and may be resorting to persistent teasing as a means of avoiding more painful emotions. As with adult groups, I strive to compose my adolescent groups in such a fashion as to avoid including any one person who in a particular characteristic is significantly different from the rest of the group. When teasing does arise persistently it is a message to the therapist that the teased person has come to represent something vulnerable to the group at that moment in time which the group is attempting to incorporate or exclude. Unless this can be more explicitly worked on the group is likely to remain uneasily stuck.

The language of the group

Early on in the life of the group, the members discover that modes of expression which are normally reserved for the peer group are accepted by the therapist as currency for the group. This often paves the way for the release of traumatic and vivid material into the group as its young members tell story after story of dreadful, personal and family events which have imprinted themselves on impressionable childhood minds. Very little so-called "analysis" is necessary during this phase of group activity. The earnest recounting of a personal story to a group of peers ever ready to respond spontaneously with anecdotes of their own or to express genuine sympathy, horror or indignation is sufficient to relieve tension, create an atmosphere of trust and allow the group to move on to a more confrontative or interpretative mode of communication.

Adolescent groups also frequently trade experiences of terrible happenings in the world at large, culled from the media and exchanged in a garbled, distorted fashion, which provides numerous opportunities for tempered therapeutic interventions on the part of the conductor. Thus stories of gruesome events reported on television, mugging, murder, rape and incest are readily introduced into the group, sometimes with a sense of urgency like the telling of a nightmare, and can immediately be related to personal fantasies and experiences just as one might work with dreams in an adult group.

Curiosity about major life events, birth, death, procreation, physical and mental illness, is often woven into highly charged personal accounts of such experiences within the family. The therapist of an adolescent group may find himself yielding to the impulse to provide factual answers to questions about such events, or correcting distorted ideas about them, in addition to encouraging the exploration of their significance in personal and group terms. In other words the therapist may at times assume an educational role, as well as an analytic one.

Adolescent groups are also quick to take refuge in the jargon of their subculture, in slang and in bad language. This may be a device to exclude the therapist or challenge him. I find it necessary to convey repeatedly to the group that I am as much a member of the group as anyone else and that therefore I demand to know the meaning of any unfamiliar expressions or phrases in use in the group at a level of simple translation or explanation. This puts me momentarily in the position of the ignoramus to whom things have to be explained and incidentally mobilises competent, caring responses from the other group members. Paradoxically it also underlines the difference between them and me and helps to retain the group in a working mode. Obscenities, bad language and so on are, like teasing, both a help and a hindrance to therapy. They can be used as a form of verbal violence and then have to be treated as such. At other times they break new ground by enabling relatively inarticulate members to enter the group and be accepted. I sometimes freeze the action by focusing on an obscenity, trying to understand its meaning in the context of the conversation and stimulating a discussion on the feelings aroused by its usage. This often leads to fruitful exploration of sexual and aggressive scenes which the therapist and group members alike can approach in a spirit of collaboration rather than confrontation. I do not believe that the therapist should resort to expressing himself in adolescent-type language in order to become more like the rest of the group. Rather, he should clearly define in what way he is different to the other members of the group and even introduce his own adult terminology as a token of respect for the group's ability to accept him as a person in his own right.

The same style of intervention, is appropriate to another phenomenon which occurs repeatedly in adolescent groups: joke-telling. Along with bantering remarks, puns, witticisms, wisecracks and other efforts at clowning, these sometimes primitive, sometimes polished attempts at communication deserve to be valued and held up to scrutiny in the group on the assumption that they provide excellent clues to the nature of the anxiety that underlies them, as well as opening up risky subjects for discussion by first peddling them in the form of jokes. Sexual, racial and cultural prejudices may come into the group by this means and the jokey atmosphere can rapidly be brought towards a serious level of communication by the therapist's insistence on examining facets of the joke in both content and form. Naturally a genuinely funny and innocuous joke deserves to be laughed at even by the therapist.

Sub-groupings

The therapist should intervene promptly to break up sub-groups both within and outside the sessions which are likely to exclude others. Secret exchanges, whispering, passing notes, getting into a huddle, anxious giggling, signalling and so on call for immediate exposure and enquiry into the nature of the underlying resistance. The therapist may be quick to align himself with the excluded party, thereby putting pressure on the conspirators to translate their communication into words that can be shared and understood by the whole group.

The pace of an adolescent group

Adolescent groups tend to move either very quickly or very slowly. In either instance the therapist has to moderate the pace in order to stay with the group. Where a group is moving with great rapidity, the therapist should feel entitled to slow it down so that the group is not flooded with material in manic style. Tracking techniques similar to those used in family therapy can be usefully adopted here. The therapist may repeat or rephrase what somebody has said, ponder its meaning, interrupt a manic exchange, question group members about the meaning of what has been said and attempt in his own ponderous way to clarify communication, often to the relief of group members who are being swept along by the tide of argument, banter, or chaotic, disjointed exchanges. For example, one girl throws out a remark that she intends to visit her sick grandmother that evening. Another girl cuts across this and asks a third girl which disco she plans to go to the same evening. Therapist [instantly intervening]: "Just a moment. I don't quite see the connection between Sue visiting her sick grandmother and you lot going to a disco." Another group member: "Well her grandmother's not going to go to any more discos is she?" (The conversation then turns to a depressed speculation that you have to make the most out of life while you can and avoid contact with sick, elderly people. Sue's feeling of responsibility towards her grandmother becomes a focus and the prevailing feeling is of anger towards sick, elderly relatives and the demands that they make.)

A very slow group may arise when the majority of members are passive, under-stimulated and emotionally inert. Adolescent groups often express a powerful wish for structure by demanding topics, entertainment and stimulation of one sort or another. Once again the therapist may provide a corrective experience by techniques which will warm the group up and stimulate communication. Questioning group members in turn without dwelling for too long on any one member helps the group out of its lethargy and passivity. Questions may be designed to provoke fantasy-thinking, along the lines of "What do you think would happen if your parents (teacher/favoured sports hero/film star) were to come into this group?" The coupling of a fantasy figure from an outside world with the here-and-now of the group is a powerful means of galvanising the group into creative and metaphorical thinking. Another technique when a group has slipped into a passive, regressive mode is to call upon group members to observe or describe their fellow group members ("What do you notice about David this morning?"). When someone timidly volunteers personal information, for example reporting a minor ailment, the passive group can be stimulated by questioning others in turn about their own minor ailments. In a short space of time a remarkable diversity of conditions can be assembled, which rapidly leads to relationship issues both inside and outside the group.

The therapist therefore constantly functions as a counter-balancer within the group, slowing it down or speeding it up to ensure that he remains an integral part of the group and that communication can deepen as well as broaden.

Co-therapy

Adolescent groups inspire a model of co-therapy for a number of reasons. Constant challenges to the boundary of the group are more easily contained by more than one therapist. Also, the model of two adult therapists in good communication with each other is a salutary one, and if it is possible to have a man and a woman as therapists then there is the opportunity to work through parent and couple-type relationships more easily. A simple, pragmatic reason for having co-therapists is that issues of dynamic administration in adolescent groups, involving as they do communication with schools, Social Services, other professional staff and the parents, are more effectively dealt with by two therapists. That having been said, it is possible to run an adolescent group single-handed, although in my experience this puts more pressure on the therapist for the reasons just stated.

Single-sex groups or mixed-sex groups?

In the twelve-to-fifteen age-range it is possible to run both types of group successfully. However, a mixed-sex group has to be carefully balanced with young people at similar levels of maturation. In my experience initial anxiety in mixed-sex groups is much higher than in single-sex groups, calling for the therapist to intervene more radically to bring down levels of anxiety to the point where a good working culture can be achieved. Nervous sexual banter, boisterous interchanges and conspiratorial sub-groupings impede the development of the group and can lead to drop-outs unless swiftly curbed. If the initial anxiety can be allayed, a mixed-sex group provides a good forum for examining and rehearsing male/female relationships, as well as activating sibling and parent transferences. Same-sex groups provide different opportunities, and in my experience they cohese more rapidly and regress more easily.

The wider network

Therapeutic groups with twelve- to fifteen-year-olds inevitably involve an interplay with families, schools, Social Services and other professionals and agencies. The therapist has to be mindful of the importance of maintaining good liaison with those who come into close contact with the adolescent. The group therapy has to be supported and there should be an understanding that there may be times when material introduced into the group may have to be shared outside it. The therapist's hands should never be tied by the constraints of confidentiality to the point of blackmail. What matters is not so much the disclosure of material from within the group but whether trust can be maintained. Sometimes a secret is brought into the group in the hope that the therapist will act as "go-between." The therapist should be in touch with other members of the team who are involved with the young person's family and this should be understood by all the members of the group. In practice, the occasion for disclosing material from the sessions hardly ever arises provided the therapist is able to represent the adolescent in broad terms to the family and other appropriate professionals.

Family therapy or therapy with parents may proceed in tandem with the group therapy. If this does not happen there is a serious likelihood that treatment will be undermined by an unyielding family system working against therapeutic change of the symptomatic part of it.

Conclusion

In some respects adolescent groups resemble groups of adult borderline patients. They call for a highly structured setting with an emphasis on containment, "support" and positive regard at the expense of "interpretation." The material offered is rich in primary-process thinking and complicated by the adolescent urge to perfect social skills and cultivate a self-image under pressure of rapid internal changes. In an adolescent group the therapist has to work harder than he does in an adult group to disabuse the group of his omnipotent and omniscient role. Paradoxically he can only do this by being more active earlier on in the life of the group and by disclosing himself more fully as a person with his own values and beliefs. Much of the analytic activity of the group takes place around its boundary. Dynamic administration involving the family, school and other professionals puts the burden of responsibility on the therapist for channelling communication into and out of the session in a way which seldom arises to the same extent in adult groups.

PART III

ORGANISATIONAL CONSULTANCY

CHAPTER FIVE

The Art of Group Analytic Organisational Consultancy: what it takes*

Gerhard Wilke

Focusing more on the group and less on the individual

The founder of group analysis had the dream that after the end of World War II applied psychoanalysis would be as successful as clinical work and make a contribution to democratising society. The ultimate aim of applying group analytic knowledge in the wider society represented for the émigré generation an inoculation programme against the recurrence of fascism. Foulkes thought that group analysts could put people into a group to learn to trust in life, other people and themselves enough to relinquish defensive manoeuvres that cut them off from the social connections that they needed and depended on. Group analytic consultancy represents, within this tradition and at the simplest level, the effort to re-connect people in groups or organisations with the social nature of their being and the inter-dependence of all the groups within the foundation matrix of the whole organisation. The message is, nothing

---

*This chapter was previously published as: Wilke, G. (2014). Group analysis in organisations: What it takes. In: *The Art of Group Analysis in Organisations: The Use if Intuitive and Experiential Knowledge* (pp. 3–38). London: Karnac.

gets done alone, and all outcomes depend on inter-dependence. In contrast the prevailing myth of the age is: it's all up to you alone and it all depends on the leader.

When Foulkes and Anthony (1971, pp. 258–260) talked of the *matrix* he meant the family and the group analytic therapy group. Here the term is used metaphorically to capture the invisible network of relationships and mutual projections that hold us together or split us apart in a group, like a multidisciplinary team. Foulkes linked his idea of the group matrix to that of a *foundation matrix* to capture the idea that each matrix is invisibly connected with a meta-matrix that is historical, cultural and social. The logic of this arguments suggests that each person, group, organisation and culture has its own and shared mind. The social anthropologist Clifford Geertz (1975) thinks about culture in a comparable fashion and argues that we all live suspended in a web of meaning that we ourselves weave through daily social interaction. A collection of such webs of meaning constitutes a culture, which is a phenomenon that is not fixed in time and space but is continually remade and preserved by people re-enacting its meaning in their various group contexts like in work, in festive rituals and meetings. If this line of reasoning captures some of the complexity of how the social order is re-created through daily interaction, then it makes sense to argue that we evolved into group beings, we depend on groups to grow up and we work and perform in and through groups. It is time to think less about the dynamics of individual development and focus on what it takes to animate and help groups develop and achieve what they have set out to do in-inter-dependence and over time. In terms of a catchy consulting phrase, an organisation changes from conversation to conversation, on contact between its parts and by paying attention to the daily interaction rituals that give it a sense of community, an identity and makes it work.

What can a group analytic consultant offer?

The fashion for heroic leadership at the end of the twentieth and the beginning of the twenty-first century created the myth that organisational performance and success depends on the imposition of the free will of the leader on the mind of a collective which follows that person. The prevailing surge of organisational modernisation, driven by transformational leaders, suggests that organisations are in a permanent fight against an adverse external environment, and the drag of tradition, outmoded work practices and ways of thinking. To be successful, these leaders split future, present and past into good and bad. Only the future is good, the past is bad and the present is part of the past. It is, albeit in a milder form, the language of the European dictators of the twentieth century and the simplest and most brutal way in which the energy locked up in human groups can be bounded and directed. What is denied, in this latest version of seeing the social world in terms of the survival of the fittest, is the inter-dependence of parents and children, families and the wider culture, leaders and their followers. Organisational teams and their departments too can only function within a wider system and culture. What is currently blanked out is the dependence of everyone on an external world that does not just threaten but also feed them. This inter-dependence within a social system and dependence on an external reality exists, not just as a result of willed visions and a wished for strategy, but is a pre-condition for any organisation to be born, to survive and to grow. The dependency of organisations on each other in a network of exchange and the inseparability of the private and public sector of the economy and the state became painfully apparent in a real crisis like the Credit Crunch and all that followed from it.

Before the crisis, the heroic leaders followed the path of hubris and denounced anyone who wanted a degree of regulation as an enemy of the free will of the market, which is simply an abstracted version of their own childish and selfish greed and desire for absolute and immature independence. In the crisis, these omnipotent and fallen leaders in the banking sector asked for mother state to rescue them from their own folly and protect them from stern, father-like politicians who might want to impose more control on their unbridled and immature greed. As is the collective predisposition of this particular professional group, they wanted to have their cake and eat it. The banking crisis exposed something else too. The foundation myth which underpins modern society—free willed and independent individuals making their own luck and regulating their own affairs via an unbridled market—has yet again been found wanting. With the unsecured credits, the illusion of absolute independence collapsed and society and its members were made aware again that human beings are social animals and can neither succeed nor fail without impact on the group or society they are a member of. It is time that we humans re-learn the facts of life—which are that we are always vulnerable and liable to need help and that we are replaceable and will die. What will outlive our self, are the groups that nurtured us, that we depended on and that we made a mark in.

Implicitly I argue that a group analyst, in the role of organisational consultant, can help people relinquish their wish to be absolutely free and learn to make choices within the limits that the outside world, and the group people work in, has set over time and in a given context. Group analysis involves the mastery of the art of the possible, not the fantastical. A group analytic consultant can translate the as-yet unnamed energy invested in the symptomatic problems identified by those who call for help—like under-performance and high levels of conflict and stress—into a shared communication about the causes of the *organisational dis-ease* and find a way out of the situation with the help of the group affected. Group analysts see problems in groups or individuals as an indirect expression of the need for an adjustment in a matrix of relationships to a changed environment. The assumption is that the problem person in a team, or the malfunctioning department in an organisation, signifies and personifies a taboo subject, which everyone colludes in keeping secret, but that needs to be aired, if everyone is to make progress. Of course, someone's underperformance can be explained in terms of the individual's personal pathology but the social environment has a trigger function in the process of this vulnerability becoming visible and having an impact on others. The analysis of the group's and the individual's involvement in the problems that organisational life generates for some members can help a leader understand what, in general and in particular, diverts the energy flow within a team from the pursuit of the task to egocentric and defensive manoeuvres that undermine responsible ways of co-operation and performance. The precondition is that consultants and leaders learn to think in terms of *social scenes* and begin to notice who reveals their character flaws, or deviates from the defined norm, under what circumstances and on contact with whom? The current fashion is to define normative ways of behaving and working so that they can be classified, quantified, measured and complied with. What I would encourage my clients to do is to resist normative and abstract ways of thinking about organisational behaviour and instead accept that, in groups, people permanently negotiate and adapt the shared norms and values, by deviating or conforming to them in each social encounter. Behavioural norms can't be fixed, just as the meaning of words can't be controlled. The human species itself and its cultural edifices are subject to adaptation and diversification in interaction with the environment.

Group analysts understand that every top down change programme results in new forms of defence and regression before it produces observable and better ways of working. During periods of rapid change in an organisation significant amounts of energy are projected outward into imagined persecutor(s), who drive the unwanted change. Many organisational managers and members adopt the position of a bystander or victim who suffers change and, by complaining, invokes sympathy and pity. Group analysts would, if they accompanied a change management process, re-open the boundary between people who see themselves as victims and perpetrators and try to understand how mobbing, scapegoating and the need for dependency and security are a normal part of human groups. We can aspire to decent and civilised behaviour but we can't always live up to the ideal. When we deviate from the ideal, it is more helpful to understand why it is happening in this group and at this moment than to blame an individual or an outside body for the non-compliance with an abstract and therefore inhuman norm. Like physicists, group analysts hate chance co-incidences and would see it as the shared responsibility of the leader and the group to notice, name, analyze and solve the problem of unhelpful dependency or scapegoating in a work team. This can be done because everyone is involved in what occurs in the group, not just the leader and the goodies and baddies. The location point is less in any one person than in their relationships with each other. Facilitated work on the group dynamic in the team will relatively quickly show that any group is performing and regressing simultaneously.

In the force field between performance and resistance three subgroups tend to form and become visible: the "yes people," the "no people" and the "do not knows." Just as in any classical Greek Drama these sub-groups embody the hero, the anti-hero and the chorus. When groups and their leaders regress into a perpetrator, victim and bystander scenario, a group analyst can be a witness and act as analyst and translator; someone who finds words to describe that, which cannot be named and gets acted out as resistance. My preferred way of doing such work in an organisation is to *accompany people* on their journey through a transition in their normal work situations. The role I adopt is that of a *life coach* who, like a basketball coach, can call time out and reflect in the moment of an important meeting on the way people are working together or how they are avoiding it. When I intervene in the work of the meeting I describe the group process by pointing out what happened, what did not happen and then explore jointly, with the participants, what sense they make of the parts that did not work and what adjustments can be made to maintain the work flow in future. It is a method of intervention which I have called *consultancy-cum-qualitative research* or *Accompanying and Action Research* as it has been named at Ashridge Business School, where I work as an Associate (Binney, Williams, & Wilke, 2012, pp. 261–278).

How can consulting, research and accompanying be combined in one approach when a group analyst is called in to make sense of unconscious group processes that seem to block effective ways of working together? Analytic consultants can do background research and, by talking to a cross-section of the organisation, capture the responses to change in metaphors that contain and hold what is felt and experienced and thereby make what is already known and perceived exchangeable through storytelling. Small and large group sessions in various combinations can help re-connect the flow of communication between different levels of the hierarchy and allow the organisation to let go of policing methods during periods of transition and find ways of adopting a learning model to change management. This approach works because it addresses the taboo of acknowledging openly that organisations are made to work just as much by the informal as by the formal system.

Recently, I was asked by a senior politician on the continent to facilitate a workshop on the theme of "Talking less about each other and more to each other." To make people aware of the fact that gossip can't be controlled, but can be worked with, I asked them to feed back to the whole group what relevant and important topics were talked about over coffee and over lunch. In the formal sessions, I had asked them to work normally on strategic issues and change implementation issues, which were in need of review. During the discussions I acted as coach and focused on how the group members helped or undermined each other. The idea being that leader, group and consultant work best together when the task and process level of a work group is recognised as of equal importance. Regular group sessions, involving frank dialogue, within a secure setting, facilitated by a skilled facilitator, who can connect the formal and informal organisation, reduces the fear of freedom, responsibility and change so characteristic of most humans. Effective work on the task and emotional levels can be achieved by accompanying and life coaching because it opens up the possibility for people to have a normal business meeting, punctuated by reflection and a post-meeting wash-up, which works through the way in which people have just engaged or not engaged with each other. The approach opens up a transitional space where, in a face-to-face meeting, the members of an organisation learn to make explicit what is normally implicit. The integration of reviews of how members of a meeting connect and disconnect, how they get real or avoid getting real on a task and process level, overcomes the fear of contact and makes power relational in the group and thereby raises levels of maturity and mutual trust. More honest exchanges oblige those involved to keep each other in mind when they make their next decision and it is this mental connectivity that enables the formal and informal organisation to exist in such a way that gossip and corridor meeting are just another method of getting the work done. The subtle acknowledgement of the official and unofficial organisation, through the compulsory reporting of the substance of their coffee break gossip, releases the energy that is often sought but not found during the implementation of strategic change. Accompanying, coupled with life coaching—that is my hunch—is much more powerful and effective than away days or massively expensive change management programs. Why? Everyone reflecting on what is held as the way we have just worked together, as an integral part of how things are done, seems to open people up to the idea that deviations from the norm, group think or the wrong decision are primarily group dramatisations, not just a single person's fault. This mind set, when it takes hold, enables an organisation to respond to a significant event, that has blown the institution off its intended strategic course, in reflective rather than panic mode and triggers a process of adaptation to altered circumstances and hence of collective and individual maturation. What such a mature process can look like, on the level of the individual, the group and the leader, was demonstrated by the way the Norwegians dealt publicly with the bomb attack and the mass killings in July 2011. The whole nation, from the Prime Minister down, suspended business as normal and engaged with a process of ritualised mourning and reflection. In this ritualised suspension of normal social time, a space was opened up in which every individual Norwegian and the nation as a very large group could ask: who are we now, what has been lost through having a mass murder in our midst and in what way can we integrate this story into our foundation myth of what Norway is and what a Norwegian stands for? In a very collectively calm and not hysterical way, the grief, the anger, the outrage and the disorientation was held and not projected outwards or translated into panic measures that made civil society worst.

From my perspective, we are at a juncture when group analysis needs to be applied in current organisations because consultancy, management and doing the job take place in a context that feels like a social survival drama. Offices without walls, teams without clear role descriptions, conflicting expectations and a flattened hierarchy can be perceived as modern, liberated and efficient by some, but are a great source of anxiety for most. In such a precarious organisational setting all those who work in it need to learn the rules of social exchange between social actors in symmetrical (equal status) or asymmetrical (unequal rank) relationships. That is, if they want to symbolically survive as an integrated human community and retain the capacity to think and act intelligently under pressure. The flattening of the organisational world has made the boundaries between hierarchies, diverse roles and the private and public world so open that work and meetings have become an ongoing group process that is ruled perhaps more by free association than structured discussions and formalised rules of behaviour. The explosion in defined and desired behavioural norms and competency lists in Human Resources Departments is a reaction against this and not the solution to anxiety engendered by open space offices, flattened hierarchies and permanently shifting objectives. Rules, regulations and prescriptive behavioural norms are a symptom of the deep unease in organisations; the unease is defended against by over-compliance, fear of the boss, fear of mistakes and manic "Actionism," lest one is seen being an underperformer or as under-engaged.

Organisational metaphors

Organisational theorists, like all social scientists, have fought an ideological battle over what an organisation is. There are roughly two camps, one is scientific and objective in orientation and the other is subjective and reflective in outlook. Each of us, working in a changing institution must become clear about the way in which we conceptualise an organisation, lest we fall into the intellectual trap of having found the key to understanding the law by which all organisations function under all circumstances. Each organisational consultant, each ordinary member and manager makes conscious and unconscious assumptions about the nature of organisational life with the help of mental images and assumed symbolic classification systems which they, like any member of any social body, project into the institutions they inhabit. This process of mentally classifying how things are supposed to work makes an organisation and our relationship to it, real for us. It also makes us feel safe and blind.

In his now classic book, *Images of Organisations*, Gareth Morgan (1986), tried to classify the mental images managers, employees and consultants construct to help them think about their daily interactions in the social context of their organisation. It is therefore not surprising that organisations, be they changing or not, possess a culture which is inseparable from a genesis myth and a collectively shared symbolic order, which classifies and categorises the order of all things. Each organisation has what we group analysts call a foundation matrix and justifies its way of working in terms of a foundation myth, like Volkswagen (People's car) or the NHS (National Health Service). These ideals rest on socially and culturally unconscious assumptions about the way social order works, what holds a network of inter-connected groups together as a social system and why it exists, how it was born, what it produces and what it delivers. It is what Christopher Bollas (1991) has called the "un-thought but known" prevalence of these unconscious assumptions, as well as the organisational diagram, the role and task descriptions and the hierarchical differentiations that hold a living organisation together and integrate it on a formalised level as a social system. Each mental image of an organisation is simultaneously a helpful way of thinking about what we rely on as a desirable state of relatedness and organisational integration and a mental prison that traps us in us and them, right and wrong and either-or thinking. This classification system, used by the organisation's members to make sense of how things are done makes it hard to envisage that other models could work equally well.

The taken for granted ways of thinking have an important psychological function and can't be changed at will as they offer the members of the organisation a sense of secure belonging and a source of pride, motivation and loyalty. Change processes come up against the boundaries of the existing and imagined self-ideal of an organisation.

In short, change and continuity are not to be thought of as opposites, but as related. If change leaders wilfully ignore the organisation's symbolic order of their evolved culture, their transformation project will probably fail as it ignores this mental map of what made the organisation in question special and adaptable. Change, like any life event in an individual's experience, has to be integrated into the existing mind map; it can't simply replace a deleted document or software programme on the hard disk. The human mind and the collective mind of a group do not work like a computer on the basis of delete and save, it is a living network of relationships that can only absorb and deal with change if it is also able to imagine, feel and master a sense of how the change and adaptation demanded fits in with the need for continuity, belonging and identity.

As a group analytic consultant I set out to work consciously with the dialectic of change and continuity in such a way that the tension between the thesis of continuity and the antithesis of change is not resolved in favour of the progressive side alone but is lifted to the synthesis level of a necessary adaptation in the light of altered circumstances. The organisational metaphors that Morgan has outlined are used in an un-reflected form by all the social actors in an organisation who try to accommodate a new experience by fitting it into their existing classification system of how the world is seen by insiders. Morgan divided these sense making classification systems into several types:

> Organisations which are imagined as bureaucratic machines that can be designed, planned re-engineered, controlled and aligned in terms of strategic intent and actual outcome by those in charge.
>
> Organisations which are imagined as brain like cybernetic systems that can be regulated by inputs, through-puts and outputs are held together by effective organizational design and an open and direct flow of communication.
>
> Organisations which are imagined as cultural and political systems in which the re-enactment of the power of leaders and a patriarchal system of cultural domination ensures that their members function through having a known place and status within a traditional and familiar hierarchy.
>
> Organisations that are imagined as bounded chaos, in which the design of work—flow processes, supply and demand chains and the recognition and adjustments of patterns of together working are the key to organizational sense making and success.

My experience of consultancy work over many years has convinced me that no organisation has a culture resting on one of these paradigms alone. What can be neatly classified into separate categories in theory gets de-constructed and re-assembled differently in each organisation or consulting process. Most organisations make up their own identity or, speaking psychologically, self-ideal by resorting to a unique combination of all these mental and mythological images. Morgan's types are like the bricks in a Lego box and can be combined in endless ways to build up a mental image of the architecture of the organisation as it is enacted daily by its inhabitants. It is a bit like the use of language by all of us. We all speak and use English and rely on the basic meaning of the words and the structure of the grammar, but, in reality, we can only function as individuals and cultural sub-groups if we evolve our own usage and mastery of the shared language.

Before we start working with an organisation as a group analytic consultant we need therefore to accept that our picture of the matrix of each team, the whole organisation and the sub-cultures of each business unit or department is of limited use for seeing what might be going on. Equally, we have to accept that by using the group analytic words matrix and foundation matrix, which describe the unconscious and invisible connections and collusive alliances between people in an organisation, we are imposing a symbolic order on a lived experience that our clients might not share and have not yet thought about. This problem represents an opportunity in that it forces us and the groups we work with, to ask: how do we jointly and separately make sense of the situation, where are the overlaps and on what basis can we find a working majority to take another step in the developmental history of the organisation? Last but not least, how can we find a shared language? This is an existential problem that surfaces every time an organisation makes a new strategy and tries to implement it. Implementation tends to fail or succeed during the transition from the old to the new when a process of confusion and re-ordering has to be gone through. Smart organisations will use the problem of insecurity to commune with people by asking them what sense and meaning can they find in the proposed changes and, having found their new sense of orientation, how would they, with the support and control of their leaders, go about the implementation of the proposed changes?

Group analysts are experts in facilitating a route through uncertain transitions, anthropologists are the profoundest thinkers about transitions among all the social scientists and that is why I would recommend drawing on these insights when organisations are faced with their current challenge of permanent transitions. It is also the reason why I work like an anthropologist when I make sense of what goes on in an organisation and use the clinical perspective of a group analyst to understand why people resist change, how they might overcome it and why whole areas of organisational life are taboo for observation and discussion. The translation of the "un-say-able" and "unthinkable" into words, as well as the construction of a setting in which people can hold each other to account face to face, are in my view the primary consulting task. With the help of the group, we can try to open up a transitional space for adaptation and progression in any organisation. To accomplish this dual task a range of methods and a combination of mental pictures is needed to begin to describe what we as consultants feel and see in response to the organisation that is trying to accept, reject or marginalise us on first contact. In engaging with the organisation in a consciously and unconsciously reflective mode, we can help make things visible and touchable by exposing the ways in which the system makes undesirable and threatening knowledge unconscious and taboo. By naming what we see, feel and think and by mirroring our own struggle to find meaning and sense in what goes on around us whilst working in the organisation a new space for thinking, feeling and relating can open up. If those who receive our feed-back sense that the descriptions and interpretations of the patterns of working in the organisation are born out of a genuine struggle to make sense, and are not part of an imposed way of seeing with the help of tools that have come off the shelf, the experience of being in a mutual sense making relationship with the external consultant can be internalised. Repeating a pattern of unconscious learning from childhood, the internalisation of a more open and less fearful way of relating and holding each other to account becomes a helpful way of letting go of familiar ways of working and embracing new and more helpful ones.

Organizational consultant as the anthropologist

Anthropologists are interested in showing the similarities and differences between and within cultures. They ask and answer the question of why humans can be the same and yet, at the same time, so different? They also make sense of connections within and between cultures or, metaphorically speaking, of social systems as communities. Organisations always operate on the level of a whole system, its sub-divisions, its single teams, its pairings and its individuals. Anthropological thinking can make sense of these inter-dependencies and how they can work to stabilise and de-stabilise the system and its culture. The Norwegian Anthropologist Hylland Eriksen (2001) has described the relationship between the social system and its culture thus:

> "Culture refers to acquired, cognitive and symbolic aspects of existence ... society refers to the social organization of human life, patterns of interaction and power relationships." (p. 4)

A current fashion among organisational development consultants is to talk in terms of complexity and bounded chaos; this evokes the image that through social interactions in a culturally informed context, the meaning, the organisation and the structure of a group or social entity emerges through interaction. Complexity consultants like Ralph Stacey (2003) quite rightly point out that planning, structures and systems based on predictable laws of behaviour are less than helpful when it comes to understanding, leading and changing organisations. Letting things emerge and trusting in the system's capacity to re-confirm what is working well, what is not quite right and adapting what needs to be changed to altered circumstances, is in this perspective, more potent and creative than all the current attempts to control and align all the details at a strategic and operational level. What complexity and chaos theorists perhaps underestimate is the extent to which human inter-actions within an organisation, from the system to the team and individual, are shaped and pre-structured by the local culture and the unconscious fears and desires of the people and the groups which are involved in holding on to their existing traditions, beliefs and ways of working together. The members of an organisation tend to be unconscious of the social and mental structures underlying their social interactions and deny that their own belonging group is not really self-contained or self-sustaining. Although the concept of the organisation as a whole is helpful to think with (in the sense of Morgan's metaphors) it must not be mistaken for a concrete social fact, as the French sociologist Emile Durkheim (1951) might have done in his book on suicide. The whole organisation is best conceived of as a symbolic representation of a shared real experience that is interpreted subjectively and therefore differently. Organisations are made up of systems within systems that, in turn, are suspended within a web of inter-dependent other systems. What holds it all together and makes it work and capable of adaptation is the existence of translucent boundaries, habits of relating and speaking, rituals of exchange, rules of conduct and the desire of people to project their needs for containment, continuity, belonging and identity into the container of their own institution. In other words, organisations are re-created in their own image when people come together in meetings and can, if the circumstances are not too unsafe and threatening on the emotional or reality level, lead to the emergence of adaptation and change when people commune.

A sense of having a place in a real organisation of fulfilling a function is also re-enforced and clarified through the exposure and persecution of deviancy. Making an example of someone unites the group and re-states the rules of the game of belonging and sharing in the identity of an organisation. The question whether an organisation is its culture cannot be answered conclusively. The person who is in the role of participant observer has to evaluate an organisation for what it is, has to judge whether one is looking at an objective reality, a subjective phenomena or a mixture of the two. I tend to avoid seeing the world in terms of either this—or that, in either-or terms. For me the organisation is an observable objective system and a subjective experience that is lived from moment to moment. It follows that a consultant needs to stand in the tradition of Relativity in Physics, Cubism in Art and Hermeneutics in philosophy. All of these practitioners of science, philosophy and art claim that the world and its observer should not be seen as separate and detached but as linked and in a relationship that exists in time and space. In this sense, observation, consultancy and organisational re-creation through social inter-action are an ongoing, interactive and interwoven group process.

The implication is that an outside consultant can, and perhaps should, assume the role of a social anthropologist who reflects on his own experience of being incorporated or excluded by the group. The process of analysing attachment and resistance experiences with clients allows us to discover and mirror, the unconscious and taken for granted ways in which things are done, not done and made socially taboo when people meet or submit to orders and impose their will on others. This means that one can try to collect and classify the phenomena, which make the individuals, and groups that embody this organisation, unique and distinguishable from its neighbours. At the same time, we can look for patterns of interaction and working that make this group universal and like all other humans. This process of learning the cultural identity of a group or system often leads to tensions with those in the organisation, who we are contracted to and who have set their mind on wrestling the culture of the organisation into shape and aligning its people with an idealised vision of the future. This clash of perspectives between what is, what has been, and what should be emerges because the anthropological perspective brings with it a concern for the integration of change and continuity, progression and regression, disturbance and integration, similarity and difference, universalism and particularism. The paradox is that consultants with an anthropological view of the world believe that the uniqueness of culture is both over- and underestimated. What the heroic leader and organisational re-engineer do not understand is that the culture of a company like Volkswagen or an institution like the NHS is less changeable than they think, but that the ways of thinking and working that are universally human are adaptable and open for development, provided it makes sense in relation to altered circumstances and with reference to the pre-existing culture.

Why is this so? Ordinary members of organisations and groups, unlike their leaders, are more interested in stability, security and safety than in permanent transition and do not want to fix or change things when they perceive them as working. In other words, consultants who see continuity and change as an inseparable and inter-linked process make uneasy bedfellows for leaders who think that the organisation and its culture are the enemy, the untamed beast that must be wrestled into submission and domesticated. The reason is that anthropologists think that it is tradition and continuity, not change alone, which makes a culture unique. Psychodynamic consultants believe that change involves loss, mourning and reparation. Neither perspective sees salvation in an endless march of progress, irrespective of reality. What happens therefore is that a consultant of this type becomes, in anthropological terms, a vertical link between the worlds of the gods and the mortals—an in-between being linking past, present and future. The task of this kind of consultant is to take on the mantle of the shaman, priest and medicine man to make it less dangerous for mortals and gods to connect and begin trading with each other. The task of the intermediary being, be it a doctor or an organisational consultant, is to explore the inter-dependence of above, middle and below in the social universe. The second task of the linking consultant is to create a setting and space in which the gods, the in-betweens and the mortals of an organisation can jointly take responsibility for the fear inducing transition from the old to the new way of working. This is best done by getting everyone involved to acknowledge that they work within a shared culture that is always evolving and diversifying, in response to internal and external pressures. Organisational development interventions attuned to the assumption that life is existentially a process of continuous change, are in my view more likely to succeed. Designed processes of social re-engineering, where people are asked to align themselves, without protest, to an idealistic and mechanistic template of social engineering, are wasteful, often doomed to failure and tend towards totalitarian forms of social organisation.

From the perspective of an anthropologist the current need to modernise and clean up the world, to make everyone conform to how they are supposed to be is a sign of moral panic, due to a sense of existential insecurity in the organization. Such organisations are pre-occupied with keeping their cosmological classification—if you like, the group's shared mind—intact. They are driven to protect themselves from threatening thoughts. It is not a failing; it is, in a fundamental way, how a group maintains a sense of self, a degree of security and order. Each attempt to fashion a new order of things, produces a new kind of disorder; each model of purity (makes us feel clean and properly adjusted) generates its own dirt (makes us feel impure and unwanted). Each age does, when its common assumptions are dislocated, develop a socially unconscious need to construct its own sense of what is dirty, what is undesirable and what is clean and desirable. The modern age, which prevailed until the third quarter of the last century, attacked anything traditional as dirty, in need of cleaning and re-ordering. The post-modern age, which has reigned since the 1980ies, views stable structures and ordinary authority as representing mortality. The age is bent on worshipping chaos, the breaking down of boundaries and the levelling of all hierarchies, which interfere with the charismatic, transforming leader and his/her dependent group. Progress, growth and social and personal happiness is reduced to cognition, behaviour, leadership, performance and identification with the brand. To an anthropologist these are the tell tale symptoms of magical thinking and religious forms of social integration.

M. Douglas (1966) thought that the notions of purity and impurity, in parallel to notions of the sacred and the profane underlie most human efforts to integrate and define the boundaries of a social system. In her seminal book *Purity and Danger* she defined dirt as matter out of place and made a link between the desire of leaders or groups to purify the social universe and a collective sense of vulnerability and uncertainty. Douglas interpreted attempts to clean the world of its impurities as an indication of a collective moral panic. In such a state the community wants to protect its leaders, the group and the boundaries of their social system from profanity, pollution and invasion. This defensive stance makes a community unable to welcome its neighbours with open arms and it becomes pre-occupied with deviancy within its own boundaries. Many leaders and their teams, which organisational consultants meet in the current world, display the symptoms of moral panic.

In the absence of holding structures and containing relationships current organisations look for salvation in the leader, the latest management tools and in a magical belief in targets and process flow charts. Far from containing the anxiety in the organisation caused by the modernisation drive, the change agents spread a sense panic by repeating the mantra that nothing is secure anymore. The very drive for cleanliness, order and perfection produces an atmosphere of fear—as if the search for the ideal order requires an increasingly restrictive and totalitarian treatment of matter or behaviour out of place. Manic actions seem to be the order of the day. Restructure first and think later is the accepted way of dealing with people and situations. In clinical terms the diagnosis must be: self-harming combined with a borderline personality. In other words, individuals and groups pre-occupied with a fear of not being good enough and therefore in danger of being annihilated. In response, the modernisers, be they leaders or change agents in other roles relate to reality in such a way that they unconsciously attack what they envy. Unconsciously, they attack as profane and unclean what they hold, unbeknown to themselves, as sacred: the old and stable organisation, containing relationships in a network of clear roles and with leaders as caring paternal authority figures. The obsession with leadership and modernisation is a symptom of anxiety and insecurity caused by the relentless need to restructure and disturb the organisations in which people do their work. All in the service of avoiding the admission that no-one has the secret key to change, development and the mastery of the unknown. Underneath the surface of the organisations we can observe a lot of panic, regression and fear. When humans panic they lose their capacity to be rational, to think and to engage in dialogue. Instead, they show their fear of falling apart and being swallowed up, by seeking salvation in what many authors since the nineteenth Century have described as a "massified" group with a charismatic leader who promises to clean up the world and forge order out of chaos. In this defensive position transformational leaders can have the effect of inspiring people when they are in their presence but leave them feeling dis-empowered and de-skilled after they have gone.

One charismatic leader I was able to see in action triggered bitter resentment in the group when it was felt that he put his own needs ahead of those of others and denied them an idealising relationship with their mother company. He ranted about its inefficiency and diagnosed it as unfit to survive, which the group heard as "he wants to make us homeless." In that situation, the group created a group fantasy that they were abandoned children and clung more desperately—in defence against the denigration—to their organisation as the embodiment of a primitive and all giving mother, on whom they could, in the end, depend. From experience they knew that the leaders embodied instability and transience. To keep the leader off their back, the group collaborated verbally with his attempt to define the future as good and the past and present as bad. To survive, they invested their emotions in the informal organisation of coffee breaks and chance meetings, in order to re-assure themselves of a degree of security in the group and the mother organisation. To work with leaders, followers and organisations in such a context requires an anthropological focus on cultural continuity and the clinical knowledge. Consultants need to pay attention to what goes on beneath the surface of conscious thinking, speaking and acting, if only to return the social actors in the organisation to a degree of sanity and restore their capacity to think and act responsibly across their divisional boundaries and in the service of the system as a whole. In the current context the capacity to hold on to the knowledge of the shared culture and the need for its sub-groups to link up and not fall back on "us and them" behaviour, so typical of distressed social systems, can make the difference between survival and extinction.

Psychoanalytic knowledge in consultancy

The dominant theoretical paradigm among psychodynamic consultants is that of the Human Relations School which has its roots in the Kleinian perspective of the Tavistock Clinic in London. This approach combines psychoanalysis and systems thinking. It conceptualises an organisation as a system, which receives demands and resources from the outside world, transforms these into products and services and returns them in the desired form to the clients. The transformation of resources into products involves the organisation of work into a hierarchical system, with clear role descriptions, a division of labour and a well-defined primary task for the whole organisation. During an organisational process, a psychoanalytic consultant looks at how the leadership style and the roles within the organisation are aligned with the primary task. The underlying idea is that the task gives an organisation a reason for existence and holds it together whilst the leadership exists to make things work and offers hope through a vision of the future. Leader and organisation must therefore make sure that the roles are clear so that the division of labour prevents waste and glues people together through inter-dependence. The perspective rests on the assumption that members in organisations are psycho-social individuals who interact in socio-psychological teams that form part of an inter-dependent network of relations between groups, which form the larger whole of the organisation. Each of these teams and the whole system operate on the conscious and unconscious level. This is the reason why organisational consultants with a psychoanalytic training have something unique to offer.

Larry Hirschorn and Carole K. Barnett (1993) put it thus, in their jointly edited book, *The Psychodynamics of Organisations*:

> "Psychoanalysis ... provides us with insights into the essentially irrational character of organizational life ... the psychoanalysis of organizations highlights in particular the frequently paradoxical quality of group life. It shows how and why in the realm of human affairs we often choose what we (consciously) hoped to avoid, or accomplish what we could not or did not expect."
>
> (Hirschhorn et al., pp. 14–15)

The biggest success story in applied psychoanalysis has historically been the Balint group. In group analysis no comparable success story of applying the psychoanalytic method in organisations can yet be told. The time has arrived to outline the hidden potential in group analysis to assist organisations in their attempts to survive and develop means of support beyond the Human Relations model. The developmental needs of doctors in their current institutional context of modernisation in the National Health Service (NHS) are a case in point. The Balint model for supporting doctors in groups, rooted in the Kleinian tradition, aimed to analyse the interaction between doctor and patient in order to find new treatment approaches by paying attention to the quality of the doctor–patient relationship. This model rested on the assumption that a doctor and a patient have a regular and consistent relationship in which transference phenomena can emerge and become part of a healing process. This model is out of date in general practice as GPs practice in groups and patients can pick the doctor they want, like consumers can buy the product they wish to possess. A more adaptable model of support for doctors in need is now required. The same applies to lawyers, architects, engineers and managers—in fact all professionals. As more and more professionals practice their craft in partner groups and not as single handed practitioners a less dyadic (doctor as subject and patient as object) and more group matrix-oriented model of professional supervision is more effective.

Reflective group sessions, without an exclusive focus on the expert–client relationship, offer a transitional space in which a modern professional can learn the skills of trusting the group enough to achieve a better level of service and care through co-operation in a multi-disciplinary team. Perhaps most importantly, during group supervision with colleagues a professional person can evolve an adjusted professional identity based on medical expertise, business and management competence and political sensitivity. The transition from one professional identity, based solely on the identification with medicine, the law, teaching or management, to a self-ideal that integrates the three roles of expert, manager and politician is indispensable to professional and organisational development today. Why should this be so? The removal of secure holding structures in organisations, like in professional partnerships, through permanent re-structuring exercises and frequent leader changes, means that people are no longer held by their leader but in relationships within work-groups and networks of inter-disciplinary projects. The ability of current organisations to survive, perform and adapt depends to a very crucial degree on the mental health and stability of the executive or partner group, located within the web of groups that constitutes the culture of the whole organisations.

W. R. Bion (1961) whose book *Experiences in Groups* inspired psychoanalytic consultancy work, concluded that each group (e.g. a team) consists of a working (conscious) and a basic assumption group (unconscious). He built on Freud's insight that the demands of the individual for self-determination and the group's need for conformity are not ultimately reconcilable. First, there is a constant push and pull between the need to conform to the norms of the group and the overall task and the leadership that is required to make it all work. Second, there is a wish to deviate from these norms, rebel against the leader and to be looked after. The leader's and the consultant's task in a group is therefore to observe how the group tries to unconsciously resist the demands of the task, the leader's authority and the group's insistence on co-operation. Bion identified three basic unconscious assumptions against the task of the work group: dependency (being taken care of emotionally rather than taking care of the work); fight-flight (picking the agreed task to bits and then avoiding the conflict that ensues) and pairing (avoiding the need for help and protection by looking for a perfect parental pair that ushers in the lost paradise of 24/7 care without the need for performance). Bion also showed how groups can self-organise and study their own ways of accomplishing or sabotaging the work, but this psychodynamic approach has had limited success in the organisational consultancy world (albeit many of the successful Business Schools have raided its intellectual larder) because the market prefers consultants to focus on technical or behavioural systems. Usually, Human Resource Departments want a quick fix that can be measured in terms of output and performance. Psychodynamic consultants subscribe to the philosophy of "slower is faster" and use methods like free association, storytelling and the verbal working through of previous organisational traumas. They can also focus on strategic adaptation, organisational survival, cultural reparation and emotional rejuvenation, but not without due attention to loss and incomplete mourning processes. The perspective offers deeper insights into experiences that can act as a guide to future action and creative endeavours.

In experiential learning groups or open space sessions, clinically thinking consultants can interpret the patterns of defensive inter-actions that fend off feelings and thoughts, which need to be aired to re-connect the parts of the organisation. Such a consultant can bring to the surface and name what is known but not said and which prevents people from working together more effectively. More open and frank exchanges will, in time, turn the leader and follower into relating subjects rather than objects of each others' manipulation. Bion's ideas were formulated against an organisational background in which the rational and bureaucratic model reigned supreme and the key relationship for the psychoanalyst of the organisation to focus on was that between the leader and the follower. In today's organisational landscapes the walls between people have been removed and a lot of employees have to hot desk in an open space office. Relatedness, group dynamics, exposure to existential risk, loss of boundaries, mental self-discipline, upside-down authority relationships and the capacity of "as if" siblings to co-operate and compete at the peer level are skills that people need to learn and master. Psychodynamic consultants must therefore go beyond Bion. The idea that an analyst comes in from the outside, interprets the pathological defences in the group against the demands of the leader and the task in a given group is too mechanistic and simplistic. From my point of view, applied group analysis can interpret regression and unconscious defences and identify developmental steps that can be accomplished and where potential spaces for creativity and change can be opened up. Psychodynamic consultants need to resist seeing organisational phenomena through the prism of a one to one encounter and desist from explaining group and social system phenomena with the help of individual psychology. In my work, I take the group as the starting point and locate individual failings and achievements in the network of relationships in which the under-or-over-performing individual is located. Group analysts call this the location principle. Taking this principle seriously allows an organisation to see behaviour in terms of economic efficiency, political power play, psychological fear and social exchange; it enables an organisation's leaders and change agents to work with how complex human interactions really are, not how simplistically they are viewed.

The consultant, who tries to integrate and model psychological, sociological and anthropological thinking needs to explore the dynamics within the matrix of a group on the vertical (leader and follower, parent and child) and on the horizontal level (siblings and peer dynamics). Consultant and client can then be helped to see that a group is dependent on a wider system and context (market, historical context, social system and culture). Each group acts, within an organisation, as a connection point between the sub-groups of the wider system. The inter-dependence that is hard to be acknowledged fully in strategy processes forces people to treat their own self, their belonging group and their wider society as a "reflexive project" (Giddens, 1991, pp. 100–108). Working together and relating has become an object of constant revision and re-construction through group interactions. In short, group analysts need, in the current organisational landscape, to be like clinicians who work with adolescents engaged in a rite of passage from childhood to adulthood; except, that full and settled maturity never arrives.

How a group and a system construct social order and how each individual maintains or loses a sense of integration and mental stability has become paramount in consulting processes and in performance management today. To put it as simply as I can, it is no longer a matter of finding out what is wrong and restoring things to a mythical state of normality but how to attain a temporary sense of order, and if you like, sanity, in a context of permanent change and adaptation. Each organisational member needs to master the psychological task of how to continue being productive with others under the relentless pressure to improve and develop. The "to be or not to be" question is: How do we maintain a degree of integrity, curiosity and creativity and avoid becoming paranoid, schizoid and resentful when our organisation is faced with the absence of existential security and stability? The slogan of the age that change is the only constant sounds clever but is a half-truth and ignores the miracle of why a society or organisation works at all and avoids falling apart.

The consultant as clinician and anthropologist can help an organisation be more effective in their maintenance of a culture of quality and accomplish its desired change by examining what is do-able, step by step and conversation by conversation. By offering safe settings in which people can reflect on how people work together and avoid it, a group analyst can help an organisation understand in more depth the dynamics between leaders and followers and the links between the individual and collective psyche that binds the organisation together. Such an exploration will also reveal the impact of risk and uncertainty on group processes, patterns of regression in the face of the task and how to resist getting sucked into manic "Actionism" and instead, learn to step back, reflect and act with appropriate consideration.

Organisational co-operation and integration

The French sociologist Emile Durkheim (1933) used non-clinical words to answer the question of how and why social order works. He distinguished between mechanical solidarity in pre-industrial and organic solidarity in industrial society. In pre-industrial society, social order is imposed through external force by scapegoating deviants and by using their public punishment as a threat to the majority. A smaller community is held together by the "social fact" that most people know each other and participate in the key annual and public rituals that enact how society and the universe are supposed to fit together and run. Small organisations and family firms can be viewed in this way when consulting with them. In our society social order depends on the invisible hand of the division of labour and the existence of collectively shared norms and values that people need to adhere to for social interactions in groups or whole systems to resemble a degree of predictability and reliability. Durkheim implies that large social systems have a collective or communal consciousness of their own. This collective mind set is not easily changeable as it is both an external set of norms and values governing behaviour and an internalised set of assumptions about a way of living and working that lends people a sense of belonging, community and identity. It makes us and our belonging group special and different from them, our neighbours. Meddling with this set of assumptions causes fundamental insecurity and distress in most people. In the modern, more complex and impersonal way of organising social order, deviance functions to discourage rule breaking and encourages compliance. In organisations this system of social control takes the form of appraisal systems, disciplinary procedures and performance reviews. Such an approach is restricted to defining abstract and external behaviour norms, which allow compliance and non-compliance to be measured but does not take account of the inner needs and emotions of leaders and employees and, if anything, undermines their sense of community. The other force that Durkheim identified as significant in modern social systems is "anomie" which occurs when the "normal" ways of integrating a social system are suspended during periods of severe crisis and instability. It is the balance between anomie, conformity and deviance that is often difficult to find. It is my contention that the current fashion for changing this balance at will, without regard for the consequences of the "engineered disturbance", causes more problems than it solves. The organisational engineering approach to change management often engenders an undiagnosed sense of anomie and "dis-ease" in organisations. It is important that consultants and leaders re-learn how difficult and miraculous it is that social systems achieve any degree of social order and that constant change, the search for charismatic leaders and the demand for compliance with visions and magical formulas of transformation represents a set of symptoms indicating anomie, loss of reality and the presence of psychological trauma.

The Tavistock perspective on organisational consultancy work has its roots in psychoanalytic and sociological thinking. It evolved before World War II and, theoretically speaking, this perspective has the bit on anomie missing. My own sense is that we used to inhabit stable modern, bureaucratic and neurotic organisations based on "organic solidarity" until the late 1970s. Ever since, post-modern, chaotic, complex and borderline organisations, displaying the symptoms of "anomie", have become the dominant form for organising work. Larry Hirschorn (1997) the psychodynamic expert from Warton Business School in the USA, argued in his book on Authority that the Tavistock model of psychoanalytic consulting is both inspired and outdated. To him this way of seeing the organisational world assumes too much predictability, control and rationality. Hirschhorn thinks that the primary task focus, which tries to align the core task of an organisation with the design of the work process does no longer describe people's experience, be they leaders, followers or consultants. Getting people to be clearer in their description of the roles people fulfil, the hierarchies that are necessary to make the division of labour "function", can't get to grips with the current organisational complexity and uncertainty. All organisations face high levels of anxiety generated by the generic insecurity induced by the over-hyped expectations of stock market analysts, the turnaround leaders in charge and the prevailing ideology that only change, short terms gains, share-holder value and the "de-construction" of traditional ways of doing things is normal and desirable. The past is therefore seen as bad, the present is part of the past and only the future is bright and good. This split way of thinking is quite "maddening" and therefore engenders fear and not hope. To relieve themselves of insecurity and fear, leaders end-up idealising their own visions and strategies and mistake them for reality. The groups that follow them become frightened and cowardly and withdraw into frustration, anger, compliance, resentment or manic "Actionism."

The breakdown of truly paternal structures in our organisations and the growth of flat and eternally young teams, without deference to age, seniority and mortality, have killed off the neurotic organisation and created internal working models in people's minds that are dyadic and governed by wishful thinking and fear. In other words, swinging rapidly between wish fulfilment (I want this done now regardless of limits) and outrage (why hasn't this been done). Paternal direction, care and encouragement, the normality of a three generational age hierarchy, the need for sibling type rivalry and co-operation and the existence of imperfection, failure and mortality are experienced by leaders and team members alike as intolerable, outmoded and not role conform. The institution that embodies these "psychotic" developments most clearly and frustratingly is the call centre. The neurotic organisation was, like a middle class person a bit conflicted about authority and discipline but nevertheless in touch with its core task. It had relatively clear role descriptions linked to a functioning hierarchy and a steady and predictable career path. Above all, it valued core skills and had a bureaucratic environment that contained the transference patterns that can turn the organisation into a substitute family or fill a meek ego with more power and grandeur through over-identification with a powerful leader, firm, profession or craft. One could be an autonomous and dependent professional and skilled worker in such an organisation, feeling secure, loved and taken care of. This holding frame is gone as an external reality but the feelings associated with it persist as an internal longing. This internal neediness could become a positive force, if enough managers, professionals and skilled workers in public or private organisations stopped colluding with the compulsion to set unrealistic targets and also refrained from deluding themselves into visions of grandeur and absolute control.

To take an example of "delusional targets": in the field of psychiatry, it is perverse, or misses the point, to set "improvement targets" for all patient groups when a psychiatric team deals primarily with people who are chronically ill, declining and often a danger to themselves and others. Over time this perversion of thinking about health targets in relation to chronically sick people leads to a serious loss of reality and closes down spaces for civilised behaviour and decision making rooted in experience and judgment. Instead of creating a new sense of humane treatment, psychiatric workers end up practicing a new form of ignoring the real needs of the patient. The need to comply with "false" targets castrates the professionals to an extent that they spend most of their time justifying their existence, through paper work, complying with their organisational parents' wishes and depriving their patients of the time that belongs to them. The result is that the whole system becomes self-absorbed in self-justification and ends up serving itself, not the clients. The employees within such a system care only for their own survival and lose sight of their primary task; to be intelligently kind to the people in their care on behalf of society.

Organisations like the NHS are in a state of a Permanent Cultural Revolution or, to use another metaphor, on a religious quest. Its modernisation cadres hang onto control, risk avoidance, the quality religion and an overly zealous complaints and evaluation procedure. Just like Mao's disciples clung to their little red book, health care modernisers repeat their mantras of permanent improvement and suffer a pang of procedural mania whenever someone makes a mistake within the system. The ideologically driven modernisers display the symptoms of a manic-depressive patient and create the dynamics of a group of borderline patients within their organisations. Whether this is good or bad is not the point. It is as it is, that is the point and the scandal. In a system without the freedom to make mistakes in order to gain new insights, it is no longer possible to have coherent thoughts. The social actors within the system become location points for a paranoid fear that turns every deviation from the carefully designed and accredited procedures, contained in "sacred" manuals, into a survival scenario. "If we don't do it in the prescribed way, we will be shamed and punished," is the primary justification.

The effect is a very high level of anxiety and a deep failure in the containing function of the organisation. Subsequently, we can witness the emergence of the kind of individual and social defences that the clinicians amongst us are familiar with from patients who fear psychosis and self-fragmentation. These phenomena are ubiquitous in the current organisations, irrespective of their function and reason for existence. It is therefore the clinician, not the handmaiden of the vision builder, the mission agent and the enforcer, that can help an organisation in a state of "dis-ease" recover its wits and ability to contain and hold anxiety levels at a level that those working in the organisation can retain their task focus. To put it less pathologically, it is the clinician who can "remind" leaders who "build" visions, missions and strategies of the fact that the future cannot be foretold. What can be done is to go through a process of taking stock, arriving at a number of "future scenarios" and having got to that point, make an informed guess about the best form of action. In other words, a clinical consultant can help leaders be "humble" enough to use strategy and implementation processes as a vehicle for the management of motivation, anxiety and commitment in their organisation.

When events in the real-world blow the leader and the organisation off the plotted course, those who do not mistake strategy for the control of the future, can use the deviation from the plan, which is bound to occur, as an opportunity to adjust "what is desired" to "what is doable" without resorting to a moral panic reaction.

Primary and existential risk at work

The enforcement approach to making people at work accountable and the attempt to encourage them to adopt new work patterns in a top down way and through the imposition of unrealistically short term targets causes more and not less anxiety. The current modernisation drive in organisations demands the permanent adoption of the adult position. The employees and the change enforcers find this, as human beings, sometimes unbearable and start to resist the pressure by getting stuck in a sadomasochistic and anal control dynamic where it becomes difficult for the infantilised employee to see what the organisational parents actually want; and, for the punitive change agents to understand what actually lies behind the withholding and immature behaviour of their resisting charges.

The most dramatic example of these patterns of thinking, feeling and acting I experienced in a nuclear power station. The CEO of a European Electricity Company, who I was coaching, asked me to work with shift workers and the leadership team in one of their nuclear plants in order to find out why they repeatedly failed to adherence to the very strict safety guidelines. The interpretation that suggested itself was that the conscious and unconscious demand for safety, which the public required, was projected into 60 volumes of Health and Safety Guidelines. The impossible task of learning the manual by heart made it ironically quite unsafe for the workers to handle the reactor, whilst complying with all the rules. The burden of expectation made them so anxious that they had difficulty in holding on to their considerable core skills and prevented them from using their judgment and common sense to deal with unforeseen events. The overriding fear was to make a mistake. In reaction people focused so hard on getting it right that they unconsciously got it repeatedly wrong. The demand from the top to be perfect was experienced at the bottom of the organisation as a lack of parental care. Getting it wrong became a preferred way of asking for help, it was an attempt to make contact and seek attention. The absence of a regular and meaningful dialogue between top and bottom, given that the task of producing nuclear energy, was potentially very dangerous made the workers feel abandoned by their critical organisational parents. Consequently, they colluded with the "disconnection" between bottom and top and felt too ashamed to seek help and check out the best course of action when something had gone wrong. Something did go wrong in small ways every day. Instead of acknowledging the impossibility of retaining all 60 volumes of safety regulations and evolving a safety system built on mutual help and trust, employees withdrew into socially isolated pockets, doing their job and hoping for the best, whilst the managers felt that safety was in the rule book. When a real incident did occur, which was potentially catastrophic, it became apparent that top and bottom acted out what they and the public feared: an unsafe nuclear power station. It happened because of a need to seek attention and the fear of failing to live up to standards that had become inhuman.

After an enquiry phase of what had gone wrong, experiential learning groups met regularly to think about the technical aspects of the job of running a nuclear power station and the emotions stirred up between people when facing that task. The group sessions revealed that, just as in society, the period of transition was the time when the organisation was most prone to "accidents." The transition from one shift to the next for example was not subject to a hand-over meeting, as would be common practice in emergency medicine. After I had suggested such a change, the hand over between shifts was institutionalised. In each meeting the group coming off a shift told the team starting their shift what had gone well, what had worried them and what they thought needed to be monitored and watched. The second outcome of this intervention in the nuclear power station was a revision of safety thinking and training because it focused exclusively on "dramatic" incidents and the introduction of the latest technology and ignored all the daily little incidents which could, if wrongly handled, get out of hand and turn into a potential disaster. These incidents now became the focus for organisational learning as we found that the workers at the bottom unconsciously "let incidents" happen and then rescued the situation very skilfully in order to unconsciously "demonstrate" their need for more care, respect and recognition from their institutional parents (managers and civil servants).

In the current context, transitions have become a way of organisational life. Their members are caught between the known and the unknown in such a way that they fear the loss of their roles, their position and security. In such an unsafe environment, an organisation's member resorts to the psychological defence mechanism of extreme splitting, projection and projective identification. In this psychological survival state very primitive social defences are used, which operate on a pre-oedipal and part—object relations level. In other words, people engage with each other at a level at which it is mentally and emotionally not possible to hold the primary task in mind and simply try to secure an existence and avoid fragmentation and eradication. In that sense Hirschhorn is right to say that analytically trained consultants should change their focus from primary task to primary risk management and begin to observe and interpret the much more "primitive" psychological defence mechanisms that are deployed to stave off the fear of fragmentation and incorporation associated with such existential risk states. The giveaway "symptom" of the presence of primary risk rather than primary task scenarios is the search for the charismatic or transforming leader and an overly idealising or resentful mass of followers; either in subservience and hysterical compliance or in a passive aggressive stance in relation to such a heroic figure. Alternatively, groups unconsciously look for a degree of comfort by creating a parental holding couple.

Organisational parenting

It is very unfashionable to talk of organisations in terms of the family or kinship, but the emotional instability of leaders and employees, engendered by the "dis-embedding" of secure structures and hierarchies does generate a need in people to be lead by people who take a caring parental attitude towards the groups they are responsible for. Those who are overwhelmed by the demands to "grow up and deliver tend to project their feelings of inadequacy and vulnerability into their leaders by accusing them of a lack of understanding and care. Hidden underneath the aggression is the wish to have containing organisational parents. The call for the strong leader is not the only wish generated by employees in distress; the call for a parent figure is equally strong. Many of the skilled workers in the Nuclear power station revealed in the support groups how abandoned and abused they felt by their projected organisational parents. They talked as if they inhabited a rule bound and restrictive totalitarian system from which one can only withdraw into a form of internal emigration. Helping the leaders and skilled workers re-connect made it possible that everyone involved could relate again in the service of a greater task and cause. In an experiential learning group leaders and employees moved in and out of the "as if" parent, child, and sibling position and practiced being dependent, responsible and in need of each other. What united them was their internalised knowledge of the family, of parents and brothers and sisters as the primary mental reference group of every human being. We all have an inner template of what it is like to be in a group, to be looked after by an authority and to co-operate and compete, based on the family. It is this inner filter that we use to process the impact of threatening, overburdening, unfamiliar or affirming experiences. As all these internal families have the same building blocks, we can use them to make sense of things that have gone wrong in an organisation in a sharable way. It is this shared unconscious knowledge that enables top and bottom in an organisation to regulate the level of engagement and distance between them and helps everyone, despite hierarchical divisions, to pull together when it becomes necessary. My conclusion that our internalised experiences of what it means to be one's self, to be familiar with patterns of relating and to be a member of a family or work group, rests on the assumption that there is a core self, that we have a sense of who we are, which can mentally be called on in order to make sense of unfamiliar experiences. Intellectually this argument is open to a wide range of criticism, but I am recording what feels to be true in experiential terms, not what is true in an abstract academic sense. The family as an internalised reference frame for processing familiar and unfamiliar experiences. This internal reference frame does tend to help work teams find a common and sharable language when facing change or other difficulties at a personal and group level.

Anthony Giddens (1999) has described globalisation as a process of dis-embedding which progressively deprives us of our "taken for granted assumptions" about social order, social space and social identity. We can no longer rely on what we learnt during our childhood or professional socialization for security to help us through the next adjustment to a changed social, political and economic environment. Being one's self as a person and as a professional has, according to Giddens, become an ongoing "reflexive project",[1] no longer something to fall back on under pressure. We have to re-invent ourselves in social situations that we cannot control and which force us into negotiations with other social actors. Any change of this magnitude produces the need in individuals, teams and whole organisations to adjust their way of working and their psychological sense of being in social time and space. Giddens describes the self as a reflexive process because the external world and its social structures is permanently disembedded. What is familiar to us is, he argues, of no help when dealing with what is new outside ourselves. For me, he describes the external changes in the social world and the ways people try to adapt their relative status position convincingly. It does not follow that the internal world must change in the same way. Indeed my work tells me that the internal world of the social actors in disembedded organisations are pushed by the external disturbance into a regressive pull, which generates the wish for dependable authority figures and a secure belonging group. In other words, the unconscious mind wants to hang on to what is universal and perhaps relatively unchangeable in the human psyche. Giddens is adapting the sociological tradition that argued that we present different selves, in different social grouping. In contrast, I argue that it is never a case of everything changing at work, but more a tension between the new and the old, the familiar and the unfamiliar and the various ways in which change experiences can be processed by individuals, located in specific social groupings and circumstances. It is not so much a case of presenting different selves in everyday life, but different aspects of one's own self in a range of social situations and circumstances.

The core of change is continuity

The way social Anthropologists conceptualise culture could help organisations work with the momentous changes we are all caught up in. Writers like Cohen (1995) say that culture (an organisation is a culture) does not exist with a capital C, out there facing the individual like the mass faces the ego in Freud's account of mass psychology and ego development. Instead, this thinker imagines that we live in a series of matrices of meaning that we weave together through our daily interactions. Interactions are ritualised and therefore familiar enough to facilitate social interaction, but the communicative exchanges are also uncontrollable enough to leave room for deviation and adaptation in the process of affirmation and contact. The shape of an organisation, an organisational culture is an act of re-creation. Change processes simply confront us with what is normal and that an organization depends on the ability of its members to re-make it in the image that they and their predecessors and leaders have projected onto it. As long as we make this fact socially unconscious, we seem to be able to deal with this labour of re-affirmation and the simultaneous creation of what is yet to come—in an unthinking and self-affirming way. As soon as we become conscious of having to do this and are being told by an outsider or an authority figure that there is no alternative and that we must submit, we regress and struggle. It is as if the command to change from someone above or outside reminds us of the sheer un-controllability of fate, and of our own mortality and powerlessness. A changing organisation that does not integrate professionally facilitated process work as a normalised and integral part of change and adaptation to altered circumstances, will be forced by the regressive and fearful response to such an initiative, to abandon the exclusive focus on the primary task. In a regressed state, the organisation will unconsciously collude with the efforts of a sub-group, within the system, to take up a defensive assumption positions against the feeling of being overburdened. The resentful sub-group members will become reliant on its leader, the angry subgroup will engage in fight and flight rituals with other sub-groups and a third type of sub-group will create a parental pair in the group or follow a charismatic messiah, who can also become the sacrificial object. In such an unconscious cultural mind set, the organisation can be helped by open group sessions or what I would call strategic conversations (resembling a free associative group process) and accompanying and life coaching work (observing and commenting on the process, whilst the work group focuses on the task). Work group meetings that reflect on their own practice of relating, getting real with each other and look at how they offer help can begin to tap into the intelligence offered by emotions during a change processes. These reflections on the emotional aspects of change can be called mourning work which is needed to cope with the transition from the old to the new.

Working with the foundation matrix of the organization

Learning to see the organisation as a foundation matrix, made up of inter-dependent smaller matrices is a very helpful way to make sense of a range of experiences in the formal and the informal organisation. Thinking about the organisation as a living network, with a superimposed formal system for external recognition offers a very different view of how problems arise and solutions can be found, without resorting to blame and punishment. What perhaps is even more important for organisational development is an experience of working with the social, cultural and historical memory, which is carried by its individual members. To give an example:

> On 8 May 1995 I sat in a large group in Switzerland with 119 members of a Consulting Firm. From the doorman to the director, everyone was present. The four large groups, planned for the day, were meant to explore why the institution had failed to compete effectively with the newly arrived consultancy firms from the USA and the UK. The management team wanted to know why people's morale had plummeted, when they had a 70-year-old history of providing services to the Swiss state and the country's major industries. The first large group, facilitated in a classic group analytic way, started with a very long silence. After about 10 minutes one could hear the church bells ringing in the town below. Whilst they chimed away, a woman began to cry. I noticed that no one was observing her grief as everyone was staring into the empty space in the middle of the group circle. As if everyone was transfixed by an invisible spot on the floor which they used to ignore the group member who was remembering something too hard to look at. I intervened when the church bells had stopped by asking: "What is the connection between the church bells, your tears, the silence and the fact that none of your colleagues wanted to see you cry?" She answered: "The church bells give thanks for Switzerland being spared the Second World War, which ended 50 years ago. The bells also remind me of the 13 people we lost during the restructuring which became necessary because our competitors attacked us and took our work away. I wonder, whether the bells will toll for us today or whether it is a day of getting real about what is happening and whether we will survive."

The location of psychological distress within a group matrix rather than an individual is the most useful concept from group analysis for an organisation when it is trying to understand why its efforts to adapt and change seem to come up against a wall of resistance rather than the desire outcome. The release of energy in the group session after the naming of the feelings of loss and mourning by the woman was astonishing. After the tears could flow a sufficient number of the staff felt spoken for and were able to face the future. They suddenly got in touch with their desire to compete, their fear of a changing reality and their need to engage in reparation and re-creation work.

What had allowed the group to move from passive aggression into a mode of wanting to fight for their survival and show their bosses and their competitors what they could do was the consultant's refusal to demand a structured discussion about their bad situation and how to move out of it in a planned and controlled way. I had started the large group with the simple statement. I wanted everyone to know why they were here and that I was giving them a protected space to commune in. I invited them to talk about their past, their present and their future and made it clear that I would intervene when people were persecuted and would confront the group, or parts of it, when they avoided the issues in the room. Furthermore, I pledged to identify developmental steps and to support those who took the risk of speaking about the issues that needed to be faced, before progress could be made. I said that I wanted to model blind trust in the group and its capacity to reflect on the problems it had generated itself through collusion, denial and the desire to keep things as they are. I tell this story because it is now profoundly important that leaders and followers in organisations learn to let go of control and accept that the best thing they can do is to meet on the level of all humans as equals in situations of uncertainty, despite their hierarchical differences. The moment to meet on an equal footing is when no one, including the leader, can know the way forward alone. Leaders who have the courage to call a meeting in order to explore how the organisation can deal with not knowing are amazed how much their authority is enhanced by taking this risk, how much more glued together the parts that make up the organisations are subsequently and how there is a sudden rush of energy for higher levels of performance and commitment.

It is not through predicting and foretelling the future that the energy flow in an organisation can be changed from negative to positive but by inviting enough representatives or key players of the organisation into a process of joint sense making. In a secure environment, thoughts and feelings will emerge that face up to the unknown and point to a path into a less frightening future. It is the existential condition of uncertainty, which all organisations now live in, that has made it necessary to talk in terms of primary risk when it comes to psychodynamic consultancy work in organisations. If Anthony Giddens is right this change is so momentous that our very own sense of self and each group's sense of identity are subject to permanent doubt. An organisation's sense of its own identity and way of doing things is now permanently under threat and in need of re-integration and re-construction in order to maintain the confidence needed to remain curious and productive in the face of fear. The implication is that organisations, its sub-groups and individual members must learn the skills of dealing with uncertainty, permanent transition and survival. These existential problems are not new and are, from an anthropological point of view, nothing more or less than the dilemmas involved in negotiating the human life cycle from birth to death. Only, dealing with transitions, altered circumstances, birth, marriage, misfortune, sudden fortune or death used to be facilitated with the help of rites of passage, mostly religious in nature but often very secular in outcome. Group analytic consultants can offer substitute *rites of passage* in the form of anthropological action research and well designed and clinically informed large and small group sessions. Professionally facilitated groups and conducted field research allows people to do the kind of experiential and reflexive learning that members of organisations need to engage in to acquire the skills of coping with the world as it now is. Why not therefore have quarterly organisational, departmental and team relationship audits alongside the budget and performance reviews? Group sessions in which people ask each other face to face how they are doing on the side of human capital and what kind of relationships they need in order to get done what needs to be done. It is this service that group analysts, who are willing to be field researchers and second-hand clinicians, are well qualified for and can offer!

Note

1. Editor's note: probably meaning "reflective."

References

Binney, G., Williams, C., & Wilke, G. (2012). *Living Leadership: A Practical Guide for Ordinary Heroes* (3rd edn). Harlow: Prentice Hall/Financial Times.

Bion, W. R. (1961). *Experiences in Groups, and Other Papers*. London: Tavistock.

Bollas, C. (1991). *Forces of Destiny, Psychoanalysis and Human Idiom*. London: Free Association Books.
Cohen, A. P. (1995). *The Symbolic Construction of Community*. London: Routledge.
Douglas, M. (1966). *Purity and Danger. An Analysis of Conceptions of Pollution and Taboo*. London: Routledge and Keegan Paul.
Durkheim, E. (1933). *The Division of Labour in Society*. New York: Macmillan.
Durkheim, E. (1951). *Suicide: A Study in Sociology*. London: Free Press.
Eriksen, T. H. (2001). *Small Places, Large Issues: An Introduction to Social and Cultural Anthropology*. London: Pluto Press.
Foulkes, S. H., & Anthony, E. J. (1971). *Group Psychotherapy: The Psychoanalytic Approach*. Harmondsworth: Penguin.
Geertz, C. (1975). *The Interpretation of Cultures*. London: Hutchinson.
Giddens, A. (1991). *Modernity and Self-Identity: Self and Society in the Late Modern Age*. Cambridge: Polity Press.
Giddens, A. (1999). *Runaway World: How Globalisation is Reshaping our Lives*. London: Polity Press.
Hirschorn, L., & Barnett, C. K. (1993). *The Psychodynamics of Organizations*. Philadelphia, PA: Temple University Press.
Hirschorn, L. (1997). *Reworking Authority: Leading and Following in Post-Modern Organizations*. Cambridge, MA: MIT Press.
Morgan, G. (1986). *Images of Organisations*. London: Sage.
Stacey, R. D. (2003). *Complexity and Group Processes*. Hove: Brunner-Routledge.

PART IV

ANTIDISCRIMINATION/FEMINISM

CHAPTER SIX

Organising for change? Group-analytic perspectives on a feminist action research project*

Erica Burman

The focus of this chapter is upon exploring the relevance of group analysis as an interpretive resource for the conduct and management of research, as a particular kind of organisational analysis. Reflecting my own political commitments, I identify some specific conceptual compatibilities and political continuities between processes involved in socially committed action research and in group analysis. While attending to process, including systemic and psychodynamic, issues have a longstanding tradition within social research (from Kurt Lewin's gestalt-influenced theory of the 1930s onwards, Argyris, 1997, to debates in feminist and anthropological research on reflexivity, e.g. Stanley & Wise, 1993; Steier, 1991; Wilkinson, 1988), my account illustrates additional critical perspectives afforded by drawing on both group-analytic and social research frameworks.

I offer some indications of the relevance of group-analytic perspectives by referring to a recently completed research project conducted under my co-direction (Batsleer, Burman et al., 2002). While my role as

---

*This chapter was previously published as: Burman, E. (2004). Organising for change? Group-analytic perspectives on a feminist action research project. *Group Analysis, 37*: 91–108.

project co-manager was informed by my training as a group analyst, I did not set out to apply group analysis to its process and functioning. Rather my comments have been assembled retrospectively to explore connections with group analysis.

Group analysis as an interpretive resource

I suggest that a group-analytic approach is useful for the analysis of research, as well as therapeutic processes because of its primary emphasis on communication and interconnection: both between groups operating at different levels within institutional systems, and between socio-cultural, political and personal dimensions.

I was particularly struck by Pines's (2002) comment, concerning what he regarded as a key legacy of the influence of the sociologist Norbert Elias on Foulkes. According to Pines, Elias identified the specific aim of group analysis (and its challenge) as maintaining a focus on introjection, rather than the more traditional psychoanalytic priority accorded projection (Pines, 2002, p. 16). This, as he indicates, offers a corrective to the individualising focus of traditional psychoanalytic approaches that abstract and posit the individual as an a priori, rather than explaining its constitution within social, historical, and cultural conditions. Such key differences have consequences for the model of the social, as well as of the psyche that it is connected to (Blackwell, 1998; Cooper, 1998). In this sense, current discussions within group analysis (e.g. Dalal, 1998) indicate compatibilities with constructionist approaches to subjectivity, and it is this outward-looking character that makes it particularly relevant for analyses that seek to go beyond individual psychic resonances in explaining institutional phenomena.

There are other contemporary connections, as in Stacey's (2000, 2001) recent reformulation of Foulkes's metaphor of the matrix as an anticipation of complexity theory, describing the intertwining network of historical and current communicational processes within groups. Like complexity theory, in group analysis the relative focus only comes to the fore according to the arena and topic of the analysis. Individual, institution and group are thus inseparable, so that concepts of identity can be treated as situated effects of broader processes, rather than distinct, inherent and static qualities. As with complexity theory, the concern with "mirroring" or "resonance" plus the key technical focus accorded consideration of questions of context, setting and organisational administration used to strengthen boundaries and promote integrity of group function (Nitsun, 1998) all invite a reading of organisational processes that grapples with shifting processes and tensions. They address the paradox, conflict, and possibilities informing the dynamics of a prefigurative action research project, where (as with therapy but at a different level) the struggle is as much to avoid only reproducing the old as it is to envisage the new.

The project design and the team

Domestic Violence and Minoritisation (Batsleer et al., 2002) was an eleven-month project[1] that set out to research gaps and barriers in service provision for women from minoritised backgrounds (specifically African and African-Caribbean, South Asian, Jewish and Irish women) surviving and escaping domestic violence. We used the term "minoritisation" (rather than "minority", or "minority ethnic group") to highlight that groups and communities do not occupy the position of minority by virtue of some inherent property (of their culture or religion, for example) but rather they come to acquire this position as the outcome of a socio-historical and political process. Our description of women as "survivors" follows current practice in highlighting women's strengths rather than victimisation, emphasising survival as a process rather than an event. Our definition of domestic violence included emotional and financial, as well as physical, abuse perpetrated by an intimate partner or family member(s).[2] Our focus on service responses to women from the said cultural/community backgrounds was to explore what issues might arise by virtue of being identified with a minority cultural community in accessing and using services. Topicalising these particular community groups was intended to be indicative of, rather than to document, the issues posed in designing and delivering appropriate services within a multicultural British post-industrial city like Manchester.

There were three main phases in the research design: generating accounts that documented (1) the perspectives of service providers, and (2) of (actual or potential) service uses i.e. minoritised women who had experienced domestic violence, while also (3) facilitating short-term support groups for women. There were two aspects of the project involving elements of active intervention, or action research. First, beyond engaging service providers (through research interviews), we convened a steering group that crossed a number of dimensions of structural differences (voluntary/statutory; dedicated domestic violence vs. general health, housing and support; culturally specialist vs. mainstream). Second, the project sought to add to existing provision by piloting three short term support groups for women survivors of domestic violence.[3] The specific demand for this intervention arose out of a previous project we had conducted on service responses to South Asian women who had attempted suicide or self harmed (Chantler, Burman, Batsleer, & Bashir, 2001). Domestic violence was indicated as a key factor contributing to their distress, and survivors highlighted the need for facilitated self-help groups as a resource that they would have found useful but were not on offer.

I should point out that my reference to "we" refers principally to the research team. Nevertheless the analysis I offer is from my own perspective, and doubtless there are others.[4] The team was composed of seven women from different institutional, professional, and disciplinary backgrounds, some identifying as similar to the racialised/cultural backgrounds topicalised within the study, and others as white, English Christian (i.e. from majoritised positions). Three members of the team—significantly the three black women—were employed (half-time) specifically for the purpose and duration of the project (with shades of institutional racism being recapitulated here), while the other four (including myself) were already employed within the university, with differential responsibilities and amounts of time seconded to the project.

It was not unreasonable to anticipate structural tensions within a project that crosses so many institutional arenas (academic vs. applied, university vs. voluntary vs. statutory sectors, culturally specific vs. mainstream services). Nor should it have been surprising to encounter a felt tension between the service development/practice work agenda (privileging innovative but safe practice) and the research agenda (privileging targets and timescales), that in turn mapped on to the elaboration of the primary responsibilities of "workers" and "managers" within the team. Simultaneously addressing an area of exclusion in terms of gender-sensitive provision and making an antiracist intervention also made this a particularly ambitious project—especially as we aimed to challenge not only the implicitly culturally exclusionary practices of some gender-specialist provision but also the privileging of "race" over gender within culturally specialist provision that marginalised the position of black and minoritised women (Burman, 1998; Burman, Chantler, & Batsleer, 2002).

Further, the focus in our research design on minoritisation disturbed the black/white divide that permeates discussions of "race," racism and anti-racism, as we included not only women from backgrounds subject to racism typically organised on the basis of skin colour but also from (usually) white minority communities that in Britain are subject to racialised oppression on the basis of cultural and religious marginalisation and discrimination (which also possibly included ambiguous visible identification).[5] On (psychodynamic) reflection, we could perhaps interpret the scope of this enterprise within what Zagier Roberts (1994) terms a "self assigned impossible task," or as omnipotence driven by persecutory internal objects. I prefer to think of it as motivated by political commitment, and arising out of the fruitful and dialectical relationship between developments in theory and practice.

Topic and process

Luc Michel (2001) draws on group-analytic and psychoanalytic ideas in his account of a research project exploring service responses to migrant communities in Lausanne, Switzerland. He describes how, unwittingly, the multidisciplinary research team in its process recapitulated aspects of the migrant experience they were researching. From an analysis of difficulties and resolutions of problems, Michel articulates both a methodological principle of flexibility and continuous reassessment of the process:

> Since our research was in a state of flux, then its framework needed to be constantly modified. At this state we were in a true situation of "action research".
>
> (Michel, 2001, p. 216)

At the end he commented on the importance of the research team being prepared to reflect upon such difficulties as a resource:

> The necessary reflection by the research team to overcome its crises is a normal part of the processes operating in this kind of action research, that is to say it modifies and enriches the very process of the action research itself.
>
> (Michel, 2001, p. 218)

Similarly, we subscribed to notions of reflexivity that inform both qualitative and feminist research (Banister, Burman, Parker, Taylor, & Tindall,

1994; Burman, 1997; Burman, 2000; Wilkinson, 1988), looking beyond our immediate personal circumstances to consider in what ways these reflected broader features of our topic, and so determine our subsequent responses. To take one example, our greater problems in identifying women survivors of domestic violence—especially Jewish and Irish women—were predictable in the sense that (unlike African, African-Caribbean and South Asian women) there were no local dedicated specialist domestic violence services to provide a network of possible contacts for us to liase with.

We could have interpreted the absence of self- (or professional) referrals as indicative of lack of demand for domestic violence services (or even that domestic violence did not exist as a problem within those communities),[6] or treated this as our failure as researchers. But, acknowledging that such gaps reappeared also within our research material enabled us to explore how to model the further steps that domestic violence services could take to engage previously unidentified minoritised women.

We drew on our various identifications. Here the position of women with "no recourse to public funds" came to the fore—women subject to the "one year rule" (currently being extended to two years) who have uncertain "leave to stay" in Britain (because their marriage to a British citizen, with residency rights, has broken up) and whose entitlement to welfare benefits or claim on public funds is therefore disallowed. This often excludes such women from all systems of support. We therefore used our engagement and positions as researchers to intervene within usual discourses of shame around abuse and violence for minoritised women and cultures, and to write an account of organisational (rather than only survivor) shame at being so helpless and ineffectual in making and sustaining changes. In doing so, we were also challenging prevailing discourses around both abuse and minoritised women.

We went on to identify institutional and policy strategies to rectify these inequalities. Through the process of the project (via the convening of the steering group and the service intervention of the support groups) we were able to facilitate links between generalist and specialist organisations across different sectors and in different regions, brokering partnerships that are likely to provide and improve services beyond the life of the project.

Hence we interpreted the general difficulties we encountered as research resources. Moreover we could also use our positions to change the landscape of interagency relations. A further indicative example was how we were able to link existing services through constituting a steering group as our consultative reference group. This steering group was composed of participants drawn from, but functioning as an arena outside, prevailing partnership fora. While the latter are typically dominated by competitive resource agendas, as a temporary project, we had no stake in this, and so the steering group made it possible for organisations to forge new or different relationships.

Similar analyses could be made of the ways we linked our responses to the distress of the survivors interviewed with the accounts of workers within the various services they had attempted to access. Here our experience accords well with other discussions (e.g. Featherstone, 1997), such as being overwhelmed, becoming numbed and desensitised; with further interpersonal and organisational effects in terms of processes of splitting and rivalry, including victim/rescuer dynamics operating between services (Blackwell, 1997).

Similarities and differences

Michel drew on a narrative of group formation to account for the shifting process and progress of his research team.

> The element of cohesion of the group became the actual object of the research—"the migrant"—and its occupation of the centre stage pushed into the wings—indeed, excluded altogether—the focus of interest and other factors which gave to each individual his own identity ... This cohesion was above all based on the elimination of our differences and the creation of a "group illusion" (Anzieu, 1981).
>
> (Michel, 2001, p. 213)

He described an initial and over-hasty cohesion which, as an idealisation, soon fragmented into sectarian conflict and "a dialogue of the deaf" (Michel, 2001, p. 214). Resolution occurred through a joint process of reflection that enabled the team to acknowledge differences based on expertise rather than power, and giving rise to a shift from a pseudo-democracy based on the denial of difference to differentiated roles, whereby the group was able to return with renewed vigour to its task.

While I am wary of developmental models due to their regulatory and normalising effects (Burman, 1994, 1996) I admit that such a model could apply to the chronology of our research team. More interesting to me though were the links made by Michel between researching migrant experiences and the submergence and resurgence of institutional and professional differences within the team.

We were like a group of siblings without parents. No reference was made to our original cultures, either professional or institutional. (Michel, 2001, p. 214)

Clearly such issues are relevant to research around minoritised women, many of whom are also immigrants.[7] There were moments when the functioning of the team seemed to be at the cost of either denying cultural, professional or specific disciplinary positions and differences or, highlighting them as insurmountable obstacles. But here two further socio-political and group dynamic factors came into play.

Our research project functioned at the interface of two competing "group illusions" (following Anzieu, 1984) or (using Foulkes) "foundation matrices" (Foulkes & Anthony, 1964, p. 292). While commentators vary in their interpretations, there is (as Dalal, 1998, also notes) scope within Foulkes's own later writings (Foulkes, 1990) for a cultural-historical, rather than evolutionary-biological reading of the foundation matrix: that is, as the political and cultural assumptions drawn upon and unfolding within a developing group process. Further, connecting Foulkes's ideas to the organisational sphere, Nitsun (1998) has put forward the concept of an organisational matrix, claiming that this "has similar qualities of containing and holding to a group matrix but also similar propensities for malignant and destructive processes" (1998, p. 251).

Applying this to the research team, it is noteworthy that feminist and anti-racist commitments typically generate different working cultures or organisational matrices. Four indications of the tensions between these working cultures emerged. Initially, the feminist commitment, including the commitment around domestic violence, seemed to be the resource to bring us together as a team. Second, as an all-women team, we reflected our topic in the sense that all our research participants (survivors and providers) were women, although—as an interesting reflection of the ways professional roles either intersect with, or obscure, gender (c.f. Burman, 2001, 2002; Dutton Conn, 1995; Featherstone, 1997)—as at least one team member noted, we talked only of the survivors as "women", referring to the others via their professional titles.[8] This collective slip also indicated something of our own ambivalences about our institutional roles as women. Third, all this underscores the history of second wave feminism as inadvertently[9] white, middle class, and Eurocentric—thereby ignoring or devaluing the positions and experiences of black, minoritised and working-class women (Carby, 1982).[10] Against all this stood the fourth tension, a commitment to antiracist work which threw all assumed commonalities around relationships between women and between feminists into question in terms of research relationships and within the team.[11]

In terms of the group matrix or (conscious and unconscious) core beliefs underpinning these two "illusions", each ethos worked in opposing directions. For, while an assumption of 1970s and 1980s feminisms was that all-women spaces were safe, orthogonal to this was the ethos of antiracist work, which typically generates anxiety between participants—out of the fear of encountering racism, or being (accused of being) racist (Cooper, 1997; Treacher, 2001/2002). This context of "race" anxiety (Burman, Chantler, & Batsleer, 2002; Batsleer, Chantler, & Burman, 2003; Chantler, Burman, Batsleer, & Bashir, 2001) could therefore be seen to function at an organisational level in terms of elaborating antithetical group dynamics to the presumed "safety" of women's groups. In this light the subordination of "women" to "worker" or professional identities can be seen to mediate the shift from collusive collaboration to more nuanced and discriminating alliances.

Conceptualising the conflict between these different organisational matrices is useful in understanding why our research team found itself in such difficulties. Perhaps unsurprisingly, these problems coalesced around the constitution of the support groups. This, significantly, was the site of three key structural tensions that also brought to the fore the differences within the research team: first, between research and service provision (highlighting different areas of strength, skill and responsibility within the research team); second, between the definition and self definition of (the salience of) racialised positions—both for participants and for research team members; and, third, between culturally specialised vs. mixed/mainstream provision. These tensions, prompted by the enormity of the task of composing and conducting these groups, at times seemed to grip us with such intensity and paralysis that this key third phase of the project nearly had to be abandoned. It was only with a lot of extra work on the part of the team that this vital part of the project was carried out.

Thus, unlike Michel, I would not see the resolution of these difficulties as only lying within a reassertion of role specialisations and acknowledgement of professional differences. Instead I would point to the marked development and change made possible within research team members by holding on to the "group illusion" of joint, but then renegotiated, feminist anti-racist commitment and responsibility for the project. Notwithstanding the differential contributions made by each member, and the gaps between expectation and reality, this commitment enabled each of us to develop confidence, experience and skills: in working inter-culturally (one team member described this shift as "from a bone of contention to a bonus"), in working with groups, and in writing; as well as seeing a complex research process through to its end. As a manager, I learned much about the structure and intersections of institutional cultures and bureaucracies, and their impacts on individual and group relations.

Refuges or prisons?

The third area of resonance (Foulkes, 1975) between topic and process concerned the dynamics of refuges themselves. Refuges are supposed to be places of safety, retreat and secrecy. Yet the practices maintaining them as safe places can also work to make them separate, isolated and stigmatised arenas. Women surviving domestic violence have typically already been subject to extreme isolation, as both a condition for, and an effect of, their abuse (since—as we documented—abusers deliberately prevented women from contacting friends, family or agencies, or even entering public arenas where such contact would be possible). As with other research, our project highlighted how minoritised women, who have often lost links with family and community in making their escape (or have been ostracised when they disclosed the violence), are even more likely to be isolated and marginalised.

The vast majority of refuges maintain secret locations as a strategy to ensure the safety of women escaping violent relationships. Although almost unquestioned as a tenet of refuge provision, this secrecy is now undergoing some critical scrutiny from analysis of US-based provision (Haaken, in press) on the grounds, first, of reproducing the separation between the refuge and (especially minoritised) communities and, second, potentially making it more difficult for (especially minoritised) women to access the networks of relationships and resources that would help them to make the transition to independent living. The penalty for transgressing the rule of secrecy is eviction.[12]

This climate of secrecy produces very intense relationships within refuges, exacerbated by the states of distress of the residents (including possibly ongoing harassment), the lack of resources available,[13] cramped conditions and inevitable tensions arising over domestic arrangements. Notwithstanding the fact that refuges often emerge as providing the only gender-sensitive anti-racist support to survivors, our interview material indicated intense (and often conflictual) relationships between residents, between residents and refuge workers, even between refuge workers. All this can be understood in terms of structural conditions alongside the effects of abuse and of working around abuse (Dutton Conn, 1995; Featherstone, 1997), as well as indicating key psychological features of the contemporary organisation of relations between women (Ernst, 1997).

In terms of our research process, some such resonances crept up upon us, including the team being used as a refuge to cope with the unbearable feelings generated by interviewing survivors, which produce a sense of enclosure or secrecy about its meetings. When the research appeared to be foundering, the dynamics of "shaming" and "blaming" associated with domestic violence also arose in terms of projected splits within the team—between the "abusive managers" and the "exploited/victimised workers". There was an ethos of "take it to the research team meetings", as if the rules of communication between research team members were bound by a therapeutic group contract. This group norm, or defence, could be seen simultaneously to mask and to covertly challenge the operation of power relationships. The very elaboration of a "therapeutic" orientation to support each other, now threatened to overwhelm the team with individual worker needs appearing to be in tension with research goals, or indeed with the well-being and functioning of the team as a whole.[14]

Like refuges, the team boundaries seemed rigid and stuck, by virtue of the same sense of ownership and commitment to the work that had sustained it earlier; but now seemed to prevent it from moving on. A group-analytic approach enabled understanding, if not direct intervention. Foulkes and Anthony (1964) regarded interpretations as only required when needed to dismantle blocks in communication, and more recent approaches have downplayed this technique further (Dalal, 1998; Pines, 2002). But through careful "dynamic administration" in the form of convening business meetings with team members that addressed structural differences being avoided between the funded and unfunded workers, some of the defensive polarisations were softened and projections defused.

Some changes of circumstances helped to mitigate the climate of distrust and defensive introspection that (like refuges) had gripped the team. First, two members of the team (one of whom was me) who had been away gradually returned, and so brought new perspectives prompting review and re-evaluation.

Second, commitments to make presentations about the project to outside professional audiences fostered different configurations of relationships and alliances, and broke up polarised positions. The steering group fulfilled this role—although at times perhaps it also represented a hostile superego, an arena calling forth the covering up of shameful fantasised inadequacies or (in fantasy) of exposure and humiliation.

Third, and crucially, one of the research team took time out and returned with a new-found commitment and energy to complete the work, and helped to enable new alliances—both within the team and bringing new members into the team.

These included, fourth, shifting what had seemed to be an intractable resistance on the part of the team to involving new people by delegating some work outside the research team. Perhaps this resistance arose from fear of being shamed as inadequate researchers. However (like women first disclosing their abuse) from plucking up courage to "talk to outsiders," this move to "trusting outsiders" conceded that, as women, we did not have to be superwomen[15]—in the sense of managing to do everything without outside support—a particular dynamic that Featherstone (1997) identified.

Experiencing the enthusiasm and commitment of these new ("outside") members was also (reminiscent of the dynamics of a slow-open group) a reminder of what we had been like at an earlier stage. Once the isolation and defensive secrecy of the team had been acknowledged and addressed and we gradually got a sense of getting somewhere with the work we felt much better, more able to be open, and so to establish a better balance of communication between inside and outside team meetings. Here we can make links both with Stacey's (1996) concept of a "shadow system" and with how Blackwell (1998) links this with the group matrix to argue that the matrix (or unconscious) is not just destructive but also a source of creativity.

Conclusions

I have drawn on group analysis as well as feminist analysis to re-politicise apparently individual dynamics; by situating them spatially (within their broader political, cultural and institutional contexts), temporally (within a chronology) and exploring part-whole relations (between individual and group, and between groups, institutions and cultures). These are all key strengths of group analysis, as Nitsun argues:

> I consider the following group-analytic principles to be the most relevant to the study of organizations: levels of the group, the group matrix, the internal-external relationship, location, the setting, communication, the individual-group relation, and mirroring.
>
> (Nitsun, 1998, p. 250)

Clearly there are other relevant psychodynamic perspectives that could be drawn upon to explain organisational processes, including those of research. Group-analytic approaches may better help in illuminating the structural paradoxes mobilised within research processes that draw on (and feeling the need to draw upon, c.f Parker, 1997) psychodynamic concepts and analyses, while warding off therapeutic analysis[16] or interpretation at the level of individual psychodynamics.[17] Writing of the limitations of current Tavistock-oriented open systems theory approaches, Andrew Cooper (1998, p. 286) highlights as his own concerns that I share about current efforts to combine psychoanalysis with organizational analysis:

> It is the value neutrality of this model with respect to the social, political and ideological dimensions of this environment which renders it unable to do the job I am interested in. I am interested in what might happen, what new possibilities could emerge within the way of thinking and working, if the view of the boundary were opened to new sorts of influences reflecting a view of the world as less self-regulating or harmonious.

In action research the goal is not stable functioning of, or exchange between, organisational units. It is a time-limited enterprise to transform via its process as well as its outcomes, including transforming relationships with research participants, also within the research team. Change is therefore not something to be managed into equilibrium, but rather to be harnessed and directed so as to use, as well as manage, it's disturbing aspects.

It may be rather far-fetched to suggest, as Pines (2002, p. 17) has done (although he attributes this to Ben Davidson) that group analysis is a "technology of empowerment"—not least because this leaves unspecified who is being empowered, who wields the technology, and crucially what power relations are recapitulated within relations of "empowerment" (c.f. Bhavnani, 1990). Yet I hope that I have illustrated how group analysis can be a useful ingredient to socially oriented psychodynamic analysis of organisational, and specifically research, processes. Far from insisting on the specificity of group-analytic perspectives, I would rather highlight their convergence with, or, complementarily to, others—such as feminist approaches. So that, without reducing one to the other—we are provided with multiple frames from which to generate further critical analysis, and so resist the closure of any single interpretation.

Acknowledgement

In addition to acknowledging the research team members for their commitment and hard work, I want particularly to highlight the contribution of my co-manager Khatidja Chantler, both to the project and to our ongoing and retrospective analyses of its processes.

Notes

1. An earlier draft of this chapter was presented at the ESRC Seminar "The Psychodynamics of Organisational Change," Manchester Metropolitan University, November 5, 2002.
2. The project was funded under strategic objective, 5:2, dossier number: 91164NW3, match funded between the European Social Fund and Manchester Metropolitan University, carried out between September 2001 and July 2002.
3. Where families are joint rather than nuclear, parents, parents-in-law or siblings may be implicated in the abuse—if not as active perpetrators—but few of our provider accounts included this within their definitions of domestic violence.
4. The process and implications of the support groups convened for the project are discussed more extensively in Chapter 8 of Batsleer et al. (2002), and in Batsleer and Smailes (in press).
5. My account was circulated to the research team for comment.
6. Both our Irish and Jewish research participants discussed ways they were identified by others in negative ways on the basis of their appearance and behaviour.
7. Typical responses we documented could be characterised within the familiar refrains of: "It doesn't happen here" alongside "They look after

their own"—both of which add up to legitimise a lack of engagement. However the British Crime Survey (1996) indicated that there is no reason to assume that rates of domestic violence differ between classes and communities.

8. I have since observed that this is also a widespread practice.
9. Clearly feminists did not set out to do this but, especially in terms of institutional practices and influences have functioned in these ways (c.f. Burman, 1998).
10. This representation has also worked to obscure so-called Third World Feminisms, whose equation and sometimes coincidence with nationalist agendas has also bolstered this (see Heng, 1997).
11. I am not sure that any of us consciously subscribed to the notion that "all women together" would be similar, safe or comfortable. My own conscious beliefs are certainly otherwise, and elsewhere I have discussed feminism as a political movement coming into being precisely because women typically have so little structural interest or incentive to identify with each other (Burman, 2001).
12. On the basis of anecdotal evidence—including some further indications encountered within the research project—it would seem that it is especially young women, and within mainstream refuges black women, who are particularly liable to eviction on these grounds.
13. Few women in refuges are in paid employment, and so are dependent on state benefits. Some refuges in our study were supporting women who were totally destitute "with no recourse to public funds." The British benefit system discourages women in paid work from accessing refuge provision, since rentals (usually paid by public funds and needed to resource refuges) are prohibitively high for an individual to pay. This contributes to the image of women surviving domestic violence (as identified by their use of refuges) as both victims (as required by current systems governing entitlement) and dependent on the state.
14. We discuss this further in Burman and Chantler (in press).
15. This is especially important for minoritised women.
16. Elsewhere (Burman & Chantler, in press) we discuss how the very "speech act" of naming organisational processes in therapeutic terms can be regarded as implicitly doing the therapeutic work of "containing" the difficult feelings but without embarking on an explicitly therapeutic analysis which would have been an inappropriate task for the group.

17. Diego Napolitani (2001) makes similar points in relation to the project of group analysis generally.

References

Anzieu, D. (1981). *Le Groupe et l'inconscient: l'imaginaire groupal* (2nd edn). Paris: Dunod.

Anzieu, D. (1984). *The Group and the Unconscious*. London: Routledge and Kegan Paul.

Argyris, C. (1997). Field theory as a basis for scholarly consulting: Kurt Lewin Award Lecture 1997. *Journal of Social Issues, 53*(4): 811–827.

Banister, P., Burman, E., Parker, I., Taylor, M., & Tindall, C. (1994). *Qualitative Methods in Psychology: A Research Guide*. Buckingham: Open University Press.

Batsleer, J., Burman, E., Chantler, K., McIntosh, S., Pantling, K., Smailes, S., & Warner, S. (2002). *Domestic Violence and Minoritisation: Supporting Women to Independence*. Manchester: The Women's Studies Research Centre.

Batsleer, J., Chantler, K., & Burman, E. (2003). Responses of health and social care staff to South Asian Women who attempt suicide and/or self-harm. *British Journal of Social Work Practice*.

Batsleer, J., & Smailes, S. (in preparation). *Groupwork for Minoritized Women Surviving Domestic Violence: Issues of Group Composition and Process*.

Bhavnani, K. K. (1990). "What's power got to do with it": Empowerment and social research. In: I. Parker & J. Shotter (Eds.), *Deconstructing Social Psychology*. London: Routledge.

Blackwell, D. (1997). Holding, containing and bearing witness: The problem of helpfulness in encounters with torture survivors. *Journal of Social Work Practice, 11*(2): 81–89.

Blackwell, D. (1998). A response to "psychoanalysis and the politics of organisation, Commentary on article by Andrew Cooper. *Group Analysis, 31*(3): 296–303.

Burman, E. (1994). *Deconstructing Developmental Psychology*. London: Routledge.

Burman, E. (1997). Developmental psychology and its discontents. In: D. Fox & I. Prilleltensky (Eds.), *Critical Psychology*. London: Sage.

Burman, E. (Ed.). (1998). *Deconstructing Feminist Psychology*. London: Sage.

Burman, E. (2000). Method, measurement and madness. In: L. Holzman & J. Morss (Eds.), *Postmodern Psychologies, Societal Practice and Political Life*. New York: Routledge.

Burman, E. (2001). Engendering authority in the group. *Psychodynamic Counselling, 7*(3): 347–370.

Burman, E. (2002). Gender, sexuality and power in groups. *Group Analysis, 35*(4): 540–559.

Burman, E., & Chantler, K. (in press). There's no place like home: Researching "race" and refuge provision. *Gender, Place and Culture.*

Burman, E., Chantler, K., & Batsleer, J. (2002). Service responses to South Asian women attempting suicide or self-harm. *Critical Social Policy, 22*(4): 641–668.

Burman, E., Gowrisunkur, J., & Sangha, K. (1998). Conceptualising cultural and gendered identities in psychological therapies. *European Journal of Psychotherapy, Counselling and Health, 1*(2): 231–256.

Carby, H. (1982). White women listen! Black feminism and the boundaries of sisterhood. In: University of Birmingham Centre for Contemporary Cultural Studies (Ed.), *The Empire Strikes Back: Race and Racism in '70s Britain.* London: Hutchinson.

Chantler, K., Burman, E., Batsleer, J., & Bashir, C. (2001). *Attempted Suicide and Self-harm, Report of a HAZ Funded Research Project.* Manchester: Women's Studies Research Centre, the Manchester Metropolitan University.

Cooper, A. (1997). Thinking the unthinkable: "White Liberal" defences against understanding in anti-racist training. *Journal of Social Work Practice, 11*(2): 127–137.

Cooper, A. (1998). Psychoanalysis and the politics of organisational theory. *Group Analysis, 31*(3): 283–295.

Dalal, F. (1998). *Taking the Group Seriously: Towards a Post-Foulkesian Analysis.* London: Jessica Kingsley.

Dutton Conn, J. (1995). Autonomy and connection: Gendered thinking in a statutory agency dealing with child sexual abuse. In: C. Burck & B. Speed (Eds.), *Gender, Power and Relationships.* London: Routledge.

Ernst, S. (1997). Group-analytic psychotherapy: A site for the reworking of the relationship between mothers and daughters. In W. Hollway & B. Featherstone (Eds.), *Mothering and Ambivalence.* London: Routledge.

Featherstone, B. (1997). "I wouldn't do your job!" Women, social work and child abuse. In: W. Hollway & B. Featherstone (Eds.), *Mothering and Ambivalence.* London: Routledge.

Foulkes, E. (Ed.). (1990). *S. H. Foulkes: Selected Papers: Psychoanalysis and Group Analysis.* London: Karnac.

Foulkes, S. H. (1975). *Group-Analytic Psychotherapy: Methods and Principles.* London: Karnac.

Foulkes, S. H., & Anthony, E. J. (1964). *Group Psychotherapy: The Psychoanalytic Approach.* Harmondsworth: Pelican.

Haaken, J. (in press). Stories of survival: Class, race and domestic violence. In: Nancy Holstrom (Ed.), *Feminist Projects.* New York: Monthly Review Press.

Heng, G. (1997). "A great way to fly": Nationalism, the state and the varieties of third world feminism. In: M. Alexandra & C. Mohanty (Eds.), *Feminist Geneologies, Colonial Legacies, Democratic Futures*. New York: Routledge.

Michel, L. (2001). Group dynamics of a research team working in the field of migration. *Group Analysis, 34*(2): 211–220.

Napolitani, D. (2001). Group analysis today. Interview with Diego Napolitani by Maria Luisa Tapparo. *Journal of European Psychoanalysis, 12 & 13*, URL. Available at: http://www.psychomedia.it/number12-13/napolitani.htm

Nitsun, M. (1996). *The Anti-Group*. London: Routledge.

Nitsun, M. (1998). The organizational mirror (Part one). *Group Analysis, 31*(3): 245–267.

Pines, M. (2002). The coherency of group analysis. *Group Analysis, 35*(1): 13–27.

Stacey, R. (2000). Reflexivity, self-organisation and emergence in the group matrix. *Group Analysis, 33*(4): 501–513.

Stacey, R. (2001). Complexity and the group matrix. *Group Analysis, 34*(2): 221–240.

Stanley, L., & Wise, S. (1993). *Breaking Out Again: Feminist Consciousness and Feminist Research*. London: Routledge.

Steier, F. (Ed.). (1991). *Research and Reflexivity*. London: Sage.

Treacher, A. (2001/2002). Ethnicity: Recognition and identification. *Psychoanalytic Studies, 3*(4): 325–332.

Wilkinson, S. (1988). The role of reflexivity in feminist psychology. *Women's Studies International Forum, 11*(5): 493–502.

Zagier Roberts, V. (1994). The self assigned impossible task. In: A. Obholzer & V. Zagier Roberts (Eds.), *The Unconscious at Work: Individual and Organisation Stress in the Human Services*. London: Routledge.

PART V

SUPERVISION

CHAPTER SEVEN

The integration of theory and practice*

Harold L. Behr

Supervision lies in the terrain between the teaching of theory and practice of therapy. As such, it allows for an integrated experience which combines the conceptual thinking of the former with the experiential learning of the latter. In supervision the supervisee's work comes under the benign scrutiny of the supervisor, enabling the two to focus together on the supervisee's skills and technique, and providing a major influence on the supervisee's overall professional development.

In the context of individual psychotherapy, supervision can be seen as a conversation between two persons about a third. However, the conversation is carefully structured, and the situation is complicated by the fact that the third person is never physically present. A series of relationships arises within a common matrix. The therapeutic relationship between supervisee and patient is brought into the supervision room through the reporting of material from the therapy sessions, and this in turn impinges on the supervisory relationship. Supervisor and

*This chapter was previously published as: Behr, H. (1995). The integration of theory and practice. In: M. Sharpe (Ed.), *The Third Eye: Supervision of Analytic Groups* (pp. 4–17). Routledge: London.

patient are destined never to meet, yet each affects the other through the intermediacy of the therapist. The purpose of supervision is twofold: first, to catalyse the therapeutic relationship for the ultimate benefit of the patient, and second to enhance the supervisee's skills as a therapist. It is assumed that the supervisor has certain attributes, be they greater knowledge, experience or "know-how", which can be imparted to the less knowledgeable, less experienced supervisee. Supervision therefore becomes a way of transmitting an accumulated body of knowledge and expertise from one generation of therapists to the next. It is a vehicle for the "oral tradition" of the school of psychotherapy which it represents.

In the context of supervision for group psychotherapy, an analogous process occurs. Here the focus moves between the supervisee's therapeutic relationship with a group of patients (referred to in a training context as the training group) and the supervisory relationship, which may be with just one person (the supervisor) or with a whole group. The supervision group can be understood as a figure-ground constellation, the foreground of which is usually occupied by the interaction between the supervisee and the training group, while the background constitutes a kaleidoscopic pattern of configurations which connect the therapeutic relationship, the supervisory relationship and the wider training setting, including the supervisee's relationship with the training institute and the supervisee's own personal therapy group. From time to time any of these may emerge into the foreground and become a focus of dynamic work.

Group supervision in the context of Group-Analytic training

It is easy to underestimate the degree of bewilderment and apprehension which engulfs trainees at the beginning of their group-analytic training. Moving uncertainly between the rarified atmosphere of unfamiliar theoretical ideas and the deep waters of personal therapy, the trainee often feels most grounded in the supervision group. Here, together with three or four fellow trainees and the supervisor, in an attitude of shared learning, group process can be looked at objectively, and techniques for intervening therapeutically can be rehearsed and understood within a dynamic matrix.

The model of training provided by the London Institute of Group Analysis offers a tripartite structure in which personal therapy, theory teaching and supervision are held within a single dynamic framework. Trainees are encouraged to regard the three components of the training as informing one another, and material from the one may become the subject of one or both of the other two. In practice, supervision is often the forum for this integrative process, since it is here that the trainees can make connections between their own work as therapists and the newly digested ideas emanating from the theory seminars. At the same time, the supervision group, composed as it is of individuals committed to an analytic understanding of groups, often captures the feelings generated by members of the supervisee's training group, reflecting them back to the supervisee and replicating a group dynamic which resonates with the patient group.

Feelings ran high in a group conducted by a male trainee after two women members of the group got into an irritable conflict over the marital difficulties of a man in the group. One identified fiercely with the man's partner, the other with the man himself. The conductor allowed the conflict to escalate, and a point was reached where one woman burst into tears and the other lapsed into a grim silence. The following week one of the women (the silent one) was absent, having sent a message that she was not well.

In the supervision, the trainee admitted to having felt paralysed by the conflict which had raised echoes of arguments between his parents when he was a child. He had justified his silence however, with the consoling thought that "the feelings were all there in the group and the group seemed to be working well with the problem". This generated a heated exchange amongst his peers, some of whom felt that he should have supported the more vulnerable-seeming woman (who had cried), others that the silent woman was more at risk of dropping out. The supervisor helped the group to look at the chain of events which had developed from the male group member's tendency to "split" the group, through to the conductor's silent collusion with the process, to a similar scenario that was being replicated in the supervision group itself. This freed the trainee to acknowledge that he had private sympathy with the woman who had cried and that he could think now about the personal significance of this for him. The way was open for an exploration of these issues in his own therapy and the supervision group could address the task of retrieving the potential drop-out.

Reconciling theory and practice

Group analysis as a subject does not lend itself readily to teaching. The problem lies in the elusive character of those concepts which can be regarded as specific to group analysis (e.g. the group matrix, mirroring, resonance, and dynamic administration) and the many non-specific concepts which inform group-analytic thinking derived from well-established schools of discourse, such as psychoanalysis and systems theory. A large number of theoretical antecedents are therefore woven together in a single fabric, making it difficult for the neophyte group analyst to discern a coherent theoretical entity.

In practice, however, the hybrid organism which is group analysis has a clear and distinctive identity which distinguishes it from other models of group psychotherapy. The principle of investing the group as a whole with therapeutic potential, while never losing sight of the individual, lies at the core of group-analytic practice. On the basis of this principle an array of techniques has been developed, each of which is by no means specific to group analysis, but which cumulatively, and within the context of group therapy, amount to a distinctive therapeutic approach.

Learning, therefore, advances along a broad front, as the trainee acquires various techniques for addressing the multiplicity of practical and dynamic issues which can arise in groups and matches them with the many facets of group-analytic theory which underlie those techniques. In supervision, it is mainly the technical aspects of group analysis which are examined: preparing the ground for the group, interviewing, assessing and preparing potential group members, protecting the group setting from incursions, managing the group boundary, coping with difficult situations as they arise, steering the group towards a more reflective mode of functioning, and helping the group to make sense of the rich, confusing and emotionally charged material which contributes to the group process.

Structure and dynamics of the supervision group

At the level of a Qualifying Course, our experience at the Institute of Group Analysis is that a mix of beginners and more advanced trainees works well. To some extent this composition of a supervision group reproduces the slow-open model of the therapy groups. Trainees have to welcome new members and say goodbye to old ones with the same ripples of feeling which run through a patient group over such issues as: "What will the new person bring to the group?" "Am I ready to leave?" "Have I done well enough?" "How will I continue to get support after I have left?" The vigilant supervisor will ensure that time is set aside to address these issues, and that the group of peers is mobilised to make its own dynamic contribution to the process.

Beginners' lack of clinical or therapeutic experience turns out to be a "non-problem", as does the fact that the trainees come from diverse professional backgrounds. The group is made up of individuals who have been through a careful selection process and who almost invariably provide an immediate and constructive input into the supervision. All trainees will have been in their own personal therapeutic groups for at least a year prior to joining the formal training programme, and come to supervision equipped with a good sense of how to function in a group-analytic setting.

Occasionally trainees have to unlearn habits acquired in their core professions, and here the diversity of professional backgrounds provides a salutary opportunity for exchange transfusions between trainees. For example, those from a teaching background occasionally have to modify a tendency towards excessive structuring and didacticism; psychiatrists may have a proclivity for medicalising therapeutic problems, being too preoccupied with diagnostic categories, or taking inappropriate responsibility for the medical care of their patients (e.g. offering "helpful" professional advice about medication, or illness). The multi-professional composition of the supervision group rapidly neutralises these professional defences and frees the trainee to think and function in a more psychodynamic way.

The frequency, time scale, and duration of the supervision sessions parallel that of the training group. The supervision group meets at weekly intervals for one and a half hours, and experiences the same rhythm of working periods and breaks as the training group. Because of the need to allow for detailed reporting of group process and discussion of group material by the trainees, it is necessary to structure the supervision sessions quite carefully. Enough time has to be set aside for peer group interaction while ensuring that all members of the supervision group have the opportunity to bring up issues concerning their training group and explore them in depth. Within these time constraints there has to be enough flexibility to accommodate discussions about the inevitable crises or acute problems which erupt from time to time in training groups. I find that the system which works best is one in which everyone has an opportunity to report on their group each session, some only briefly, perhaps for no more than a few minutes, others (not more than two) in substance and in depth, while anyone can claim additional time to deal with more pressing issues. Through a gradually rotating system of turn-taking for "major" and "minor" presentations, each trainee has a regular "slot" for detailed attention to his or her group, and all are kept in touch with one another's groups. This does mean, however, that the supervisor has to be especially watchful of the time boundaries, and mindful of when to "cue in" the peer group, when to invite a pause in the presentation (or "freeze the action"), and when to offer comments.

Listening to the material from a session, I try to place myself in the trainee's shoes, monitoring my own possible interventions alongside those of the trainee's. What might I have said at that point? Would I have intervened just then? If our paths seem to be diverging, I might recapitulate the process as I have understood it and invite a response from the peer group. This opens up fresh dynamic insights and often achieves the reconciliation of contrasting perspectives.

It is especially important to acknowledge therapeutic competence. If a training group is functioning well, or if a trainee seems to be handling a particular situation effectively, I look for an opportunity to draw attention to this. Trainees feel affirmed by a supervision in which their strengths and skills, as well as their blind spots, are recognised. The awe of the training situation and the confusion intrinsic to group interaction can sometimes lead to unjustified feelings of pessimism and self-doubt, which positive feedback by the supervisor helps to counteract.

The actual reporting of material is as varied as the personalities of the trainees. Beginning trainees are given a structure in which they are encouraged to record as much of the raw material of the sessions as they can hold on to, capturing it in sequence as far as possible, and not bothering to analyse or "package" it in theoretical terms. That task will be left to the supervision group. Trainees sometimes have to be prompted to remember and record their own interventions. Not infrequently a beautiful process account of a session is presented, from which the conductor's participation is conspicuously absent!

Trainees are encouraged to plot the group's attendance record week by week, from which it becomes possible to see at a glance the pattern of attendances, absences and late-comings. This provides a useful chart of the group's course through the turbulent waters of arrivals, departures, holiday breaks and other group events. Schematic representations of group sessions showing how people seat themselves can provide a useful prop for the presentation and can help the supervision group to visualise interpersonal interactions. In general, however, I discourage handouts which list biographical details of the individual group members, or record complicated psychodynamic or diagnostic formulations. Too often a preoccupation with this kind of information gets the supervision bogged down in a welter of facts which contribute little to an understanding of the group-analytic process.

As trainees become more experienced, the supervision group comes to feel more like a group of colleagues, sharing thoughts with one another about the complexities of group analysis. The group being presented becomes a focus for comparing notes on counter-transference and technique, and the realisation dawns that there is no definitively "correct" intervention at any given point. The collective voice of the supervision group speaks clearly, as it does in a patient group.

I occasionally proffer my own experiences as a conductor (for better or worse) to the supervision group, setting them alongside those of the trainees. In a well-functioning supervision group the trainees come to realise that the training is designed, not to create clones of some imaginary, idealised group analyst, but to encompass a diversity of styles, techniques, and approaches.

The demolition of myths about Group-Analytic technique

Whether or not they have had previous experience of psychotherapy prior to entering their group-analytic training, most trainees bring with them assumptions about the sort of behaviour which constitutes good therapeutic practice. In their early endeavours as group conductors, they attempt to implement techniques which, by their reckoning, will move the group in the direction of the ideal. The supervision group has to provide a corrective learning experience without undermining the trainees' confidence in their skills. Often this amounts to no more than a nudge towards greater flexibility, allowing the pendulum to swing towards the midpoint between two polarities. Anxious beginners are notoriously rigid in their application of real and imagined rules. In a field as nebulous as group psychotherapy, it is always tempting to adhere to clear and dogmatic assumptions and to deal with uncertainty by adopting a handful of monolithic formulas in the hope of bringing some order to the confusion.

The reticent therapist

One of the commonest pitfalls facing the beginning group analyst lies in the tendency to withhold interventions to a point where the group starts to move in a counter-therapeutic direction. Sometimes this well-intentioned position is governed by an overzealous adherence to the group-analytic tenet that "the group does the work", forgetting that the conductor is very much part of the group, and failing to realise that the group members, for all their inherent therapeutic capabilities, depend heavily on the conductor to actively mould the therapeutic culture towards an attitude of openness and interpersonal exploration, especially in the group's formative stages.

Another reason for therapeutic reticence lies in a misguided translation from psychoanalytic technique into group analysis, of the notion that the therapist should furnish a "blank screen" to draw out transference projections. This therapeutic stance is sometimes fuelled by the therapist's genuine anxiety, a fear of saying or doing something that might interrupt a delicate process, and perplexity about what is really going on in the group. When in doubt, it is often easier to take refuge in silence, especially if one's silence can be justified by some respectable professional axioms.

Preoccupation with the group as a whole at the expense of the individual

Related to the problem of excessive reticence is an attitude which assumes that the therapist should confine interventions to pronouncements about the group as a whole. Often these pronouncements take the form of interpretations, another technique borrowed from classical psychoanalysis and from some forms of psychoanalytic group psychotherapy, and often used inappropriately or prematurely in an effort to hold the group to a psychoanalytic mode of functioning.

The problem with predominantly group-as-a-whole interventions, as with excessive reticence, is that individual group members are often left feeling unheld or unrecognised. Anxiety and frustration are increased, and group members find it more difficult to interact freely with one another in a mutually therapeutic mode or tolerate one person holding the focus for very long. Such groups tend to be affected by an increased drop-out rate and function with an anxious, compliant culture. Supervision in such a situation concentrates on encouraging the trainee to recognise the importance of acknowledging individuals, modelling dyadic interactions within the group, and increasing the repertoire of interventions to include not only interpretations but other forms of communication, and especially to feel free to ask occasional questions and offer affiliative comments. The challenge to therapeutic omniscience is, not surprisingly, often greeted with relief.

Preoccupation with individuals at the expense of the group

A contrasting, but equally hazardous course which some trainees embark upon is the overactive engagement with group members to the point where the rest of the group is forced into the background and loses effectiveness as a therapeutic agency. When a particular group member is chosen as the focus, the trail in supervision quickly leads to the conductor's counter-transference. It often becomes clear that the trainee's over-identification with a group member, or with a sub-group (the men, or the women, for instance), is shadowed by over-identification with a larger, archetypal symbolic representative of that person or sub-group, for example, "the helpless little boy" or "the vulnerable mother". Equally, confrontation over the tendency to ignore some individuals and sub-groups may reveal a negative counter-transference. These counter-transference issues can then be usefully explored, along with other counter-transference issues, in the trainee's own therapy group, having been opened up in the supervision group.

It is difficult to know when to focus on the individual and when to focus on the group. The group-analytic concept of the group as a figure-ground constellation, offering ever-changing configurations of dialogue, provides a useful working model and serves as an anchor for trainees who feel themselves tossed from one interaction to another in the group. In the end, the trainee usually comes to realise that "good-enough" therapy depends not so much on knowing what is going on, but on being able to hold the setting, providing oneself as a containing presence, facilitating open communication between all in the group (including the conductor) and protecting the group from buffetings which threaten its predictability and safety.

Steering between the Scylla of the "Here and now" and the Charybdis of the "There and Then"

Group analysts vary somewhat in the extent to which they facilitate the exploration of interactions between the group members themselves, as opposed to the exploration of material deriving from group members' relationships outside the group and past experiences. Excessive preoccupation with either mode can constitute a group defence against open communication. Some trainee group analysts have a tendency to polarise along this spectrum as a means of resolving difficult therapeutic dilemmas. As group analysts, we have considerable power to influence the direction which a group takes, and it is not sufficient to plead that one should be guided by the group in this matter. Supervision helps the trainee to steer a middle course through these uncharted waters.

Quite often the supervision session is occupied with helping trainees to turn the rudder away from the "here and now" (an interactional field which has much fascination for professionals but is usually of little interest to "bona fide" patients), and steer the group towards material which brings alive the group members' own worlds outside the group. The introduction of this material into the group makes it available for therapeutic work and almost invariably engages the group. From time to time the rudder has to swing the other way, particularly when a group changes its membership, or when a group event, such as conflict between group members, intrudes into the process. But for the most part, groups function well in an atmosphere in which all can feel able to bring their outside lives and inner worlds into the space of the group to be held, looked at and worked on by the whole group.

The virtues of small talk and humour

Trainees often feel an obligation to maintain their groups at a "profound" or "analytic" level of communication. In practice this often leads to the creation of an unduly oppressive, solemn atmosphere in which group members feel uncomfortable about bringing to the group any material other than their most serious life problems or their most premeditated thoughts. Light-hearted or humorous comments may be frowned on as frivolous, or construed, implicitly or explicitly, as "defensive".

In supervision, I go to some lengths to foster a welcoming attitude towards humorous, joking, playful, or bantering interactions, redefining them as the adult equivalent of childhood play. I encourage trainees to look at them as creative opportunities for entering the transitional space of the group and I show them how to amplify such communications within the group, and how to induct group members into an exploration of their therapeutic significance. By the same token, trainees often have to be helped to elevate mundane forms of communication such as casual observations, exchanges of trivial information, gossip, generalisations, conversations about social and political issues in the world at large, seemingly petty remarks and throw-away lines, to the level of important contributions, with inherent therapeutic potential. It is not too difficult to demonstrate how any such interaction in the group, if grasped, can lead through a maze of associations, to deeper, emotionally charged levels of communication. Supervision also helps trainees to discard the assumption that it is analytically correct to withhold their own playful impulses and humorous inclinations.

Interpretation or interruption?

Trainees generally experience relief as they come to appreciate the fundamental group-analytic tenet that the licence to interpret is granted not only to the conductor, but to individual group members, and to the group as a whole. The formal, elaborately constructed interpretation of classical psychoanalysis is replaced by a gradually emergent group response to group members' material. The concept of "ego training in action" takes pride of place in the therapeutic repertoire, superseding interpretation by the conductor as the main therapeutic instrument. Moreover, as mentioned earlier, if interpretation is offered as the only therapeutic intervention by an otherwise inscrutable conductor, a passive, regressed group dynamic is cultivated, weakening the therapeutic potential of the group as a whole.

When the conductor does venture an interpretation, timing is of the essence. Trainees and seasoned therapists alike struggle with this problem. Too early an intervention, delivered with a ring of finality, and conveying all the power and authority of the therapist, can stifle an emerging dynamic. Similarly, an interpretation given as a means of effecting closure over a messy, unresolved interaction, can be experienced as a gratuitous offering, and may be aimed more at reducing the conductor's anxiety than at moving the group forward. The so-called "plunging interpretation", an attempt to link group associations with primitive levels of communication before the group itself is ready to make the connection spontaneously, is another common, tempting but generally unhelpful intervention, and can be experienced by the group more as a puzzling interference than a facilitating contribution.

Trainees are also sometimes inclined to pull communication insistently towards themselves, in the belief that the conductor should be the central transference object. Conductor-centred interpretations may well be indicated, especially early in therapy, when an individual or the group has to be coaxed from an attitude of dependence towards a more mutually interdependent mode of communicating, but trainees often struggle to get the balance right between centrality and marginalisation, and inappropriately resort to making transference interpretations as a means of asserting their position in the group.

A group being held in a large psychiatric hospital was briefly interrupted when the door opened and an unkempt, bewildered-looking man wandered into the room. The conductor ushered him out, and one woman remarked indignantly that it was disgraceful that people could get lost like that in a hospital with no one nearby to keep an eye on them. A man in the group facetiously remarked that the man could have been a psychiatrist. This was greeted with peals of laughter which broke the tension, and a series of rapid-fire associations about how "crazy" psychiatrists are and how, according to one group member, they are even more "weird" than their patients. There was more laughter and joking, with references to the cannibal psychiatrist in the film *The Silence of the Lambs*. Someone remarked drily that she did not consider herself a tasty morsel for any psychiatrist. The conductor delivered an interpretation to the effect that the group was coping with the anxiety of chaos and fear of madness by projecting this onto himself, the therapist. This was greeted with a long silence which was broken by an apparent non sequitur when someone remarked that time seemed to be going by very slowly and this seemed like one of the longest sessions he could remember. The session ended with two members announcing that they could not be there the following week because of family commitments.

One group member mentioned that she would have to collect her young son from a friend since he could not find his way home by himself.

In the supervision, the trainee's peers reflected back to him that they felt angry on behalf of his group. The supervision session helped the trainee to focus on a number of issues: the group's anger at the intrusion into their setting and the conductor's failure to protect them from this, their identification with the man who was manifestly an inpatient at the hospital and therefore in need of more intensive therapy than they themselves required, with all the fears and wishes associated with this, including the fear of madness, which was indeed reflected in their attempts to project this on to the powerful figure of the psychiatrist/therapist. The supervision group debated the pros and cons of breaking into the jocular mode of the group with a solemn interpretation which had effectively widened the distance between the rest of the group and the conductor at a moment when the group was perhaps attempting to reconcile stereotyped differences between "sanity" and "madness".

Coping with critical moments in the group

The supervision group sometimes functions as a shock absorber when a training group experiences a crisis, or when a group event occurs which shocks or traumatises the group, such as the suicide or attempted suicide of a group member, the sudden appearance of severe mental disturbance or serious illness in a group member, or an episode of destructive acting-out behaviour.

A woman trainee telephoned her supervisor to ask for some urgent advice. She herself had been telephoned by a distressed group member who informed her that she had been found to have a breast lump which had proven to be malignant, and that she might have to undergo surgery. The group member doubted whether she could share this with the group, her manifest reason being that another group member's mother was critically ill with cancer, and that she did not want to add to that person's burden. She even wondered whether she would return to the group at all. The trainee herself had misgivings about this, fearing the impact on a group whose membership she was already experiencing as precarious, of a group member with a serious, potentially life-threatening illness. The supervisor supported the trainee in her decision to offer the group member an individual session as a prelude to returning to the group, and the supervision group encouraged the trainee to retain the group member and help both her and the rest of the group to deal with the shock of the news, the mourning of the loss of good health, the anxiety about the future, and possible repercussions on other group members. In fact, the group worked well with these issues, and the trainee was able to reflect on her own sensitivity to the effect of illness on family life, arising out of a personal experience with a chronically ill parent.

Less traumatic but nevertheless stressful incidents may arise through disruption of the group setting (for example, through abrupt changes in the group room imposed by the institution hosting the group or through an assault on the group's boundary). Many and varied are the ways in which groups can be encroached upon to render them less effective as containers. An important ingredient of supervision throughout the training is the emphasis on "dynamic administration", another core concept of group analysis which refers to the necessity for the group conductor to attend assiduously to all the details that surround the establishment of the group setting. These include selecting and preparing the group members for the group, structuring the group in time and place, and ensuring that communications taking place outside the group are ultimately woven into the dynamic context of the group itself and used to advance the therapeutic process.

When a crisis or shock does occur, the supervision group holds the trainee in a supportive way, much as a therapeutic group would, and provides the necessary space to reflect on the event. Appropriate therapeutic interventions are jointly rehearsed and the trainee is helped to understand that such occurrences are an inevitable part of therapy, and that the therapeutic group carries within itself the potential for working through and repairing the process.

Supervision beyond the training context

Trainees often come to experience supervision as a necessary concomitant of therapeutic practice. Once the training has been completed and the trainee emerges into the hurly-burly of professional life, the loss of supervision is felt with a pang of uncertainty, even a feeling of deprivation. In practice, very few group-analytic therapists are able to build into their professional activities a slot for supervision. Indeed, it is an open question whether supervision should be construed as an essential element of the work routine, or a luxury for which few can afford either the time or the money and which belongs indispensably to the student role.

For more experienced therapists, the term "supervision" itself feels uncomfortable. The notion of being looked at from above is less appropriate amongst trained peers than it is within a training context, and it would be good if some other term (perhaps "paravision"—looking at one's work alongside another person) could gain currency. But leaving aside the problem of jargon, it would seem that those therapists who are able to gather together with a few of their colleagues and meet regularly to discuss their groups and exchange ideas, are few and far between but fortunate indeed. Group analysis rests on the assumption that interpersonal disturbance comes about through isolation. The corollary of this is that a group which fosters open communication provides an antidote to isolation. If this is true of therapeutic groups, it should be true of groups in which fellow therapists contemplate their work together.

PART VI

EDUCATION

CHAPTER EIGHT

Beyond the unconscious: group analysis applied*

Jane Abercrombie

Mr. Chairman, ladies and gentlemen, or as I would rather say, Malcolm, and other friends, I need to crave your indulgence for my boldness in agreeing to give this lecture in a series which honours the memory of Dr. Foulkes. My title may seem a pretentious one. "Beyond the Unconscious" may give you a spooky feeling, as perhaps "infrared" or "ultraviolet" may do—rays which are neither red nor violet: we have no bodily senses to perceive them with, but only know them as unseen powers. And "Group Analysis Applied" may also seem grandiose. Dr. Foulkes himself saw group analysis as having possible relevance to many fields of human behaviour, just as does psychoanalysis, which also developed out of observation and treatment of the mentally sick, and has made its contribution to our understanding of many aspects of so-called normal human behaviour, influencing for instance the way we bring up our children. My own experience, however, is limited to the application of group analysis to higher education, though I think that similar methods can be applied to many other fields.

*This chapter was previously published as: Abercrombie, M. L. J. (1981). Beyond the unconscious: Group-analysis applied. *Group Analysis, XIV*: 2–14.

I shall be talking, then, of helping students to become more effective in their chosen academic fields by getting better understanding, and therefore better control, of those relevant parts of their behaviour that originate outside their own conscious awareness and are therefore not subject to their own evaluation. This dabbling with the unconscious is not a recognised aim of most higher education, but stated in this crude simplicity, it is not very different from that of most psychoanalytically, or depth-oriented psychotherapists, whether practising with individuals or with groups. Their aim is to make the unconscious conscious. But the unconscious they tackle is the result of repression in the service of avoiding psychic pain in infancy and childhood. The unconscious processes that affect seeing and thinking in later life are the results of habit, of familiarity with processes and things that can be handled without taking thought. We have learned to save nervous energy by relegating to the unconscious our ways of handling events that have occurred repeatedly and can be expected to continue so, in order to focus attention on new or unexpected events. Comparison with the so-called "autonomic" or "vegetative" nervous system is relevant. It gets on quietly with its work of controlling the movements of the gut, vascular system and other viscera without our needing to take thought. But we can learn how to regulate its activities by taking thought; to do this we need to become sensitised to its working and to get feedback of the results of consciously controlling it.

The human brain has been described as the best and cheapest general computer, assembled by unskilled labour. I feel that as users of it, we are all unskilled labourers. Let me remind you of the complexities of our computer. The brain of each of us contains many millions of nerve cells. Each has richly branched extensions which make contact with other cells. One such cell can make contact with a thousand or so others. The possibilities of different communication routes within this neural network are enormous. I believe that group analysis can help us to make better use of such diversities. Perhaps I should now describe how I came to apply group analytic methods to teaching. As a young teacher of zoology my aim was, as is conventional, to hand over to the student a body of knowledge, the fruits of my own labours of learning what others had learned from others or themselves discovered. This was to be done in such a way that the student would be able to observe accurately and comprehensively himself and draw reasonable conclusions from what he saw, and would go on learning and finding out as a resourceful, competent, independent scientific worker. But I noticed that students sometimes behaved otherwise. If, for instance, they were drawing something they saw under the microscope, they would often draw what they thought they *ought* to see, whether it was there or not. If they had identified the object correctly, their drawing would be a mixture of what others could agree was in that specimen, and a textbook diagram of it, which would have been made as a composite of many specimens treated in various ways. They were confirming what they knew, had been taught, not reporting on what was exposed to their *own* eyes. In similar manner children drawing an apple with a knitting needle stuck through it will often show the whole needle as though the apple were transparent.

I came to see that the difficulties of seeing a thing as it really is are related to the manner in which the observer relates his present sensory experience to his past, his store of memories of similar or relevant experiences, including what he had been taught. His relating present and past is connected with his relationship to teachers. It seemed to me that one was handicapped in trying to help students to come to terms with past and present in the ordinary relationship of the student to his teacher, that of one dependent on an authority figure. So I started to experiment with group discussions, in which relationships between students, peers, were strengthened.

In attempting to train preclinical medical students in scientific method using discussion groups, I came across the distressing response of some students of intense hostility to a teacher who tries to liberate them from their dependence on authority figures and become self-reliant in learning. (This was in the early post-war years, when many ex-service students were in the medical school.) I chatted about my experiences with a colleague at University College London, saying it was something like reports about group psychotherapy (of which I was very ignorant at that time). He told me of a friend, Dr. Martin James, who was treating skin patients in groups, and arranged for me to visit one of his clinics. I just walked into a little room where there were some patients in blue hospital uniform and some out-patients. I was strongly impressed with the social atmosphere in which Dr. James conducted the group, and I realised that if teachers could achieve something of this in teaching groups, half the difficulties could be overcome. Dr. James introduced me to his teacher, Dr. Foulkes, and I joined one of his group analytic psychotherapy groups, and began to apply some of his techniques in teaching. I did this first with preclinical medical students, then with students of architecture, and then with university teachers who wished to improve their use of small group methods.

In these three projects the institutional circumstances were different, as were the specific teaching aims. In the first project the aim was to help students to be objective, scientific in their tasks of diagnosing and treating patients; in the second to help architecture students to prepare themselves for team work with other members of the building team—with builders, engineers, quantity surveyors, clients, etc. and perhaps most difficult of all, with other architects over the design process itself. In the third, collaborating with a colleague, Paul Terry, we tried to help teachers to achieve the changes in their role which are necessary for group teaching.

As to the institutional circumstances, the first project, running for ten years through the fifties, took place in a Faculty of Radical Sciences of international renown, much preoccupied with research, comparatively little concerned with students as persons, so that the clubbable atmosphere of the discussion groups showed as a marked contrast. A student said, "We're tickled pink you know our names".

Five years later in a School of Architecture with a very innovative Head, the second project started in a quite different educational climate. The post-war convalescent calm and confident prospect of expansion of the universities was succeeded by energetic criticism of the methods used to teach the increased university population. Students were much less biddable than their predecessors and in the late sixties all over the globe exploded into active rebellion. I set myself the task of trying to engage the teachers in developing a climate of adapting to change and in particular to encouraging autonomous learning. This could perhaps be seen as comparable with the therapeutic community philosophies which Dr. Foulkes himself had used in his Northfield experiment.

By 1972, when the third project started, many teachers had realised that advances could not occur only by curriculum development and the application of educational technology, and that they needed to look into the importance of their highly personal contribution to the teacher/student relationship. Comparatively few had seen as yet the importance of student-to-student relationships.

All projects were similar in that I saw my job as one of setting up the means by which participants could talk freely about their current behaviour in relation to the specific educational task, in such a way that their relevant basic assumptions, or expectations, or attitudes, of which they were not aware, could become clear to them by comparison and contrast with those of the other participants.

Authority and dependence

Before I describe in more detail how I set about this, I need to spell out more precisely how I see the influence of older people on one's learning.

In Rembrandt's sketch of two old women with a child learning to walk, the child wears a padded hat in case he falls: the women do not *teach* him, so much as encourage and support him—they help him into a future of conditions unfamiliar to them, beyond their imagination. In a photograph of a child pushing a full-sized wheelbarrow, we see him imitating a grown up and supporting himself with a grown-up's tool—he can hardly walk on his own. A two and a half-year old watching his father mend a toy has every muscle tense. Would that students paid such fascinated attention to what we would like to teach them! In Picasso's "Young Acrobat on a Ball" the youth is practising in the presence of his father, a monumental seated figure, seemingly not actually watching his son, but massively *there.*

Some significant observations were made (Harlow, 1959) on the effects of an artificial mother figure on the behaviour of baby monkeys. The baby monkeys were reared on two kinds of models equipped with milk supplies, one made of wire, the other padded and covered with terrycloth. When a baby was put in a strange situation, a room with interesting objects strewn around, he would retreat to a corner, hiding away in fear if no mother surrogate or the wire model, were present but if the padded model were there he would rush to it and cuddle it as though rubbing comfort into himself. Then he would turn and look at the interesting things around, and finally make little excursions to one or the other, returning at intervals to the mother base. In the presence of the comfortable model the baby got support enough to learn and explore, which he was unable to do without it, or with the wire model. Teachers in plate-glass-and-concrete universities have commented on the large number of students who bring teddy bears with them.

Lee (Lee, 1957) reported that children's rates of learning at school were related to the *perceived* distance between home and school.

For journeys taking the same time, the children who could toddle along to school did better at school than those who lived so far away that they had to be taken in car or bus, and could not get back on their own.

It will be noted that in the case of learning motor skills, the child gets feedback from his own body, he can *feel* and *know* whether he's walking, or balancing on a ball properly. The same immediacy of feedback occurs with the satisfaction of natural curiosity, as in the two and a half-year old watching his father, and the monkey exploring his strange environment. But with factual information, other people's experience conveyed verbally, the child gets no feedback from himself—he cannot test the truth of the teacher's statements, nor whether he has learnt from them what the teacher intended. I recall how, when I was taught geography, we traced several maps of Australia, coloured to show mountains, towns, rivers, crops, or industry, etc. But I could never check with my own sense organs, whether what I'd learned was true or not, nor did it ever occur to me to try to do so. We never did anything so revolutionary as happens in some schools now, of letting children learn the geography of their own neighbourhood. I never dreamed of finding out with my own sense organs, using a compass or the sun, whether the house I lived in faced north, south, east, or west.

The set up for teaching "factual" knowledge as distinct from motor skills is indicated in a picture of a mediaeval school room, which is a caricature of the setup in many modern school rooms or lecture halls. The authority of the teacher is exaggerated by several features which are strictly speaking extraneous to his scholarship. He sits on a higher seat than the pupils, wears a high hat, has a bigger book propped up on a lectern which also serves to separate him from the children, and has a birch to beat them if they are naughty and an assistant to ridicule them with a donkey's head if they are stupid. It is an asymmetric relationship—the teacher talks, the children listen and occasionally speak to him (usually only if spoken to) but are not supposed to speak or listen to each other. If they have learnt the lesson, they can reproduce what the teacher said to his satisfaction. They have no other ways of knowing right from wrong. The acquisition of knowledge becomes intimately associated with the students' relationship to the teacher, and to other authority figures. In a wood carving from East Africa, mentor and child are sharing one head in an affectionate relationship. This is O.K. in times when the dogma received in childhood will last a lifetime, but is not good in times of rapid change.

I think this close relationship of teacher and taught is the answer to the question Dr. Foulkes often asked with various tones of wonderment or exasperation "Why is it so difficult to teach and to learn?" I guess it's all a matter of our old friend and enemy, the transference relationship, inevitably ambivalent. It follows from the above that the authority figure does not benefit the situation by simply absenting himself, as some teachers think. In their anxiety to encourage autonomous behaviour in their students, some teachers set up group projects for the students to get on with on their own. This is often unsuccessful, no doubt partly because the project is unsuitably adapted to the students' level of competence, but also, I guess, because of the students' adverse reaction to what they see as rejection by the teacher. The comparative failure of educational technologists to get teacher-less methods (televised lectures for instance) accepted in the brave attempt to cope with an expanded student population in the 1960s, is part of this picture. In the Department of Radiology in which I now work we have a collection of slides and taped seminars from USA, which is intended for students working in groups, and gives an excellent introduction to the basics. But at first students did not make much use of this alien facility. When, however, the radiology teachers deliberately identified themselves with it by referring when relevant to the material covered by the seminars, and dropping in occasionally on groups of students using them, the attendance rate went up.

I have been talking so far about the general conditions of relations with adults that predispose a student to learn or not to learn. The effect of the transference situation is important, each student being powerfully affected in his individual way by how he personally perceives the teacher. I guess that if one can, as a teacher, one should try to avoid arousing negative responses, but you are bound to come across instances. I remember in my first project, a young man who made it clear by largely non-verbal behaviour that he bitterly resented me and my doings. The course was a voluntary one, but this student attended regularly to spit venom and cast the evil eye so that I felt tempted to suggest to him that the course was voluntary, he need not come, but I never actually did so. At the last meeting he dallied at the door and turned, giving me a very broad wink and said "Better luck next time". On another occasion, far away in Australia, I witnessed another change of heart, not towards me personally, but towards teachers in general. The group was of final year students of education, on the brink of entering their chosen profession. In the first meeting we discussed the word "submission" (at their choice), and they talked from the viewpoint of downtrodden students, rather than that of teachers to whom others submit. Later they derided their own teachers, the Diploma of Education course, the Government's mean attitude to education, the schools in which they were practising, the teachers, pupils, parents, buildings, and equipment. They began to wonder what would become of them when they were teachers. But in the fifth and last seminar they began to tell of teachers, however bad, to whom they had been able to talk, pupils who were not impossible to teach, parents who cooperated, a headmaster who was tolerant and tolerable, a grandfather who was learning the New Maths with his granddaughter. And, turning their faces towards their professional role, they had already begun to redesign a Diploma course which was too late for them but would help their successors.

Receiving information: assumptions and context

I should like to turn now to discuss briefly some of the other factors that affect our learning, but without our being conscious of them. I shall be using visual examples to illustrate how we select information from an experience, but the same factors affect the receipt of information by the other senses also. It will be convenient to consider these under two headings, our personal store of information, and the context of the stimulus pattern.

I should like you just to look at this (The Rotating Trapezoid) and chat about what you see to your neighbour. What most people see is a window swinging continually from right to left and back, as though on a hinge. When a wooden rod is hung on the frame, very strange things happen. One sees the rod move independently of the frame; at one moment it is at right angles to the frame, at another parallel with it, and pressing so hard against it that it suddenly breaks through and appears on the other side. A small red cube attached to an upper corner of the window also appears to have independent movement. One may see it slide up and down the top edge of the window, or circle the frame like a satellite.

The apparatus consists of a trapezoidal piece of cardboard cut and painted to look like a rectangular window seen in perspective. It is mounted on a rotating spindle fixed to the middle of the bottom edge.

If we change our position relative to it by tilting it for instance, we can immediately see that it is rotating, not swinging backwards and forwards. The explanation of this error of observation is that we are from the cradle bombarded with the images of rectangles—common in industrialised buildings and most artefacts—but most of the images thrown onto the retina at the back of the eye will be trapezoidal not rectangular, because the objects are seen in perspective. So we equate trapezoidal images on our retinas with rectangles in the real world. Of course actual trapezoids also throw trapezoidal images, but they are rare, especially among windows. As the trapezoid rotates its shorter side comes to the front, but we cannot see it at the front, because this would conflict with our assumption that it is a rectangle—so we see the short side always at the back, further away, and the long side always at the front, so the window seems to swing as though on a hinge and not to rotate on a spindle at its middle. We cannot see the trapezoid as it really is, nor the rod or the cube when we see them in relation to it, because of our assumption that it is a rectangle. People (e.g. Zulus) who do not live in a rectangle dominated world do not experience the illusion as we do.

I want to emphasise that we are quite unaware of the assumption that we are using, and therefore cannot evaluate its effect on our perception, on our understanding of what we are looking at.

A photograph of the boiler of a battleship illustrates the same thing. You see the small bosses, convex rivets which hold the metal plates together, and the large irregular dents, concave, made by shell fire. Turn the photograph upside down, and the rivets become dents and the dents blisters. In normal life the light comes constantly from above, whether from run or moon or artificial light. We learn to interpret shapes with a shadow at the top as dents, concave, and those with a shadow below as bumps, convex. Perception depends on relationships.

Another example of our tendency to expect constancy of frequently experienced events: some doctors working with a primitive tribe, educating the people about diet, were asked: "But why do white men eat babies?" White men were seen to eat a lot of food out of tins with a label illustrating the contents such as tomatoes, beef (a cow's head) and … a bonny baby's smiling face on a tin containing puree of apricots and rice.

This propensity to store experiences which occur frequently in such a way that they unconsciously influence present experiences can help us to interpret and react swiftly to a recurrence of the same or similar events. But they may lead us astray in rapidly changing conditions, where they may be used inappropriately, and help us to be resistant to change. It is common for inventions to retain many features of their predecessors, e.g. the first electric cab looked like a horse-drawn vehicle; our remote ancestors who learned to make pots on a wheel would mark them with the impressions of the baskets in which they had previously been moulded; an early Picasso (most inventive of painters) called Science and Charity, could easily be confused with a pre-Raphaelite painting; it was painted when he was an admirer of Burne-Jones.

Here is an example of how past experience can help you to interpret an apparently meaningless pattern.

Most of you who have not yet seen this picture will see only a meaningless pattern of black and white shapes, but it is called "The Hidden Man". A few people see the man immediately. For instance a girl who had grown up in a convent and had a picture of Christ on her bedroom wall asked "But what's hidden about him?" and admirers of Che Guevara may also see the man immediately. [*The same picture is shown*] how an artist saw him. The same image was present on the back of the eye, whether you saw a man or saw a black and white muddle. Now that you can see him, look at two black marks: one which represents his left eye and the other a meaningless blot, almost level with it at the edge of the picture, which was one of the many that the artist left out altogether. When you saw the man it was at the cost of ignoring, becoming unconscious of, a lot of the pattern—the background—and giving very different special meanings to other blots—the "figure". This is done through your "schema", an organisation of your store of images of bearded men's faces, which helps you to interpret stimulus patterns which are similar. If your schema is strong and sufficiently appropriate you will use it spontaneously, but you may need to be prompted by other people's description of their schema, either verbal or pictorial, which evokes your own. This information can be regarded as part of the context in which you look at the stimulus patterns.

You will recall how in the mediaeval schoolroom picture the children's perception of the teacher would be affected by his context—clothing, furniture, birch and donkey's head. During the Second World War, discussion groups became a recognised medium for further education, but as is shown in a painting in the Imperial War Museum, Spurrier's "Discussion Group", the symbols emphasising authority are still present. The teacher still sits behind a table on which books are strewn; he faces one way and the pupils the other. There is a greater distance between him and the nearest pupil than between neighbouring pupils. The set up is very different from that favoured by Dr. Foulkes (see the emblem on the cover of *Group Analysis*).

A clear effect of context on perception is demonstrated in an experiment in which subjects looked at ten photographs of people and ranked them on a five point scale for energy and well-being. Some people did this in a beautiful room and others in an ugly one, drably furnished, dirty and unkempt. The mean scores for energy and well-being given to the same ten photographs was higher when they were observed in the beautiful room than in the ugly room. The psychologists who administered the test worked alternately in the two rooms and each day did the test themselves. After three weeks the means of their rankings were also higher in the beautiful room than in the ugly one. They were shocked to learn this because although they disliked working in the ugly room, feeling not on top form themselves, and even disputed as to whose turn it was to use the ugly room, they had not thought that their judgements were affected (Maslow & Mintz, 1956).

Sometimes such unconsciously registered contextual influences work against educational objectives, for instance students of dentistry must learn to treat the whole mouth, but it is reported that when they are practising in the department of conservative dentistry, they tend to fill cavities in the teeth, ignoring the soft parts, and when in the department of periodontology to attend to the gums and ignore the teeth.

A photograph of a baby was used in a tutorial about observation in a department of paediatrics. Students were asked to consider what the matter with the baby was. They described its large eyes, long lashes, sad expression, etc. but were amazed when the paediatrician told them the photograph was of a dead baby. Some students had noticed two clues which might have helped them to recognise that the baby was in the mortuary—but one said he thought the parents were callous to photograph the baby uncomfortably against a brick wall and another had noticed the frills on the burial gown but thought it was a frilly nightie. It's likely that if they had been given the problem in the post-mortem room instead of in a paediatric seminar where most babies discussed are alive, they might not have censored these contextual clues.

Time also affects perception, as can be seen in examples of children's drawings of Father Christmas on 6th, 21st and 31st December. He is shown biggest on 21st December and much shrunk on 31st after his "main" function has been served.

Egocentricity

We now turn to consider differences between people and the essentially egocentric nature of perception. Each of us has an individual constitution, even at the physical level, and throughout life we can be identified by our fingerprints and our hearts can be exchanged only with great difficulty because of biochemical incompatibility. As children we are psychologically egocentric. At the age of five or so a child can show you his own right hand, but if asked to point to *your* right hand when you are facing him, will point to your left, his mirror image. Up to the age of nine or so, a child will think the world looks the same spatially to other people as it does to him. When a child is asked how a child seated opposite to him or to his right or left would see a model landscape with a high mountain at the back, and in the front a lower hill with a house on one side and an even smaller one with a cross on it on the other, he thinks the others see the same spatial relationships as he does himself, the high mountain at the back, the hill with the house on his left, that with the cross on it to his right. He cannot put himself into another's shoes and visualise that a child opposite him would see the snowy mountain in front, and the hills reversed from right to left. As we grow up we grow out of this crude spatial egocentricism, but although we know that a person does not have our own attitude to such basic things as, say, religion or politics or sex, we still find it difficult to visualise just how he thinks about them. We cannot put ourselves in his shoes. And it is (occasionally) quite funny to see ourselves as others may see us.

A picture of Escher's—"Hand with Reflecting Globe", illustrates our egocentric position. He draws himself looking into a spherical mirror. He can see more of the room, the part at the back of his head, can extend his knowledge of his little world with it, but however he moves around exploring different parts of it, he will always be at its centre. Escher has another useful drawing of three globes—"Three Spheres II". Again, he is looking into his spherical mirror, but there are two other globes reflected in it. If these were mirror globes held in the hands of other people, he could incorporate their egocentric pictures into his own. (For reasons of copyright we are unable to reproduce these two illustrations here, but "Hand with Reflecting Globe" may be seen in (Abercrombie, 1979).

Making use of egocentricity

We can make use of differences between people in helping each member of a group to become aware of his own egocentric position by comparing and contrasting his idiosyncratic behaviour with that of others. Note that the comparisons are made with other students, his peers, not with the teacher. He is presented with several interpretations of the same event, and is required to unravel the complex web of associations of ideas, more or less relevant, that unconsciously contribute to his judgement and he must consider their validity. The aim of this kind of teaching is to help the student to explore his own memory store and get better command over the parts of it he uses unconsciously when making scientific judgements. In the conventional student/teacher relationship, if his judgement is not consonant with the teacher's, no such exploration of his own unconscious behaviour is evoked; he simply changes his mind to agree with the teacher, simply changes wrong for right without learning how he came to his judgement. The end result is corrected, not the process.

I would like to give an example of how this worked in my first project. The course on observation and reasoning consisted of eight weekly meetings of groups of twelve students lasting one and a half hours. After an introduction of the main points about perception as illustrated above, each session began with an exercise at which students worked individually before coming together as a group for "free" or "associative" discussion. In one exercise a copy of an article describing an experiment which the author claimed demonstrated that excess of Vitamin A in the diet causes diarrhoea in domestic animals was given to each student. He was asked to read this and then to design an experiment himself to test the hypothesis that excess Vitamin A causes diarrhoea in dogs. In the subsequent discussion it was clear that the students had a good grasp of experimental method and were well equipped to criticise the author's experimental set up and correct its deficiencies. However, when asked what they thought would be the outcome of their own experiments, some thought their dogs would certainly get diarrhoea, some sat judiciously on the fence, and a few reacted so strongly against the article that they thought their dogs might get constipated. How could these seemingly competent scientists come to such different conclusions? In the rambling discussion about the various reasons for the various judgements of the validity of the author's conclusions, it became clear that many of the reasons given were not, strictly speaking, relevant to the scientific data. Different students had picked up different clues which we might call contextual factors. For instance, some thought that the journal in which the article was published was a reputable one (his own professor read it, one said), others that it was not—it was "only a weekly". The author was a woman and some thought women can't do good research and others that only very good women could get into research at all. The author worked in a department of genetics, which some thought unsuitable for physiological experimentation, while others thought genetics was a very rigorous subject and only good work could be done there. She was an American and the Americans can't do research—or can, because they have lots of money and good equipment. Some believed that the pressure to publish (especially prevalent in the USA!) led to a lot of work being reported prematurely, others that the editor would have sent the manuscript to be refereed by experts and who were we to doubt their judgement? We got down to questioning the fundamentals of belief in human nature, some saying people are conscientious and truthful, others dubious about the extent to which one could rely on this virtues.

At the end of these courses students who had attended them did better in tests of perception and reasoning than their class mates who had not yet taken the course. They made more descriptive and fewer inferential statements; the same number made true inferences and fewer made false inferences; more made alternative inferences and fewer were inappropriately "set" in response to one exercise by experience of a previous one (James, Johnson, & Venning, 1956).

The most usual favourable comment made by students on the course was that it made them think and that they went on thinking long after the discussions. In some cases it was possible to detect changes in a student's attitude during the course by studying the transcript of the recorded discussions.

An example (Abercrombie, 1969) is that of Mr. X who in the first meeting appreciated the far-reaching implications of the discussion involving radiographs of two hands, but defended himself against them:

> "It's so long that we have taken for granted what we're told that to turn round not only what we're told but everything ..."

He was sharply critical of the method of teaching as being too destructive. In the third discussion he accused me of asking the students to throw away the key they could use, before they were able to use another (he referred to writing music). Later he insisted:

> "... one still keeps the hard core—the majority of assumptions work in the majority of situations ... The hard core of our living, our day-today living, is secure, and I stick to the word very firmly, and that we do question, we question a lot, but on the periphery, where our knowledge is expanding into new ground. And we're so taken up with this expansion into new ground, and get so worried that some of these assumptions are being questioned, that we tend to work backwards and question the whole of the hard core. And in fact it's very, very stupid to do so ..."

Two other students responded to this, as the teacher might have done in other circumstances (note that her abdication was effective already in this third meeting).

> Mr. Y "All you know is that the assumptions were secure as far as you know, and are now as far as you know, whether they will be or not ... Whether some of these basic assumptions will suddenly be altered tomorrow you don't know, lb call them a hard core gives them a sense of permanence which they shouldn't have if you're going to be able to question these ... fringes as you say."
>
> Mr. Z "These are certain assumptions which work in a greater number of cases than other assumptions and therefore you can call them a harder core than the rest, but you can't say that every, any particular assumption works in absolutelyevery instance, because surely that is what we saw with the revolving window frame. We thought that was an assumption which always worked, well it obviously doesn't. And we may, might have thought it to have been one of the assumptions that make up a hard core, and realise that even a basic assumption like that is destroyable."
>
> Mr. Y "If I can bring in an analogy you seem to be as if when learning to skate, trying to find a nice hard piece of ice which you can stand upright on instead of trying to learn how to move on it. You continue trying to find something, some foundation piece which will not move, whereas everything will move and you've got to learn to skate on it."

In the fifth discussion Mr. X. talked of people having their experience in boxes, and these boxes must be broken to let new experience in; he seemed to complain that I was not permitting them to do this, behaviour which is scarcely compatible with what he had complained of before.

In the final discussion Mr. X said:

> "... I think the thing about it is that our basic assumptions are as important in medical subjects as the actual knowledge ... therefore to a medical student, as important as acquiring knowledge of anatomy, is the examination of pure basic assumptions and the realisation that these must be made to grow and develop along with your knowledge."

Mr. X expressed his fears and criticisms openly from the beginning, and throughout commented freely on his own changing perceptions of the course, using different symbols with his changing mood. Mr. X's schemata concerning the relation of teacher and pupil, and his own relation to the external world in general, had been activated by the discussion, but he had preferred to keep them separate from those concerning the subject matter of the course.

In the second and third projects the small group discussions did not begin with individual work at an exercise in scientific method but were concerned with participants' current experiences. In the second project, with architectural students discussion was based on spontaneous reporting of goings on in the school, (the organisation of the course, work in the studio, personal reactions to designing, teamwork, assessment) and in the third project, in their teaching in small groups (*see e.g.* (Abercrombie & Terry, 1978a; Abercrombie & Terry, 1978b)).

The discussions in the third project came nearest to group psychotherapy in that they aimed to help teachers to get better control of their behaviour in groups, which involved reconsiderations of their early behaviour as students and their present relations with authority figures and peers as well as in those with their students. Four functions of group discussion could be differentiated to serve the specific purpose—that of offering mutual support; providing opportunities for getting increased awareness of one's own behaviour, helping to develop greater empathy with their students (being in the position of students themselves) and serving as a model for one kind of behaviour that can be developed in teaching groups.

Teaching and psychotherapy

I would now like to compare and contrast this work in higher education with group analytic psychotherapy. Briefly, I like to think of it simply as a further step in the same direction as Foulkes took in his own progress from psychoanalysis to group analysis. He wrote in one of his last papers (Foulkes, 1975) that compared with the psychoanalyst in the two person situation

> "The conductor is not so much concerned with interpretation but with the uncovering of the unconscious part in the here and now of the therapeutic situation. We analyse the ego in action. We analyse the individual in the group in actual on-going behaviour and reaction".
>
> "The most powerful factor in bringing about change and the possibility for further and future progress after the group has ended is based on this ego training in action and not so much on the insight and interpretation based on words as such as upon the on-going corrective interaction with others. This is the main spring of the mutative experience in group-analytic psychotherapy".

Corrective interaction with others is I believe also the main factor improving behaviour in academic matters. In teaching, as in group psychotherapy, we recognise the tremendous power of the transference relation but we do not use its interpretation as the main medium for change. Rather perhaps we see it as an important and ever present constituent of the "group situation" which we engineer to encourage interaction among all members of the group.

The group is not a group of strangers, as it is in strict group analytic therapy, which I think is an advantage in the potentiality it gives for the direct transfer of what is learnt in the group to experience in practice and for the strengthening and spreading of change in the work situation. And by no means should the conductor be a stranger to the group. On the contrary, I think one must be steeped in the educational microclimate of the group, the department, the institution, should be aware of the conceptual and attitudinal problems of the discipline, and sensitive to the larger context of educational thought.

I think the difference in technique used by teacher and therapist all derive from differences in aim. In education, by contrast with psychotherapy where the whole person is the target for help, we focus the attention of participants on specific aspects of their current academic work, and bring to light those processes of which they are unconscious. It is worth noting, however, that participants often reported peripheral changes in their own behaviour. Some medical students for instance said that the course influenced their general philosophy of life; and some teachers reported that their lecturing improved, not only their small group teaching, and that they got on better with their colleagues, not only with students.

I think in teaching it helps to behave in a socially acceptable manner and avoid increasing students' anxiety above that inevitably induced by the profound changes in role, theirs and the teacher's. One must avoid the temptation to outsmart a student (which transference interpretations are prone to do) and in general be prepared to refrain from making a crucial point, because if you wait long enough the students will probably come to it. At the same time it is important to show signs of listening, learning and remembering, and to prepare yourself, when chaos seems overwhelming or at any time when students ask for it, to describe the themes, and comment on the processes that have occurred. Therapists are prone to criticise this softly softly approach, but I believe there is enough anxiety in overcoming the natural resistance to change, in the whole situation of being a student, of learning to become autonomous, and tolerant of ambiguity and doubt.

In this work the teacher acts less like the one in the mediaeval school room, more like Rembrandt's old women supporting a child learning to walk, knowing that he may fall and hurt his head, providing him with a crash helmet and pointing to the future, his, that they will never see. Or even like a wheelbarrow, a grownup's artefact that a toddler can lean on and learn how to manoeuvre.

References

Abercrombie, M. L. J. (1969). *The Anatomy of Judgment*. London: Hutchinson.

Abercrombie, M. L. J. (1979). Studies, concepts and research: The uses and abuses of boundaries—perception: The structure of space and group process. *Group Analysis, 12*: 30–40.

Abercrombie, M. L. J., & Terry, P. M. (1978a). Reactions to change in the authority-dependency relationship. *British Journal of Guidance and Counselling, 6*: 82–94.

Abercrombie, M. L. J., & Terry, P. M. (1978b). *Talking to learn: Improving teaching and learning in small groups*. University of Surrey: The Guildford.

Foulkes, S. H. (1975). A short outline of the therapeutic processes in group-analytic psychotherapy. *Group Analysis, 8*: 60–63.

Harlow, H. F. (1959). Love in infant monkeys. *Scientific American, 200*: 68–74.

James, D. W., Johnson, M. L., & Venning, P. (1956). Testing for learnt skill in observation and evaluation of evidence. *Lancet, 2*: 379.

Lee, T. R. (1957). On the relation between the school journey and social and emotional adjustment in rural children. *British Journal of Educational Psychology, 27*: 101–104.

Maslow, A. H., & Mintz, N. L. (1956). Effects of esthetic surroundings: Initial effects of three esthetic conditions upon perceiving "energy" and "wellbeing" in faces. *Journal of Psychology, 41*: 247–254.

PART VII

COMBINED THERAPIES

CHAPTER NINE

Combined therapy—a group analytic perspective*

Jason Maratos

The group of therapies

Psychological development progresses through interactions of the *self* with the *other* from the beginning of life. Some of these interactions will be growth promoting, some will be damaging and others will be corrective or in other words, therapeutic. In this sense, any therapy can only be combined.

Combined therapy existed, probably, long before it was written about. Hobdell (1991) cites Foulkes (Foulkes & Lewis, 1944) as the earliest author on the subject. In the early days of group analysis, there was uncertainty about the effect, ambivalence about its advisability and concern about its effect on each of the two combined therapeutic modalities. One concern was that the combination may detract and dilute the patient's efforts and that one therapy may "contaminate" the other. The same concern was expressed, as late as 1980, (Scheidlinger & Porter, cited by Praper, 1997) by focusing on what they saw as the potentially

*This chapter was previously published as: Maratos, J. (2000). Combined therapies—a group analytic perspective. In: S. Brooks & P. Hodson (Eds.), *The Invisible Matrix* (pp. 128–148). London: Rebus Press.

damaging effect on transference within the group. Such reservations are understandable when group therapy, as a new therapeutic modality, was not yet secure in its own identity. Perhaps even today, some of the reluctance of therapists to recommend combined work may be related to their own uncertainty about their identity as therapists and to seeing the 'other' intervention as a threat.

A boost to combined work, however, came from the therapeutic community movement. Hobdell reminds us that in the first therapeutic communities, there were many therapeutic influences taking place at the same time, such as community groups, small groups and individual work; combined therapy, therefore, seemed to be the norm. Is there a rank order of therapies? In considering combined therapy, one needs to address the issue of rank ordering of therapies. As rivalry and splitting are endemic dangers in combined therapy, rank ordering has to be taken into account and, certainly, is not to be dismissed with a facile statement such as "all therapies are of equal importance." Some highly experienced therapists operate under a conscious (or even unconscious) rank ordering of therapies. The primary therapy is occasionally thought to be individual psychoanalysis followed by other psychotherapies and by counselling.

Though rank ordering is important in the choice of one therapy, in the case of combined such considerations become paramount. Interestingly, a training analyst with the Society of Analytical Psychology (Hobdell, 1991) writes that:

> … in conducting combined groups I have always worked from the major premise that the group is primary … the integrity of the group has to be maintained at all times.
>
> (Hobdell, 1991, p. 141)

In the same spirit, Hobdell named the individual sessions "the satellite group." In the case of combined therapy, this clear position is not without its risks. If we use the metaphor of a surgical operation, one therapy may be considered like the work of the surgeon while the other is reduced to that of a theatre nurse who hands him the instruments.

Some professionals feel demeaned or despoiled if they are expected not to address the internal world of their client directly; they may see themselves as "hand maidens" of the primary therapist. The basis of competition for primacy would lead to actual re-enactment of a real external split and its transfer into the internal self of the patient as an internal conflict.

Is there a more important and a less important therapy? Ideally one would wish to see all therapeutic interventions as mutually enabling and potentiating, but in reality, it is difficult for therapies to operate at this finely balanced point. Therapies acquire different significance at different times. For example, there can be occasions where the interactions within a group are too intense for a borderline patient to manage. In this case, individual therapy may be the setting in which more direct therapeutic work is carried out; work which brings about change by itself and not only through enabling the group therapy to continue. Readers are aware of examples where the opposite is the case.

This temporal rank ordering is different from that which exists in the minds of some patients and therapists. Rivalry internal and external, between therapists and between those offering therapy proper with those offering interventions with a therapeutic effect is a dynamic which if left unaddressed may lead to anti-therapeutic consequences. This rivalry may be expressed (or experienced) as idealisation or denigration of therapists or of therapies.

Implicit in the notion of combined therapy is the understanding that two forces act on the same subject. These two forces will need to be considered and managed if they are to work together, for the same purpose without undermining or duplicating each other. Porter (1993) (cited by L. R. Benjamin & R. Benjamin, 1995) takes the optimistic view that "combined therapy offers the twin advantages of complementarity and potentiality" (the latter taken to mean enhancement of the effect of one by the presence of the other).

Difference from concurrent, parallel, sequential and incidental therapies

In the literature on combined therapy one encounters terms which are used with different meanings. Some reserve the term "combined" only for the case where both therapeutic modalities are delivered by the same therapist (Praper, 1997) while others consider therapies which are concurrent or even sequential as combined. Praper uses the definition of two therapies by different therapists as conjoint; a term which has been used for description of therapy of one unit (say a family) by two therapists present at the same time in the same sessions. It is only with time that terminology will crystallise; the present author will not attempt here to impose his own understanding; this would be a futile exercise. Instead, we will only highlight the issue in order to prevent misunderstandings from arising. The dynamics of therapies by the same or different therapists obviously vary, as do the dynamics of therapies with essentially similar philosophy from those based on widely different principles as, for example, the combination of a psychoanalytical variant of therapy with systematic desensitisation for a specific phobia.

Dynamics of combined therapy

The parental metaphor, though hackneyed, retains its usefulness. The child may benefit from the differentness of her parents; may feel and become enriched by their different qualities if the parents themselves value and enjoy their diversity. If, on the other hand, the parents relate in a conflictual, antagonistic manner then the child will be placed in a position of having to choose one instead of the other. The result will be internal poverty and conflict. The same principle applies to combined therapy irrespective of whether it is carried out by the same therapist (in which case the potential for destructive conflict is between the therapies) or by different therapists (where the potential for gain or loss is even greater). The potential for splitting is so well recognised that it is unnecessary for me to add further to the existing literature.

The special case of group therapy

It is worth considering how two concepts developed by "individual" analysts apply to group therapy; these are the related concepts of self-object and transference.

A key concept in the psychology of the self is that of the self-object (Kohut, 1971; Maratos, 1996). Aspects of the therapist's self may be internalised by the patient; these will form the patient's new self objects. One can see that in the case of group therapy the sources of self-objects are more than one, and in the case of combined therapy even more. If the patient is to avoid some internal chaos, disorganisation, fragility and enfeeblement, some effort needs to be directed at enabling the patient to select and organise his new self objects. Without such effort, the self will not be able to function effectively and will be vulnerable to fragmentation and breakdown.

Freud introduced the concept of transference (Freud, 1912) as an unconscious perception of the therapist and the unconscious experience within the therapy situation of feelings which originated in early childhood and are misapplied towards the therapist. In an analytical group, there are more therapists in addition to the conductor and such misapplications occur in many forms. Porter (1993, cited by L. R. Benjamin & R. Benjamin, 1995) refers to "multiple transferences" which can be explored simultaneously. Patients often "see" other group members as persons of their early life and relate to them as such. Resolution of these transferences is a cornerstone of therapy.

In the case of combined therapies, especially in the case of two therapists, transference acquires a further dimension (Dagg & Evans, 1997; Horwitz, 1994). Some hold reservations that transference may be diluted while others see that in combined therapy there is the unique opportunity for the development of transference towards the therapeutic couple. Porter (1993) (cited by L. R. Benjamin & R. Benjamin, 1995) warns about the danger of what he termed as "transference splitting" a process through which different therapists/therapies are idealised or denigrated. Transference towards two therapists may be problematic, if the original parental couple had an antagonistic or conflictual relationship. The patient may experience a transferential wish to get therapists together. Such transference could be considered as a possible source of resistance towards combined therapy and as a possible destructive **force** within it. Resolution of such transference will add a further dimension to therapy. There is always the danger, though, that the prevailing transferences may be more than the single patient can process at one and the same time.

Acting out in combined therapy

Acting out refers to the enactment of unconscious feelings either within or without the therapy setting. Combined therapy is a rather more open system than unimodal therapy and therefore lends itself more easily to the enactment of affectionate, sexual or aggressive feelings. Attempts of patients to create an "unholy" alliance with **one** against the other therapist or to get the therapists together may represent transferential acting out. We have referred earlier to the phenomenon where pre-existing splitting of the internal world is acted out in the external world of therapists who may become unwitting participants in this anti-therapeutic process.

What is appropriate material/or individual sessions and what for group?

The received wisdom is that individual material is dealt with in individual sessions while relational material is dealt with in groups. Such a notion may serve as a useful rule of thumb, but can be anti-therapeutic if applied too rigidly. Relationships with other group members may need to be discussed in individual sessions if the group member is too anxious to explore or negotiate them within the group setting. If the process were to stop there, then there would be no indication of a real resolution; there would be no experiment which would validate the theory. If the exploration in the individual session is followed by exploration and negotiation with the other group members then the therapeutic objective will have been accomplished. Indeed, the issue of feelings towards the other group members is a very good example of how combined therapy can help a patient over an otherwise insurmountable block to therapeutic resolution of internal difficulties and an example of how individual can complement the group work. Boundaries are there to be negotiated not to block treatment.

The mirror image of the above eventuality is the case in which early personal or dream material arises within the group setting. Normally this would be considered material for individual sessions. Nothing would be further from the truth. Many group therapists have encountered sessions in which group members share early material which (to their surprise) has striking similarities. Such material had been brought into consciousness by the intensity of the shared group experience. This is one therapeutic objective achieved in groups (making the unconscious conscious). Group members can develop a deep and full understanding of each other's intensely personal material thus achieving a second therapeutic objective: acquiring a new understanding of previously unconscious material.

What group members often find striking is that in a group session they present a dream, which they think of as an exclusively private experience, only to discover that other group members had similar dreams. This is a powerful therapeutic experience on many dimensions but the one I would like to stress here is the experience of the communality of human nature. This T am not alone—even in my private moments' feeling is not only restorative of the sense of self but also is formative of new bonds; both powerful therapeutic forces.

Dr Hobdell (1991) introduces another dimension of combined therapy: that it reinforces the idea that therapy happens "in a couple." Freud himself (1910) alluded to this in his uniquely fresh style: "To-day things have a more friendly air. The treatment is *made up of two parts,* out of what the physician infers and tells the patient, and out of the patient's work of assimilation, of 'working through', what he hears," (my italics). This notion of the co-operation of "the couple" needs to be explored (and can be explored constructively) openly in therapy (both in the group and in the individual sessions). The couple, in this case, is the couple of therapies as well as the couples of subjects and carers. The dyadic nature of therapy is similar to the dyadic nature of development. The basis of development is the dyadic relationship of infant and maternal care. It is this relationship which led Winnicott to utter, at a scientific meeting of the British Psychoanalytical Society (circa 1940), the extraordinary phrase, "There is no such thing as an infant" (cited in Winnicott, 1985).

The internal world of the therapist

Counter-transference is being understood by different authors to mean not only the unconscious feelings which the therapist experiences specifically in response to the patient's transference (as Freud originally intended 1910) but "the whole of the analyst's unconscious reactions to the individual analysand" (Laplanche & Pontalis, 1983). A whole host of feelings, irrespective of whether they arise out of the therapist's own experiences or in response to the patient's transference can be included under the same term reducing, in this way, its specificity and usefulness.

We use the term "internal world" at the heading of this section in order to highlight that feelings and beliefs, conscious, pre-conscious and unconscious play a determining part in relation to combined therapy. For example, some therapists feel more comfortable with uni-modal therapies; some have difficulties in sharing while others prefer combining approaches and efforts. These elements in the internal world of a therapist will influence whether they engage in combined therapy themselves, whether they recommend this kind of treatment and whether they accept to see patients in this context. The L. R. Benjamin and R. Benjamin (1995) claimed that their relationships with the group members who they did not treat individually as well, were not as intense, and express the view that it may have been preferable if instead of combined, they offered conjoint therapy. It seems to me that such a contribution, which contains feelings and thoughts of the authors, is valid and should be distinguished from counter-transference.

The feelings of a therapist towards a patient in combined therapy in response to the patient's transference may be initially unconscious (and, therefore true counter-transference) and, in due course, be brought to consciousness by the experienced therapist or in supervision. Hobdell advocates that therapists need to beware of the possibility of recommending combined therapy out of counter-transferential hate. One can see how a therapist, troubled by such difficult feelings may seek the comfort of sharing these feelings in a wider therapeutic circle (with other therapists or other patients); such a move may not be counter-therapeutic in itself; it may indeed be a way of making feelings which are intolerable for the therapist more manageable and therefore no longer a hindrance to analysis. The danger is that a referral for combined therapy made on this basis may be defensive and may lead to avoidance of such feelings and may, therefore, compound in the therapy situation the client's original trauma.

Therapists who are about to recommend additional therapy could do well to consider that it is possible that their recommendation arises out of a whole spectrum of feelings arising from the patient such as feelings of not being a good enough therapist, of not being "contained" enough, feelings of intense depression as well as the above mentioned feelings of hate. A recommendation arising out of such feelings is nothing short of acting out on the part of the therapist. Therapist acting out is not often cited in the literature, but therapists who work unsupported, isolated, stressed or who are newly qualified and may be poorly supervised, are all liable to such behaviour.

Issues around combined therapy

It is unusual for clients to be referred for combined therapy immediately after assessment. The most common pattern is to recommend one treatment modality and during its course, recommend the addition of a further therapeutic modality because of difficulties or lack of progress.

Perhaps it is more difficult for a therapist to recommend that a patient devotes every week 50 minutes in individual therapy and 90 minutes in a group than to recommend that he/she devotes 150 minutes (the equivalent time total) in three times per week individual therapy or analysis. Although the explanation may be more complicated, when there is a clear understanding of what the combined therapy has to offer that is specific to the needs of the particular client, the recommendation may flow more naturally. Starting therapy in the combined mode may prevent early therapeutic "drop out" and may save the client (and the therapist) from unnecessary angst.

Modulation of level of arousal

A neurophysiological finding, often ignored by some therapists, is that an organism is in an optimal position to learn and to negotiate the environment when at a reasonable arousal level. Too low arousal, as in relaxation or sleep at one end, or too high arousal, as in the case of panic, are not conducive to learning. Too high arousal is painful, and the subject will direct his efforts to reduce it or avoid the arousing environment. Therapy cannot be sustained if the patient (or the therapist) is persistently excessively anxious within the sessions; it is equally unproductive if the client is too relaxed and "cosy."

A therapist aims to make a judgement about this factor during assessment. If a client is likely to experience arousal at either extreme of the above continuum, then combined therapy may enable him to shift to a workable level. Such a consideration remains valid both before the beginning of treatment as well as during therapy of any modality. Combined therapy can serve both to increase anxiety by confronting the patient with neglected aspects of his self as well as reduce anxiety to workable levels in patients who feel too threatened or exposed in a unimodal setting. Hobdell (1991) advocates that combined therapy is initiated when anxiety in the group therapy sessions is so high that it inhibits the therapeutic process. He suggests that it should be available to all who can afford it.

The notion of expenditure in therapy is well worth separate consideration. Therapy does not represent only something that is provided to the patient. In order to access it, the client needs to expend time, effort and, often, money. Therapists often ignore this factor and interpret a client's reluctance to undertake therapy (or more extensive therapy) as resistance or defensiveness. Some therapists are puzzled about why those who need therapy most, are less likely to avail themselves of it. One of the reasons may be that they are near the point of exhausting their resources. I hope I will be forgiven if I use a simplistic metaphor, which in spite of its simplicity illustrates this point quite clearly: we, as therapists, are on a ship; we see a person overboard struggling to stay afloat. The person is moving about in the water in a way that causes him to expend a lot of energy without making much progress towards safety. We know that the only way they can stay afloat is if they learn to swim. We shout instructions on what to do, but he is too tired and too anxious (maybe in a panic) to follow them. In real life, we are not always in the position to throw a life-saving rope and then instruct in swimming, even though this course of action is highly desirable! Therapy can only provide the equivalent of swimming instruction and the therapist who attempts to be a life saver and an instructor at the same time often drowns with the patient.

Combined therapy is often thought as a mode of treatment that is more "expensive" than unimodal therapy. It is easy for one to forget that it may also represent a "saving" of expenditure in cases where the patient would have otherwise needed more intensive treatment as, for example, in-patient treatment. Combined therapy does not always represent more therapy. Combined therapy represents a specific mode of intervention with its own dynamics (strengths and difficulties and risks); it should be engaged in for the right reasons—neither as a cheap alternative to treatments which though more costly would be more appropriate for a particular patient at a particular time, nor as an unnecessarily costly over treatment when briefer interventions would have met the patient's treatment needs.

Diagnostic categories are often useful if they are used not as absolute rules but flexibly. Borderline personality organisation is such a category which has been thought to be more likely to respond better to combined therapy (Wong, 1988). Review articles, such as the excellent paper by Praper (1997), refer to the work of numerous authors who have considered the advisability of combined therapy for patients suffering from obsessive compulsive disorders, from excessively schizoid personalities, those in a manic phase of a manic depressive illness, those who are severely masochistic and those in an acute crisis. But, while some authors refer to these conditions as indications for combined therapy, others refer to the same conditions as contra-indications. The reason for this apparent inconsistency in the literature is, I relieve, that each diagnostic category includes a wide spectrum of disturbance, both in terms of severity but also in terms of variation. Even the most psychotic patients may have relatively healthy parts to their personality, which sustain them in therapy (and in life).

Rather than indications and contraindications, the present author would advocate the use of the following guidelines: combined therapy can be engaged in by clients who are able to use or are likely to respond to psychotherapy, and have (or are likely to have) difficulties in unimodal therapy which will lead them either to drop out, to stagnate or to leave areas of their personality unaffected (untreated). Awareness of the above factors may take place before or during one form of therapy and introduction of combined therapy may proceed respectively, from the beginning or during the process of one therapy. The decision will depend on numerous, and not only dynamic factors.

Consideration of factors extraneous to the patient

Various authors often advocate that the decision for a particular treatment should only depend on the needs of the patient. This objective is-as idealistic and desirable, as it is often unobtainable. Therapists live in the real world of funding, contracts, policies of insurance companies' and priorities of health services. It would be unrealistic to ignore all these factors, especially when a major objective of therapy is to enable the recipient to make the most of their real life (rather than feel unhappy because their situation is far worse than that of others or of their hoped-for or imagined world).

Extraneous factors are not only practical/material but also those related to the therapist or the institution or agency responsible for the care of the patient. Management of therapist or institutional anxiety is one of the factors which is often thought of as an inappropriate consideration. Obviously, one should not simply over-treat a patient for the sake of reducing therapist or institutional anxiety, but alternatively high-handed advocating that the therapist should manage their own anxiety independently of their patient is equally unrealistic. One cannot forget that therapist anxiety is rarely independent of the state of the patient, and may be a healthy signal of patient needs. Therapist and institutional anxiety should neither dominate clinical decisions nor be ignored but needs to be seriously considered as a signal of the dynamic between client and therapist, and to be taken account of in the complicated process of deciding to engage in combined therapy. Therapist anxiety is a powerful factor influencing the level of arousal within therapy, a parameter which has already been considered briefly in this chapter.

How to set up combined therapy

Equally important to the selection of patients is their preparation for combined therapy. Boswood (1976) highlighted the need for the establishment of a good "bond" between therapist and patient if therapy is to be sustained. The concept of a bond is very complex but it contains at least two elements: the first is some degree of liking or affection and the other is some degree of trust. The therapist needs to earn a reasonable level of trust from the patient. Just as the therapist assesses the patient during the early interviews so does the patient assess the therapist.

The present author believes that trust is best when it is only reasonable and not when it is absolute. When patients tell me that they trust me, I become anxious. Absolute trust (especially when genuine) implies that the patient has handed a large part of their thinking or critical power over to the therapist and this is not a helpful step. I make a point of telling my patients that 1 approach them having "done my homework" and having acquired a reasonable level of competence (and when appropriate, that I have no intentions of taking advantage of them), that I am reasonably "good" (meaning competent and well intentioned). But I also point out to them that I am human, that, often, my interpretations will amount to hypotheses for them to consider and that they should accept them only if they think that they really apply to them. Therapy is inconceivable without the active and critical participation of the patient. Absolute trust is equally unhelpful as its opposite, paranoia. This paragraph should not be read to mean that I advocate that one should generate unnecessary anxieties in one's patients.

Trust is, at least, bi-dimensional. Trust does not imply only that "the other" is perceived as benevolent but that "the self also is perceived as competent." Persons with a seriously damaged self find it virtually impossible to experience trust because they perceive themselves as incapable of coping with any conflict of interest. These persons find it very difficult to establish the reasonable trust required for therapy to begin and if they do engage in it, they run the risk of ending it prematurely.

A large part of the art of psychotherapy is taken by the therapist's efforts to develop in the client a sense that he/she is competent enough to cope with the vicissitudes of therapy and that the therapist and/or the group (that is, the therapeutic setting) are reasonably "good."

Blanket statements about the safety of the group or of therapy often fail to reassure clients—quite justifiably. The therapy situation (individual, group or combined) can be as safe as the landing of an aircraft in a storm; it is exciting and usually safe but only if the pilots are "good." In group therapy, there are more than one pilot and it has always been recognised that the process can be constructive as well as destructive. Statements about the therapy situation being secure or safe serve only to reduce the credibility of the therapist.

Reassurance can only be reached after a thorough investigation of the client's anxieties about therapy. Will therapy unleash pain, which the patient will not feel able to cope with? Will the group members detect the clients' unacceptable internal world? Will the other group members place demands which the client will not be able to meet? Will the client have to fight to get any attention? Will there be repetition of earlier traumatic experiences, like scapegoating or manipulations? One cannot give a false reassurance that such dynamics will not take place—they do. A more realistic approach is that such dynamics can occur in groups as in real life and that the setting of client-group members-therapist operates with an interest, common to all, that of therapy. It is the common objective, the shared interest, which gives to the therapeutic situation greater security than life, which is at least perceived as full of actual conflict.

In recommending combined therapy, one gives the impression that one therapy is not enough! Such a recommendation may, thus, become an anti-therapeutic move. Especially when additional therapy is recommended, this may be a statement of inadequacy of the first and that something "better" needs to be brought in for the rescue of treatment. Care needs to be taken because this perception is partly true; one therapy or unimodal therapy has indeed been considered inadequate for the needs of this particular patient. It is very difficult for patients to differentiate between the notion that a combined modality is more appropriate for them and the perception that one form of therapy is a poor therapeutic tool. The risk is that the therapy that is introduced second is seen as the more "real" or "powerful" method, that the client will dis-invest or de-cathect from the original therapy and will end up receiving only the second therapy, thus defeating the whole objective of receiving combined therapy.

Timing

Hobdell (1991) recommends that clients already in group therapy, could be offered combined therapy if their early material cannot be adequately explored in the group or if the analysis of their dreams may take time at the expense of the group. Other authors recommend that group therapy be added when there is a need for the client to develop their way of relating to others.

A number of authors advocate that individual therapy should added if there is a need for exploration of early material and personal material, like dreams, while group therapy is added when there i need for the client to develop their way of relating to others. Such approach implies that the internal world is separate from the way which a person relates to others. How could this be so? How could I relationships not be based on the internal world and how could I internal world not be shaped by relationships? One is a function of t other; perhaps not an equation but certainly a function.

Therefore, neither can we accept the notion that a group patient offered additional individual therapy in order to address early material nor that an individual patient be referred to a group so that they c develop their relatedness. The deciding factor in considering the timing of the introduction of an additional therapy is not the therapeutic target but the method. Relatedness can be helped in individual setting, and dreams are analysed in group settings. Additional therapy is considered when the client finds it very difficult to make progress in the existing therapy.

The same or different therapists

The aim of this section is not to conclude with a recommendation about the preferable method but to touch upon the different issues highlighted by the two approaches. We will refer to confidentiality between the settings later on but here we can point out that information in the min of the therapist is obviously optimal in the case of same therapist combined therapy and there is no problem of communication towards the therapist. Attention needs to be paid to the type of information, which the therapist can disclose to the group. The patient may well be anxious that the therapist may inadvertently disclose to the group information before the patient is ready to disclose himself. Such anxiety may act as an anti-therapeutic force in the individual session. A therapist who sees a number of her group patients individually will be taxed to remember what material to which she is privileged she may use in the group setting and what not. As the group members are the therapists, they will need to know material which may be relevant to them so it is the timing of the disclosure which is important more than the fact that information is disclosed or not.

As the relationship between patient and therapist will be different in the two settings, the same therapist will be experienced differently in the two therapeutic situations. The exclusively attentive therapist of the individual sessions may be unresponsive and may be perceived as withholding or depriving when in the group sessions. Such difference may be puzzling for the patient who will need some help to think this through before it gives rise to pathological dynamics. One most obvious misinterpretation may be that the therapist is not genuine, or two-faced. It is difficult for some patients to understand how the same person can behave differently towards them in different settings and maintain the same relationship.

The experience of the differentness of the same can be quite a useful introject for some patients, who feel that they can only be true to themselves and others if they behave in the same monolithic way in all situations. Such persons tend—for example—to treat their children or their seniors at work as their friends, with counterproductive consequences. Such persons also have difficulties in differentiating what is private and what public and when it is so. Introjecting this experience will enable them to adopt appropriate roles in diverse settings and feel honest with themselves at the same time.

Relationship between the therapists

The concept of splitting was introduced by Freud (1940) and further developed by Melanie Klein in 1932 (1975a) and referred to an unconscious process internal to the psyche of the patient. This attempt at coping with internal ambivalence by perceiving one person as good and the other as bad (my apologies for this simplifying expression of this complex mechanism) can be projected with such force that it can be adopted as reality by the perceived subjects. In a combined therapy situation, there is a risk that one therapist will see herself as the good object and will think of the other therapist as the bad one. A therapist runs the risk of falling victim of this process, and the present author is no exception to this, especially if he is the recipient of benevolent projections. One is less likely to wish to re-examine perceptions of oneself as a bad therapist than as a good one.

In the combined therapy situation, one is faced with a multi-dimensional counter-transference: the feelings of each therapist about themselves, about each other and about their patient. If this counter-transference remains unconscious it can be experienced by the therapists as conflict between them. If therapists do not know each other well or if they do but do not hold each other's skills or theoretical orientation in high regard, then the risk of actual conflict is even greater. The patient's splitting can then be mirrored and enhanced by the therapists' rivalry. The destructiveness of this process is obvious.

Not all conflict between therapists is counter-transferential in origin. Attributing all differences to the shared patient is nothing short of a "therapeutic cop-out." The two therapists are bound in the same venture of treating one patient. Their professional identity and reputation depends on the good outcome of the treatment. If one feels that their work is undermined by the work of the other he will not be satisfied with interpretations of splitting and counter-transference. There will be times when the client is deteriorating or simply not making progress. It is possible that one or other therapist intervenes in an unhelpful way. This is precisely the time for therapists to communicate with each other.

Communication between therapists and therapeutic situations

Confidentiality is of equal value to good communication when more than one therapeutic situation is involved, even though one is opposite to the other; the one withholds while the other imparts information. Withholding information opens the road to manipulation, splitting and other unhelpful defences, which ultimately delay or work against treatment. Without confidentiality, the patient feels inhibited and cannot use the session properly. Openness of communication compromises the privileged position of the therapy session.

The patient in combined therapy is, therefore, faced with a dilemma: openness inhibits, secrecy delays resolution. This is true in the case of different, as well as same, therapist combined therapy. Cohn (1986) seems to favour confidentiality of the individual session, but accepts that group material can be dealt with individually.

It seems to me that in this situation, principles and guidelines are more useful than rules. The first principle is that the patient needs to feel that she is in control of who she imparts information to, and when. This is the essence of confidentiality and a cornerstone of therapy. The second principle is that withholding information from either therapeutic setting deprives the therapists of an opportunity of becoming helpful and is therefore to be avoided. The "working formula" could be that the patient will maintain control of information but will aim to share material which is thought to be relevant.

One needs to define what is relevant. This task is impossible in absolute terms; a few attempts towards definition ended in unhelpful tautologies. My rule of thumb is that material is relevant if any of the involved parties experience ambivalence or unease about the "confidential" information. It is precisely for such unease that individual sessions can be an invaluable complement to group therapy. Such ambivalence cannot be resolved within the group, as such a move would break confidentiality. Such ambivalence may not arise in individual sessions. In situations like this combined therapy genuinely offers something that neither single modality can provide.

It is precisely in such situations that the therapists need to be able to hold a frank and honest exchange of views. The unease may arise out of defensiveness or manipulation by the patient but may also spring from an erroneous approach by one or other therapist. Mature therapists can benefit from the combined therapy situation because by having an opportunity to discuss their shared patient they can acquire an understanding which may be deeper and more thorough than they could have reached thinking through the patient's psyche on their own. Even in supervision, the supervisor would not have the same wealth of information as the other therapist and therefore may not be able to reach such a deep understanding.

Communication, which may involve criticism, but may also involve the sharing of the feelings of the therapists, can be a source of genuine support for the therapists as well as an experience that promotes professional growth.

Some risks of combined therapy: contamination and dilution

Some practitioners are concerned that the therapy they provide may be contaminated by another. Such fears have been expressed that the purity of therapy will be lost and that the patient will be confused by ideas and interpretations which may be incompatible. In such situations, the "other" insights are seen as "foreign bodies" to the "real" therapy. 0 course, neither therapists nor therapies are clones to each other and differences will arise. Such differences may be conflictual; it would be defensive of combined therapy (probably a manic defence) if we did not recognise that this is a real risk. Differentness does not always automatically lead to complementarity; it may do so but it will require some active thinking through.

A more benign concern is that the combination of two therapies may make it difficult for a patient to engage wholeheartedly in one and that the experience will be diluted. The patient runs the risk of thinking that the real therapy will take place in the "other" session and thus spend considerable time being "in between" therapies. Any patient who has intensive therapy runs the risk of "stretching" the therapy and as a result may have long but not intensive therapy.

The above mentioned are only risks and should not be seen as disadvantages of combined therapy. They are stated here to caution against a false sense that more is necessarily safer and better; combined therapy can be so but only if the risks are negotiated appropriately.

The effect on the whole group of added individual therapy for one patient

A very disturbed patient absorbs considerable time and energy from the group; the group members are relieved when additional therapy addresses some of the personal difficulties of one patient. The group is pleased when it is able to work better. Hobdell (1991) found that in his groups, patients occasionally recommend that a member has some individual sessions as well.

Naturally, one does not expect group members to consider matters always in such a mature manner. Feelings of envy and rivalry will almost inevitably arise as well as feelings of superiority in those who are not thought to be so disturbed as to need "extra" therapy. In a setting of private practice, the feelings of envy for those who can afford additional therapy will bring to the surface earlier feelings of fairness or otherwise in early years. For patients who still confuse equality (having equal amounts of everything with everyone else, at least, within the sibship) with fairness (meeting the different needs with different amounts and different kinds of care) can learn a lot from the experience.

Unfortunately, "things" are neither equal nor always fair in real life and re-enactment of this simple truth in therapy provides an added opportunity for the patient to learn how to progress without being overwhelmed by feelings of envy, sadness, loss and anger. If negotiated successfully, the combined therapy of one member can be therapeutic for the whole membership of the group.

Who is "the case"?

With the influence of family therapy and systemic thinking, the notion of "who is the case" has taken a wider dimension. For a family therapist, the case is the family, just as the couple is for the marital or sexual therapist. Although the case can be the family, treatment need not always be of the family as a whole through sessions in which all the members are present. In some families the dysfunction may be addressed by separate sessions in which one therapist sees the child on her own while another sees the parents, at least for a phase of the treatment. If the "case" is the family, then this approach is combined therapy. If the family re-unites in conjoint therapy, then the dynamics mentioned above may prevail and inhibit progress, if they are not negotiated constructively. This is particularly so in the case where one section of the family received therapy of a different approach and philosophy than the other.

Pace of therapies

The pace at which therapy progresses is a concept which is often talked about, but not written on. This is probably due to the difficulty in defining this concept. Patients refer to feeling under pressure when the therapist or the group expect them to change before "they are ready" to do so—whatever the term "ready" may mean. Pace has to do with change, and living organisms are affected both by no or too little a' well as too much of it. No change can only mean death and 'too mud-leads to stress and breakdown. Change is an inevitable part of development, but the change which is part of therapy requires greater adjustment and energy as it aims not only to promote growth but also to "demolish and reconstruct" patterns which have proven to be unhelpful in the past. Parting with even painful patterns can in itself be painful, and there is only so much pain that a person can process at any one time.

Ideally, the pace of change in therapy is negotiated Jointly between the various parties. The therapist and the group read the signals of distress from the patient and "ease off the pressure." The emergence of primitive and pathological defence mechanisms are often such signals of distress. Unfortunately, the need to 'ease off is not always recognised nor is it always respected by group members (or even over-ambitious therapists). In combined therapy the opportunities for this fine tuning to go wrong increase, the patient may feel that she is "persecuted" from both group and individual therapy situations and may suffer a counter-productive response. This is the risk of making combined therapy "too much therapy." The ambitious therapist(s), the over-anxious group or the uncontained disturbed patient in the group can become for an individual patient a re-enactment of early trauma from parents of similar psychopathology.

The case of training

It is highly likely that most existing courses prepare trainees in the use of combined therapy rather inadequately. Some courses devote one seminar to the subject and I doubt that any offer supervision to trainees engaged in combined therapy. To my knowledge, experience in conducting combined therapy is not a requirement for qualification in any course and a requirement that trainees should experience combined therapy as subjects is almost unheard of. A number of training courses expect their trainees to gain experience in more than one mode of treatment irrespective of the focus of the course. Trainees in group analysis in London are expected to gain supervised experience in individual psychotherapy and other authors (Dagg & Evans, 1997) recommend that trainee psychotherapists be exposed to group psychotherapy. The same authors advocate that trainees should do so in co-therapy. In the group setting, the authors claim, unconscious processes are more visible through the interaction of participants with each other. Furthermore, the trainee can observe in group therapy the different aspects of the patient's self, gain a more whole/total understanding of the patient and carry over this learning in their work with individuals by expecting that their individual patients have aspects of their self which may not be apparent in the individual analytic situation.

The co-therapy setting is an approximation of combined therapy, in the sense that it gives rise to some of the dynamics prevalent in combined therapy but in a setting which is safe as it takes place in the presence of an experienced therapist.

Conclusion

Combined therapy adds an extra dimension to unimodal therapy; it may enable, enrich and sustain therapy; it carries its own risks and places special demands on therapists and patients alike. In the case where one of the interventions is group therapy the demands and the rewards are to the other group members as well.

References

Benjamin, L. R., & Benjamin, R. (1995). A therapy group for mothers with dissociative disorders. *International Journal of Group Psychotherapy, 45*(3): 381–403.

Boswood, B. (1976). The letter to Dr. DeMare. *Group Analysis, 9*(2): 81–82.

Dagg, P. K., & Evans, J. B. (1997). The synergy of individual and group psychotherapy training. *American Journal of Psychotherapy, 51*(2): 204–209.

Feldman, L. B. (1988). Integrating individual and family therapy in the treatment of symptomatic children and adolescents. *American Journal of Psychotherapy, 42*(2): 272–280.

Foulkes, S. H., & Lewis, E. (1944). Group analysis, studies in the treatment of groups on psychoanalytical lines. *British Journal of Medical Psychology, 20*: 175–184 [reprinted in *Therapeutic Group Analysis*, London: George Allen & Unwin, 1964; London: Karnac, 1984].

Foulkes, S. H. (1948). *An Introduction to Group Analytic Psychotherapy*. London: Heinemann. [reprinted London: Karnac, 1983].

Foulkes, S. H. (1964 [1991]). Group analysis and psychotherapy services. In: J. Roberts & M. Pines (Eds.), *The Practice of Group Analysis*. London: Tavistock/Routledge.

Freud, S. (1910). *The Future Prospects of Psycho-Analytic Therapy. S. E., 11*: 144–145.

Hobdell, R. (1991). Individual and group therapy combined. In: J. Roberts & M. Pines (Eds.), *The Practice of Group Analysis*. London: Tavistock/Routledge.

Horwitz, L. (1994). Depth of transference in groups. *International Journal of Group Psychotherapy, 44*: 271–290.

Laplanche, J., & Pontalis, J.-B. (1983). *The Language of Psycho-Analysis*. London: The Hogarth Press and the Institute of Psycho-Analysis.

Pilkonis, P. A., Imber, S. D., Lewis, P., & Rubinsky, P. (1984). A comparative outcome study of individual, group and conjoint psychotherapy. *Archives of General Psychiatry, 41*: 431–437.

Porter, K. (1980). Combined individual and group psychotherapy: A review of the literature 1965–1978. *International Journal of Group Psychotherapy, 30*: 107–114.

Porter, K. (1993). Combined individual and group psychotherapy. In A. Alonso & H. I. Swiller (Eds.), *Group Therapy in Clinical Practice* (pp. 309–341). Washington, DC: American Psychiatric Press.

Praper, P. (1997). A case of combined therapy: Some developmental and object-relations phenomena. *Group Analysis, 30*: 331–348.

Scheidlinger, S., & Porter, K. (1980). Group therapy combined with individual psychotherapy. In: T. B. Karasu & L. Bellar (Eds.), *Specialised Techniques in Individual Psychotherapy*. New York: Brunner, Mazel [cited by Praper, 1997].

Winnicott, D. W. (1985). *The Maturational Process and the Facilitating Environment*. London: The Hogarth Press.

Wong, N. (1988). Combined individual and group treatment with borderline and narcissistic patients. In: N. Slavinska-Holy (Ed.), *Borderline and Narcissistic Patients in Therapy*. Madison, WI: International Universities Press.

PART VIII

RESEARCH

CHAPTER TEN

A ten-year study of out-patient analytic group therapy*

Barbara M. Dick

Introduction

Since Kurt Lewin (1936) first used the phrase "group dynamics," Gestalt, Encounter and T-type groups have proliferated on both sides of the Atlantic and have become the focus of high expectation of positive outcome on the part of their participants and leaders. This enthusiasm for the group experience has not been widely shared by psychiatrists, many of whom have been disquieted by the lack of a definite basis of theory and practice, although paradoxically some have hoped to achieve a saving of therapist time by group therapy. A study by Bovill (1972) to test this assumption did in fact show that the readmission rate for a sample of 36 neurotic patients in combined day-hospital group, and relaxation therapy was one seventh that of the control group, with an equal expenditure of therapist time. A detailed evaluation study of group psychotherapy by Sethna and Harrington (1971) included fifty-three in-patients and day-patients involved concurrently in daily analytic or supportive group therapy and other therapies related to Day

*This chapter was previously published as: Dick, B. M. (1975). A ten-year study of out-patient analytic group therapy. *The British Journal of Psychiatry, 127*: 365–375.

Hospital care who completed treatment. Improvement was assessed by both patients and therapists and a comparison was made. The objectives of the study also included an attempt to assess patient suitability for group psychotherapy. The results are described by the authors as "modest but worthwhile," although of the thirty-five patients receiving only group psychotherapy, twenty-four continued with individual or group psychotherapy as out-patients.

Evaluation studies of analytic group therapy are few. To some extent this is attributable to the considerable extent to which psychotherapists depend on their conviction that what they do is valuable. Developments within the group sessions are frequently marked and dramatically reinforce the conviction of a powerful therapeutic agent. It is consequently tempting to avoid the challenge of scrutiny and research and to repress the awareness that potency may be for good or ill, or consist of a placebo effect.

Home (1966) has indicated the important implications of Freud's view that the symptoms of the neurotic patient convey meaning and are the individual creation of the sufferer. Creativity has long been recognised as difficult to evaluate, for it concerns the sharing of individual experience and defies objective scrutiny. To study objectively the psychotherapeutic relationship is to attempt to face this difficulty, but it could be as inappropriate as to attempt to measure music in metres. The nature of group phenomena is equally elusive. Kurt Lewin offered a useful analogy from Einstein: It was not the charges, or the particles, but the field in the space between which was essential to the description phenomena. The therapist, however, unlike the physicist, is required to be both observer and an integral part of that which is observed, and the elusive nature of the dynamic forces which operate in the "field" of a psychotherapy group remains.

While scientific objectivity is unattainable, and in spite of these difficulties, the study and evaluation of the outcome of group therapy in terms of its effect on patients and of patients' suitability is essential for further appraisal of its therapeutic potential.

A recently published study by Lieberman, Yalom, and Miles (1973) of a student population involved in thirty hours of intensive group therapies of a variety of types has evaluated the outcome in terms of change in the participants on a number of parameters. Evaluation has been made in terms of the positive and negative change in participants experienced by themselves, their leaders, co-participants and outside friends. The authors found that one-third showed positive change, one-third were unchanged, and one-third were negatively changed at the end of the group. Six months later, three quarters of the changers had maintained their change. Changes were most noticeable in areas of value, judgement, and self-image. Such changes, however, in a student population must be attributed to some considerable extent as the authors accept, to the developmental and maturational changes characteristic of this age group.

Elsewhere Yalom (1970) has described the neurotic patient as "… frozen into a closed position; he is not open learning, generally searching not for growth but for safety". This description precisely describes the patients in this study of ninety-three neurotic and borderline psychotic patients, few of whom could be deemed to be readily accessible to maturational change.

Objects and Methods

Objects of the study

These have been two:

1. To test the assumption that closed analytic group therapy can be an agent of maintained positive change from the status of chronic patienthood to that of an ongoing and coping person, independent of psychiatric help.
2. To define factors: (a) relevant to patients' suitability for analytic group therapy; and (b) to define group structure suitable for patients conditioned to expect therapeutic failure.

Outline of study

Ninety-three neurotic or borderline psychotic out-patients, fifty-two female, forty-one male, aged between nineteen and forty-five years and with a history of from one to ten years of unsuccessful psychiatric therapies, have been involved in the study (Tables 1 and 2). Fifteen patients had previously been in-patients and fifteen had made one or more serious suicide attempts.

There have been eleven groups over the ten-year period from 1963 to 1973, held in the psychiatric department of a district general hospital.

All patients were initially referred by consultant colleagues or by G.P.s for assessment as to suitability for individual or for group analytic psychotherapy. The writer, a psychiatrist with a Jungian analytic training, working under the N.H.S., has been the therapist throughout the study.

On referral, each patient was involved in five or more individual psychotherapy sessions with the therapist with a view to appropriate selection for either individual or group therapy.

Task of therapy group

The primary task has been that of facilitating change from patient status to that of an ongoing person. As group psychotherapy has frequently been seen to be the end of the therapeutic road by those making the referrals and those referred, it has been of primary importance to avoid a reinforcement of therapeutic failure. A selection based on patient suitability for analytic group therapy has involved the therapist, the patient and patients' key relations.

Selection of patients

(a) Therapist's selection criteria

1. After brief individual therapy, therapist selection has been made where the symptoms appear to be both the cause and the effect of the long-standing dependency role, both maintaining the past child/parent relationship in the here-and-now situation and continually reinforcing this. Such patients describe stress in the whole range of relationships with parent-authority figures and in situations where they themselves are involved in the exercise of authority and responsibility. In relationships with bosses, senior colleagues or work mates, and at home in the role of spouse or parent such patients appear to be compelled to fail to fulfil their potential as adults and continue to maintain themselves as dependent children.
2. An additional therapist requirement has been that members should be currently working either as housewives or outside the home. This has ensured a reality-base for analytic therapy in an out-patient setting where no other therapy has been offered other than medication already assessed by the patient to be only marginally effective.

3. Reasonable expectation that a patient will be locally domiciled for the 18 months of group therapy is also sought by the therapist.
4. An upper age limit of 45 has been selected as giving optimum potential for change.

(b) Patient's self-selection

This is based on motivational strength towards change. It must be sufficiently strong to cope with the considerable and necessary tension involved in analytic group therapy and the processes of change. All potential members are informed that therapy offers no easy option and that during the 18 months they may frequently feel worse rather than better. This is also indicated to their G.P.s.

Motivation has also been assessed by the patient's acceptance of the "group contract." This outlines:

(a) Regular attendance at weekly sessions for eighteen months.
(b) Total confidentiality concerning all group transactions.
(c) The requirement to bring painful material and feelings and current life events to the group.
(d) A ban on socialization between members outside of group sessions.
(e) The cessation of individual contact with the therapist.

This last requirement has had particular relevance in that the thirty-eight of the ninety-three patients had previously had eight to twenty-five individual therapy sessions while awaiting a group place. The graduation from the one-to-one relationship to a shared one is challenging to a patient and a further test of motivational strength (Wolff & Soloman, 1973). Those who opt for group therapy have been encouraged to feel highly privileged, and the majority have come into the group with considerable hope, which in itself is significantly correlated with positive therapy outcome (Goldstein, 1962). Some patients have been stimulated to find a job in order to qualify for group therapy.

(c) Family involvement in selection

The collusion of a key relative or family nexus in preserving the status quo of patients, is of crucial importance in failure to maintain therapy. While spouses and key others may assert their support for therapy, they frequently manipulate or unconsciously prevent its action. An attempt has been made prior to final selection to explore the strength of this collusion with the key relative and to enlist their

> positive support. In spite of this, owing to the unconscious nature of the collusion, family stress has been common during group therapy. The expectation has been that the excessively vulnerable and those too enmeshed in collusively restrictive outside relationships will be daunted either by the forecast of storm and stress or by the opposition of the collusive partner.

No persuasion has been offered to such patients in order to avoid a further experience of failed therapy.

It will be seen that the patient's suitability for therapy has been based on self-selection, which in turn has been based on the therapist's selection of appropriate criteria conducive to positive outcome. The assumption has been made that the appropriate matching of a patient to therapy is as important as the matching of pharmacological or other therapies to diagnostic criteria. Truax and Carkuff (1967) have indicated that a treatment mismatched is potentially untherapeutic.

Symptoms of patients accepted for group therapy

Patients in this series suffered from the full range of symptoms listed in the Hamilton Anxiety Rating Scale. In addition patients were included with obsessional compulsive symptoms, sexual difficulties

Table 1. Treatment prior to group therapy.

Treatment		*Number of Patients*
Pharmacological only		38
Pharmacological + 8–25 individual Psychotherapy sessions*		38
ECT	O.P .8}	
	I.P. 4}	12
Behaviour therapy		4
Hypnosis		2
Leucotomy		1
Total treatments		95
1 patient had previously had ECT, behaviour therapy and leucotomy		

*All patients had 5–8 sessions of individual psychotherapy for assessment purposes prior to Group Therapy. Individual psychotherapy session = 30 mins fortnightly.

Table 2. Length of duration of symptoms prior to group therapy.

	Under 1 yr.	*1–2 yrs.*	*2–5 yrs.*	*5–10 yrs.*	*10+ yrs.*	*Total*
Number of patients	1	15	38	27	12	93

Table 3. Predominating presenting symptoms.

	Depression	*Phobic anxiety*	*Psychosomatic*	*Sexual*	*Obsessive compulsive*	*Anxiety*	*Agressive anti-social*	*Paranoid delu- halluci-nating*	*Alcoholsm*	*Total*
Number of Patients	40	9	8	9	6	10	4	5	2	93

and deviations, uncontrollable antisocial or aggressive behaviour, and alcoholism. Thirteen borderline psychotics were also included who described severe paranoid ideas, delusions and hallucinations both auditory and visual of variable duration, but who fulfilled criteria for selection (Table 3). The symptom most stressed by the patient at referral was accepted as the predominant one. Symptom removal has not been seen as the primary task of therapy, however. Symptoms have been regarded as an integral part of the constellation of failure to achieve full adult potential, and the primary task, as stated previously, has been that of basic change of status. Overall management of symptoms has therefore been explicitly handed over to the patients' G.P.s with a request for encouragement of maintenance of attendance.

Group composition

Foulkes and Anthony (1957), Whitaker and Lieberman (1964), Yalom (1970) and others share the clinical sentiment that the heterogeneity of patient's symptoms and conflict areas and patterns of coping facilitates the process of change in interpersonal transactions. Whitaker and Lieberman stress in addition the importance of the homogeneity of patients' vulnerability to anxiety. "The greater the span between the polar types (diagnoses and disturbances), the higher the therapeutic potential, if the group can stand it"—is the way that Foulkes sums this up. This approach to group composition has been used with all the groups reported here. In addition, in this series the attempt has been made to include in each group a range of educational, social and occupational backgrounds, in order to facilitate an exchange of thinking, feeling, intuition, and sensation transactions within the group (Juno, 1923). Each group has also included some borderline psychotics.

The eleven groups have contained an average of nine members, with a balance of the sexes as far as possible. Since the early groups, no new members have been added after three sessions.

The average number of sessions per group has been sixty-three, held over a period of eighteen months (Four patients in the first three groups started late and continued with the next group).

It has seldom been possible to realise our theoretically conceptualised model of group composition, as in the psychiatric department of a district general hospital the pool of suitable patients at the start of a group is limited in size. This, however, in the writer's opinion, in no way invalidates the importance of a facilitating group composition, and the reverse of this can be damaging to a group, as reported on later.

Group setting and structures

These groups have met weekly in the evening to avoid disruption of working life. Two groups have usually run concurrently but at different stages of development, one at 6.30–7.45 p.m. and another at 8.30–9.45 p.m. thus allowing some comparisons to be made. The setting has been a room in the out-patient department at times very basic in its fittings. Each group has included a non-participating regular recorder, who has recorded sessions verbatim in abbreviated longhand. From this recording and discussion, recorder and therapist have evolved the Focal Conflict and resolution for each session, based on the model of Whitaker and Lieberman (1962). From these summaries it has been possible to monitor group development on a cognitive level. The recorders' contributions here have been invaluable apart from their explicit function, and the availability of support and discussion of counter-transference has facilitated a balance between anxiety and smugness. The experience of recording in a therapy group has offered a valuable opportunity for training for group therapists, and been sought after eagerly.

Group process and content

The group analytic model of Foulkes (Foulkes and Anthony 1957) has been used with all these groups. The therapist role has throughout been that of facilitator of understanding of self and key others in the here-and-now situation. Swapping of symptoms as such has been discouraged, and the group has been encouraged to look for meanings. The regular attendance of medical student and social worker observers has provoked the expression and further examination of concealed paranoid feelings and has provided a link between the outside world and the "inside" world of the group. In addition to its function of testing motivation for membership of a group, the group contract has had an additional importance. Group patients who experience relationships as transference largely ones have highly ambivalent feelings towards parent and authority figures. The breaking of contract rules has been usual and invariably flagrant. Developing groups have acted out their rebelliousness and ambivalence to authority and parent figures in the here-and-now, and this flagrancy has enabled the group to experience their conflicting needs for the all-powerful parental control and support, and for independence and potency. Rebellions within a group herald the desired basic change but involve therapist and recorder in the acceptance of this. The Focal Conflict schemes have at these times proved invaluable, as also when groups appear static.

Termination of group therapy

At termination each patient has been seen individually by the therapist, the recorder and latterly by a third member of staff. Information has been sought on the eight parameters reported below, together with the member's appraisal of the group experience and of the here-and-now life situation by questionnaire. This has requested information about changes in key relationships. They have then been offered three possibilities: (a) an appointment in six weeks' time; (b) an appointment in three months; (c) an appointment made by the patient if requested at a later date. Few have requested the first, and like those who have requested the second, few have kept their appointment, citing pressure of outside life as the reason. Ex-patients have occasionally phoned in for an appointment, but this is exceptional. Further therapy has been discouraged by the therapist in view of the objectives of group therapy, and in spite of counter-transference feelings experienced by therapist and recorder, as in all psychotherapy in depth.

Method of assessment of change following group therapy

The specific areas of disturbance of patients were identified from an early stage as related to eight areas; it is on these eight parameters that estimation of change before and after group experience has been made. (A further study reporting on the results of a Repertory Grid given initially, mid-way and at the group-end is in preparation.)

The parameters chosen were: 1. Marital (or in single patients) patient-parent relationships; 2. Work; 3. Sex; 4. Physical health; 5. Leisure; 6. Self-image; 7. Self-understanding; 8. Symptoms. The Sethna and Harrington study used four dimensions based on those of Hartley and Rosenbaum (1963) which to some extent overlap those used here.

The first three of these parameters are based on Freud's description of successful outcome to therapy—"to be able to love and to work." Physical health relates closely to these. Leisure involves the dimension of self actualization as opposed to survival (Argyris, 1968; Goldstein, 1940).

Prior to therapy, distortion and conflict have been seen to be most marked in the areas of relationships, self-image and self-understanding as indicated earlier, and effective therapy in this study implies the ability of the patient at the end of therapy to see himself and others appropriately in the here-and-now. Symptom evaluation has been included specifically to enable patients to evaluate dependence on psychiatric treatment. Ratings are as follows:

A.	The acceptability to the patient of all aspects of their life situation.	8
B.7	The acceptability to the patient of aspects of their life situation.	7
B.6	The acceptability to the patient of aspects of their life situation.	6
B.5	The acceptability to the patient of aspects of their life situation.	5
B.4	The acceptability to the patient of aspects of their life situation	4
B.3	The acceptability to the patient of aspects of their life situation.	3
B.2	The acceptability to the patient of aspects of their life situation	2
B.1	The acceptability to the patient of aspect of their life situation	1
C.	All aspects are unacceptable to the patient.	

The rating before the start of group therapy has been made by the therapist and derived from the clinical notes. Since all patients had an initial five sessions of individual psychotherapy, these areas were specifically explored. The post-group rating was made at the termination interview by discussion with patient, therapist, recorder and where possible, a non-involved member of the department.

Change here has been seen to be largely global in character, as opposed to the view taken by Sethna and Harrison. One parameter would appear to affect another and throughout the centrifugal effect of each on all other parameters has been marked. All parameters have, therefore, equal ratings.

Ninety-three patients were rated in terms of these eight aspects of life, acceptable to them, before the start of group therapy; fifty (53.7 per cent) were rated C (all aspects were unacceptable; sixteen (17 per cent) only were rated above B 2. No patient was rated higher than B.4 (4 aspects acceptable) (Table 4).

Results

Results of the assessment at the termination of group therapy

Seventy patients (75 per cent) were assessed at the termination of the group and these included 64 who completed the full group life and 6 others who terminated before the end of the group by agreement with the group and therapist and who had attended more than 30 sessions.

Table 5 shows the rating of these seventy patients after group therapy. Sixty-seven (90 per cent) were rated above B.2, by contrast with 17 per cent who were rated above B.2 before group therapy.

From Table 6 it will be seen that sixty-one patients (87 per cent) showed positive change from their pro-group rating; 8 (11.5 per cent) showed no change, and one patient showed a negative change. Change was recorded as equivalent to alteration of three or more points in rating.

Negative changes

The potential for group therapy to produce negative change is illustrated here. The patient (K.S.), a thirty-four-year-old housewife, was presented before group therapy with depression, anxiety, and obsessional rumination about her IQ. The onset had been eighteen months earlier, when she had become involved in an affair with her Group Leader in a W.E.A. Group. There was history of lifelong difficulties in personal relationships. She was rated B.4 at the start therapy, along with only six other patients in is study.

In the group she set herself up to be the leader, and was obstructive and destructive to members and therapist. Eight members left this group in all and several unsuccessful replacements were made. At the thirty-fourth session she became acutely psychotic and paranoid and attempted suicide. She was treated with phenothiazines and ECT as an in-patient, and subsequently attended as an out-patient for two years on phenothiazine medication. She was surly and resentful and the marriage was under considerable stress. She refused further medication or treatment after two years, but in response to a third follow-up questionnaire requested an appointment. She reported herself better than she had ever been in her life, and this was endorsed by her husband, who said her whole personality had changed for the better. He stressed that their marriage relationship had always been disastrous because of her destructive belittling of him on account of his inferior job and education. Both felt that the group experience, although highly painful for her, had enabled her to discard her old personality which the group had reflected back to her, and she was immensely grateful. At the same time she expressed a good deal of anxiety about her own destructiveness to the group. Her offer of help at the social club for patients was accepted, and for some years she has been a much valued helper there. Recently she has again shown paranoid symptoms and ideas of reference and has resumed phenothiazine medication, but has shown considerable insight into the causal factors involved and has been able to continue with her job and work with the social club. This patient would seem to have experienced a psychotic illness precipitated by group therapy, and, although it seems probable that she must maintain her medication, her warmth and her ability to relate both inside and outside the family since the group therapy is noticeable. Such patients provide a painful learning experience for the therapist.

Table 4. Pre-group rating of total series.

Rating	*A*	*B.7*	*B.6*	*B.5*	*B.4*	*B.3*	*B.2*	*B.1*	*C*	*Total*
Number of patients	–	–	–	–	6	10	15	12	50	93

Table 5. Post group rating of 70 patients (75%) who completed G.T.

Rating	*A*	*B.7*	*B.6*	*B.5*	*B.4*	*B.3*	*B.2*	*B.1*	*C*	*Total*
Number of patients	4	21	18	13	5	6	1	–	2	70

Table 6. Change* in pre- and post-group rating.

	Positive change	*No change*	*Negative change*	*Total*
Number of Patients	61	8	1	70

*Change = an alteration of 3 or more points in either direction, e.g. C-B.3 or B.4–B.1.

Unchanged patients (Table 6)

Of the eight unchanged patients at the end of group therapy, one received behavioural therapy after the second follow-up, after clearly defining acute anxiety symptoms in social situations. These responded rapidly to behaviour therapy, and she married shortly afterwards. Group therapy would seem to have either changed or clarified the nature of her symptoms. Another unchanged patient (B.D.) appeared to demonstrate a manic-depressive pattern during and after group therapy and was referred for lithium therapy. He complained that this dampened down all his feelings, and later he declined it. At the third follow-up he reported himself well and grateful for the insight he had gained in group therapy, which had enabled him to perceive that his severe depression was related to the end of an important extra-marital affair when the girlfriend married. He had previously considered himself to be a gay Lothario in his love life and was surprised to discover himself as deeply emotional and with a vulnerable personality concealed by a superficial bravado.

A further patient unchanged on post-group rating and who never replied to follow-up questionnaires was reported on by his G.P. 3 years later as being well and not in need of psychiatric treatment. He appeared to have come to terms with a sensitive autonomic nervous system.

Three patients appeared totally untouched by the group experience in spite of exceptionally regular attendance, but they do not appear to have sought further psychiatric help. Two were alcoholics and one was obtaining considerable secondary gain from his marriage partner through his psychosomatic symptoms.

First follow-up

Six months after the group's end, patients were asked to complete a further questionnaire. Of the seventy patients assessed at the end of the group, fifty-three (75 per cent) replied to the questionnaire. Three had improved on their end of group rating; forty-eight had maintained their positive change. In addition to K.S., who was still a negative changer, two others had negatively changed. One became severely depressed after the end of the group and was treated by EGT and antidepressants. The marriage relationship had completely changed, the patient having become self-sufficient after years of dependency. She made an excellent recovery, but the marriage problem remained and the husband subsequently became severely depressed. This couple later received joint marital therapy. The second negative changer was at this time awaiting a mitral valvotomy operation. She recovered well, but her marriage ended in divorce which she had previously refused to envisage, and she then showed positive change.

Second follow-up eighteen months after the group's end

Questionnaires were received by sixty-one patients; forty-five (73 per cent) replied. Three patients showed increased positive change on their previous rating, and these included the two negative changers at first follow-up. B.D., the only negative changer at this stage, recovered shortly afterwards, relating his depression to the girlfriend's marriage.

Third follow-ups two and a half years after the group's end

At the time of this study fifty-four patients were eligible to be followed-up, and forty-four are accounted for. Twenty-five patients completed forms, two had died, five were known to have left the area, and nine were reported on by G.P.s. Other information was available concerning three. G.P. reports showed no symptoms or visits which suggested psychiatric illness. The twenty-four patients who completed forms and two of the patients about whom other information was forthcoming all showed maintained positive change. One patient was referred to the department with symptoms identical with her original ones. The whole family nexus and the G.P. were highly involved in this patient's illness and she is currently receiving a variety of medications eight years after the end of the group. She is one of three patients who completed group therapy and who are currently receiving intermittent therapy. Follow-up was confined to questionnaire or indirect enquiry to avoid encouragement towards further psychiatric referral.

Patients' description of change

All questionnaires invited comment from patients in addition to specific assessment on the eight parameters. These comments indicated patients' cognitive understanding of the group experience and their awareness of change in themselves. Four examples are illustrative.

> ... I feel the group experience helped me to a better understanding generally. I do cope; my tiredness does pass and I no longer collapse; nor do I over-eat. (A compulsive eater and highly obsessional woman.)
>
> ... Most important, I now realize I am not "special" in the way I thought I was. In being special to one person (the patient is now married) the importance of promoting myself as unique or superior has diminished. (A repeatedly suicidal 27-year-old who feared homosexuality and was discharged from the Army as a schizophrenic.)
>
> ... When I say I have been helped I mean I now understand my marriage, husband, family, etc., much more clearly, but I do not feel that I have changed at all. I am still the same inconsiderate, demanding, selfish person as before—but I perhaps now feel more guilty about it .... Things have settled down beautifully for us. I have an enjoyable and interesting job and I am relieved of a great many domestic responsibilities which overwhelmed me (she has five children). We are managing to face the unsettled future of my husband's job. (32-year-old woman with obsessional dislike of, and aggressive feelings towards, one child who was referred to the C.G. Clinic for behaviour disorders.)
>
> ... How does one accept the unacceptable? Before group therapy it would have been impossible. (An obsessional ruminator and transsexual.)

Cognitive understanding appears to play an important part in 'the corrective emotional experience' and a positive outcome of therapy.

Changes in family relationships

As indicated previously, change in a patient appears to involve the family in considerable stress. Twenty-one patients (30 per cent) described severe disturbance in their key relationships concurrent with or at the termination of group therapy. In all, fifty-seven of the seventy patients assessed at the end of the group experienced life situational change immediately after or during group therapy. Nine divorced or separated, ten spouses sought marital counselling, and two single patients left the parental home for the first time. Eleven married or formed a stable partnership. Seven housewives started work or training. Eight changed jobs for promotion reasons. Seven changed their place of domicile. Two achieved a desired pregnancy, and a further patient took her children out of care. These major life situational and relationship changes would seem to validate the assumption that group therapy is an agent of maintained change.

Early terminators

Twenty-three patients (24 per cent) failed to attend for the thirty or more sessions on which the patients have been assessed in this study. Four of these left the area; two became acutely psychotic. The remaining sixteen left for a variety of reasons. Ten of the early terminators attended twenty+ sessions.

Eight (30 per cent) of the early terminators were in the same group, seven of whom attended less than ten sessions. As only two other patients in the whole study attended less than ten sessions, this group's composition was felt to be significantly related to fall-out. This group contained patient K.S. referred to earlier, who became psychotic after the thirty-fourth session, having been aggressive and destructive throughout. Another patient withdrew from this group with psychotic symptoms, becoming severely depressed at the sixteenth session. Patients were added to this group to replace the early terminators, but the tension was too high for cohesion to develop. This group offered a further learning experience for the therapist, as it illustrated the capacity of the group to be an agent of negative change where group composition provided too little security for patients. Patients who terminate early or show psychotic or disturbed behaviour may, however, facilitate change of a positive nature in the other group members, if group composition promotes sufficient cohesion.

Follow-up was done on the twenty-three patients who were involved in fewer than thirty sessions. Information was received about sixteen. Seven (44 per cent) have since sought psychiatric treatment and medication from G.P.s or psychiatrists, as compared with 7 per cent of those who completed treatment. Those who completed questionnaires and have not sought further treatment show little cognitive awareness of the group experience or change in self-understanding.

There is no indication of how many hours in therapy enable a given patient to obtain "the corrective emotional experience" to break a repetitive pattern of failure or to gain understanding of what has taken place, which appears to be an important part of the therapy. A minimum of thirty sessions was arbitrarily chosen in this study for the expectation of change, as was the eighteen-month length of group life. Patients appear to need this time, though charge has frequently developed transiently at a much earlier period and been followed by repetition of the old pattern. There appears to be a need to consolidate the learning experience. It is, however, possible that patients also unconsciously regulate their processes of change to fill the time offered to them.

Discussion

Patients in this study who before group therapy have lived considerably disabled fives within the closed society of their families, their G.P.s and subsequently their psychiatrists and social workers, have been exposed to the "open society" (Popper, 1945) of an analytic therapy group, and following this the majority appear to have been enabled to become independent of the psychiatric services and to become involved in a process of change.

Post hoc is not of necessity *propter hoc,* and as in all relationship therapy there is the inevitable "contamination" factor in that the therapist has been involved in the assessment and the spectre of this "contamination" no doubt plays a part in the paucity of psychotherapists who undertake the scrutiny of their effectiveness.

Patients here have been encouraged to seek their own evidence of change, and additional objective evidence has been provided by the maintenance of independence from the psychiatric services during 2 J years and by the reported changes in life situations and relationships.

While it is true that in this study the therapist has been a constant factor, it would seem a paradox to stress this. Change is the therapeutic endeavour in analytic group therapy, and with the widening experience of ten years of the conducting of therapy groups, it may be hoped that both therapist and therapy have changed.

The decline in response to questionnaires over the two and a half-year period of follow-up is in keeping with a familiar pattern, but may to some extent be attributable to the declared policy in this study of discouraging patients from maintaining their relationship with the psychiatric services. However, efforts have been made to ascertain that ex-patients are not "doing the rounds" of the psychiatric departments in the N.H.S., though this does not, of course, preclude use of the voluntary counselling agencies.

It is impossible to compare the number of hours of therapy or their cost in terms of therapist time with those spent before the group experience as we would like to do in terms of a control study. There is, however, considerable evidence that chronic depressive and anxiety states lead to severe disablement of the patient and disruption of family life, their consequences being more disastrous than those of severe psychosis (Bransby, 1974). The phenothiazines and antidepressant drugs, together with lithium and EGT, offer a basis of hope for the sufferer from psychosis. At the present time neurotic patients must share with John Donne (1623) the protest "But I do nothing upon myself and yet I am mine own Executioner". This study offers encouragement for the assumption that analytic group therapy with selected patients may change this state of hopelessness.

"Group therapy" is a generic term, and reports of its results often avoid definition of the expectation of outcome of therapy and of the value and direction of therapist training. An analytic therapy group has the expectation of intrapsychic change, and the facilitation of this requires therapist awareness of his intrapsychic and interpsychic functioning, and the awareness of counter-transference involvement. There is, therefore, need for the experience by therapists of membership of an analytic therapy group, and in addition for supervision groups, workshops, and symposia. These are at present not readily available outside London. The method evolved here in which a therapist–recorder partnership monitored sessions through the Focal Conflict Scheme of Whttaker and Lieberman has been helpful in the absence of formal supervision and support groups. A therapist can take his group only as far as he has gone himself, and expansion of the facilities for training of therapists is a priority need for psychiatrist training schemes.

Acknowledgements

These groups took place initially at Salford Royal Hospital and later at the Lancastrian Clinic, Hope, I thank my colleagues Dr. Hugh Freeman and Dr. Michael Tarsh for their help in referring patients, and Dr. Hugh Freeman and Professor David Goldberg for help and advice with this chapter. In addition, I acknowledge the considerate help and challenge derived from the recorders Mrs. R. Milner, Mrs. B. Banning, Mrs. M. Bayncs, Mrs. B. Henkstenberg, Mr. B. Minty, and Mr. H. Hall.

References

Argyris, C. (1968). Conditions for competence and acquisition therapy. *Journal of Applied Behavioural Science, 4.*

Bovill, D. (1972). A trial group psychotherapy for neurotics. *British Journal of Psychiatry, 120*: 285–292.

Bransby, E. R. (1974). The extent of mental illness in England and Wales. *Health Trends, 6*(3): 56–59.

Donne, J. (1623). Devotions upon emergent occasions XII. In: *Complete Poetry and Selected Prose.* Hayward.

Foulses, S. H., & Antony, E. J. (1957). *Group Psychotherapy.* Penguin Books.

Goldstein, A. P. (1962). *Therapist-Patient Expectancies in Psychotherapy.* Pergamon Press.

Goldstein, K. (1940). *Human Nature in the Light of Psycho-Pathology.* Cambridge, MA.

Hartley, E., & Rosenbaum, M. (1963). Criteria used by group psychotherapists for judging improvement in patients. *International Journal of Group Psychotherapy,* *3»8c-3.

Home, E. J. (1966). The concept of mind. *International Journal of Psychoanalysis, 47*: 42–49.

Juno, C. G. (1923) Psychological types. *International Library of Psychology.*

Lewin, K. (1936). *Principles of Topological Psychology.* New York.

Lieberman, M. A., Yalom, I. D., & Miles, M. B. (1973). *Encounter Groups: First Facts.* Basic Books.

Popper, K. R. (1945). *The Open Society and its Enemies.* Routledge & Kegan Paul.

Sethna, E. R., & Harrington, J. A. (1971). Evaluation of group psychotherapy. *British Journal of Psychiatry, 118*: 641–658.

Truax, C. B., & Carkhutf, R. R. (1967). *Towards Effective Counselling and Psychotherapy.* Aldine Publishing.

Whttaker, D. S., & Lieberman, M. A. (1964). *Psychotherapy Through the Group Process.* Prentice Hall.

Whttaker, D. S., & Lieberman, M. A. (1962). Methodological issues in the assessment of total group phenomena in group therapy. *International Journal of Group Psychotherapy, 12*: 3.

Wolff, H. H., & Solomon, E. C. (1973). Individual and group psychotherapy; complementary growth experience. *International Journal of Group Psychotherapy, 83*: 2.

Yalom, I. D. (1970). *The Theory and Practice of Group Psychotherapy.* New York: Basic Books.

CHAPTER ELEVEN

Evaluation of ward group meetings in a psychiatric unit of a General Hospital*

Jason Maratos and Margaret J. Kennedy

Introduction

Since the beginning of the century, group methods have played an increasingly important role in the treatment of patients suffering from psychological or physical disorders.

Although group methods had been used long before the Second World War, it was during that period that they matured as therapeutic tools.

Most of the published work in this field reports effects of group psychotherapy (Stein, 1971), or of therapeutic community methods as a whole, with few attempts to evaluate the effect of ward meetings *per se*, or to support their observations with objective evidence (Abramczuk, 1966; Woods, 1970).

The aim of this study was to measure the effect of ward group meetings held in a psychiatric unit of a general hospital. The hypothesis was that a measurable improvement in patients' behaviour would result.

---

*This chapter was previously published as: Maratos, J., & Kennedy, M. (1974). Evaluation of ward group meetings in a psychiatric unit of a General Hospital. *The British Journal of Psychiatry, 125*: 479–482.

Method

Description of wards, patients, and staff

Two of the four mixed open psychiatric wards in a general hospital in central London were involved in the study. Each had twelve female and eight male beds.

Patients on both wards were adults of mixed diagnoses. Their socio-economic background was similar, as the wards drew their patients from adjacent catchment areas in the same London borough. The majority of patients were admitted by the Senior House Officers, who admitted patients to the various wards according to the area in which they resided.

Turnover of patients in the two wards differed. As shown in Table 1, there were significant differences in the number of admissions and female admissions over the period.

Each was under the overall supervision of a consultant psychiatrist, each with similar training background. One Senior House Officer was attached to each ward for approximately half his stay in the unit, and then changed to another ward. This changeover fell between weeks thirteen and fourteen of the study, the investigator concerned (J.M.) moving from Ward A to Ward B. During this period, there were no major changes in nursing staff.

Description of meetings

Hour-long meetings were held weekly at mid-day, when both shifts of nurses could be present. All in-patients and day patients and all staff on duty were asked to attend. Participation was not compulsory, but the nurses encouraged patients to attend. None of the

Table 1. Number of admissions during present study.

Ward	*Male*	*Female*	*All admissions*
A	29	58	87
B	26	27	53
x^2	.16	11.30**	8.26*

d.f. = 1 for all comparisons.
*p < . 01; **p < .001.

participating staff was a trained psychotherapist, and there was no supervision by a psychotherapist. There was no set agenda, and no attempt by the staff to select topics. The meetings were not intended as formal psychotherapy, and the patients were discouraged from discussing individual personal problems if they were thought to be of no interest to the group as a whole; e.g. delusional material. On the other hand, discussion which might be helpful to others was encouraged; e.g. fears about the side effects of ECT. Staff meetings were also held weekly to discuss the ward meeting and inter-staff and staff-patient problems.

Plan of the study

The study lasted for twenty-two weeks. During weeks one to nine, meetings were held in Ward A only. During weeks ten to thirteen, no meetings were held in either ward. During weeks fourteen to twenty-two, meetings were held in Ward B only. In this way, each ward served as a control for itself and for the other ward.

Evaluation measures

Ward incidents. An "incident" was denned operationally as any event in the ward considered sufficiently out of the ordinary by the nursing staff to be entered on their records.

Ward Atmosphere Scale. The Ward Atmosphere Scale represented an attempt to quantify the impression received on entering the ward by a person familiar with the patients and staff. It includes estimates of noise and movement levels, socialisation, complaining and hostile behaviour, and the reaction of staff and patients to the rater. The scale was completed at random intervals throughout the twenty-two weeks of the study, approximately once a week, by one of the investigators (**M.J.K.**).

Attitude Scale. The Attitude Scale was devised to elicit feelings about ward meetings, including the subject's opinions on whether ward meetings are helpful or harmful to patients or to staff; whether they improve or worsen relationships between and among patients and staff; and whether they improve or worsen patients' behaviour. It was administered before and after the experimental period to both patients and staff.

Results

Content of meetings

At the ward meetings, the level of discussion varied from superficial topics, such as the washing-up rota, to more significant ones, such as social attitudes towards mental illness, problems of friendship and loneliness, and others relevant to ward life itself, including authoritarianism of staff and sharing the space with acutely disturbed or violent patients.

At staff meetings, members explored inter-staff problems and staff-patient relationships, and attempted to clarify motives underlying patient and staff behaviour and the patterns of group behaviour, at a different level from that of the ward meeting. For example, the topic "side effects of drugs" was discussed in a factual way at the ward meeting, but in the staff meeting the possibility that the topic might represent repressed hostility towards staff was explored.

Ward incidents

In both wards, the holding of meetings was associated with a significant reduction in the number of incidents recorded, as shown in Table 2.

Although fewer patients were involved in causing incidents under the experimental conditions on both wards, the differences were not statistically significant, as shown in Table 3.

Table 4 gives a summary of the main types of incidents recorded, and their frequency. The greatest changes were in the number of times patients refused medicine or absconded from the ward, but changes occurred also in most of the other categories.

Table 2. Number of ward incidents.

Ward	*Condition*		x^2
	Meeting	*No meeting*	
A	48	81	7.94*
B	29	49	4.62*
Both	77	*3°	13.06**

d.f. = 1 for all comparisons.
*p < .005; **p < .0005.

Table 3. Number of patients causing incidents.

Ward	*Condition*		x^2
	Meetings	*No meetings*	
A	14	17	.29
B	9	11	.20
Both	23	28	.49

d.f. = 1; ns.

Table 4. Incidents, by type, both wards combined.

Type of incident	*Condition*		*d.*
	Meetings	*No meetings*	
Absconding from ward	21	48	27
Refusing medication	10	23	13
Breaking objects	3	8	5
Attacking staff	3	5	2
Requiring emergency Medication	16	18	2
Attacking other patients	6	5	–1
Harming self	7	5	–2
Other	11	18	7

"Other" incidents were mainly physical complaints, real or imagined, which necessitated calling the duty doctor. Changes in the opposite direction in two of the categories were too small to be statistically significant.

Ward Atmosphere Scale (WAS)

Scores on the WAS were remarkably stable over meeting and no-meeting conditions, with mean scores of 4.38 and 4.4, respectively. Analysis of variance showed no significant difference between treatments (F = 10.138, d.f. = 2, n.s.) or between wards (F = .215, d.f. = 1 n.s.).

Table 5. Staff attitudes before and after meetings.

Ward	*Attitude*	*Before meetings*	*After meetings*
A	Favourable	5	0
	Unfavourable	2	2
B	Favourable	6	7
	Unfavourable	2	1

Attitude Scale

Analysis of Attitude Scale scores showed no changes in patients' attitude towards ward meetings. Staff attitudes changed in a negative direction on Ward A, and remained positive on Ward B, as shown in Table 5.

Admission and discharge rates

Turnover rates were not influenced by experimental conditions.

Discussion

The most objective measurement of patient behaviour, the number of incidents recorded, was the only one to show significant changes in the expected direction. The types of incident most affected (refusing medication and absconding from the ward) can be interpreted as expressions of hostility to staff, and the change suggests that such feelings can be expressed verbally instead when given an outlet such as a relatively unstructured meeting.

The fact that the number of incidents returned to its original level as soon as meetings stopped indicates that this effect is not a long-term one. It also suggests that the effect on the patients is direct, and not due to resultant changes in staff techniques.

As the Ward Atmosphere Scale is an un-standardized instrument, it is not possible to say whether the results mean that it is not sufficiently sensitive to changes in behaviour, or whether ward behaviour as a whole was indeed unchanged by the experimental conditions. The reliability of the scale could be questioned on the grounds that the scoring is largely subjective, and that the rater knew which of the wards was currently holding meetings.

The Attitude Scale proved to be difficult for patients to complete, as most of them had never considered ward meetings, did not know what they were, and really had no opinion to express. Because of the high patient turnover it was not possible to measure pre- and post-meeting opinions of the same patients.

The scale appeared more useful in reflecting the attitude of staff to ward meetings. It is interesting to note that the unfavourable attitude of staff on one of the wards seemed to have no effect on the relationship between meetings and incidents. This suggests that the effectiveness of ward meetings is not dependent on enthusiastic co-operation of the majority of the staff.

The study would have to be replicated in different settings to determine whether the findings have general application. This is partly because both the parameters of the meetings and the measurement of their effectiveness include soft data liable to subjective interpretation.

Conclusion

The data collected in this study give some support to the hypothesis that patients' behaviour in a ward improves if they are given a chance to participate in a series of unstructured, permissive meetings, and to express their feelings about other patients and staff verbally without having to resort to acting-out behaviour.

The effect on the patients appeared to be a direct one, and not *via* better management by the staff. Previous training in psychotherapy, supervision by a psychotherapist, or positive attitude of staff towards ward meetings do not appear to be necessary to achieve this effect.

Acknowledgements

This study was carried out at Hackney Hospital, where one of the authors (J.M.) was S.H.O. and the other (M.J.K.) Senior Psychologist.

Thanks are due to Dr. Trevor Silverstone, who suggested that we should undertake this study, and who encouraged us in all stages of our work; to Dr. J. L. Reed for his permission to hold (and withhold) meetings on his ward; and to the nursing staff and patients of the Psychiatric Unit for their co-operation, and for putting up with the stress that these changes must have caused them.

References

Abramczuk, J. (1966). Reports from Poland: An experiment in the development of a therapeutic community in a psychiatric unit. *International Journal of Social Psychiatry, 13*: 309–314.

Stein, A. M. D. (1971). Group interaction and group psychotherapy in a general hospital. *Mount Sinai Journal of Medicine, 38*: 89–100.

Woods, L. W. (1970). Group psychotherapy in a general hospital. *Canadian Psychiatric Association Journal, 15*: 357–360.

CHAPTER TWELVE

Setting the world on wheels: some clinical challenges of evidence-based practice*

Chris Mace

Introduction

I had better start with some explanation of the title of this article. Warwickshire, where I work, cannot fairly claim to be a hub of evidence-based practice. But it is the county where William Shakespeare was born, and it is to his works that I have turned for some images with which to begin.

During *The Two Gentleman of Verona*, Shakespeare invokes the image of a world set on wheels which, like all good images, outlives its origins and is refracted by our expectations. The original reference, naturally enough, is to the world as in "everyone" and to the spinning wheel. A world set on wheels comprises a seeming infinity of pedalling figures, each separately hunched forward over identical apparatus. It carries an extraordinary premonition of what loomed in the future, the industrialisation of life. To us, other images may be conjured up also. We are familiar with the world as a physical object that can be

*This chapter was previously published as: Mace, C. (2006). Special section: Setting the world on wheels: Some clinical challenges of evidence-based practice. *Group Analysis, 39*: 304–320.

photographed like any other object. We can picture it as a sphere that could be set upon wheels, even if the necessity or function of these wheels is not wholly clear.

Already, two different kinds of picture capture some of the anxiety that attaches to this business of evidence-based practice. With the first, there is the personal worry of being pressed into a treadmill as a bureaucratic dystopia takes hold. Such anxieties don't take long to surface when talking with a group of therapists (or even student therapists), i.e. "There is only one way to do this, it must be the same way for everyone, it's what we decide, it's quick and it's cheap." The other kind of world on wheels points to the broader professional concern of whether, if the machinery of science is brought to bear on the world of group psychotherapy, this does result in a reformed and ultimately more helpful set of practices—rather than one where, paralysed by "guidance," it is no longer able to revolve at all.

First, I would ask each reader to question where he or she stands with such anxieties. Then ask the same question again, after reaching the end of this chapter. It is time to move from images to thought. But in order to get very far, we shall need to understand a little more about evidence-based practice. It can be described in terms of its aims and its procedures.

Evidence-based practice: some principles

The essential aim of evidence-based practice is to improve the benefit which members of the public can expect to result from consulting health professionals. This is understood to depend on the quality of the interventions that these professionals offer, whether these are physical treatments or psychotherapies. The range of available interventions in any area of practice might be summarised by Figure 1.

At the periphery, are interventions (usually a small proportion) that are counterproductive or harmful, although we may not know it. In the centre are other interventions (also, usually a small proportion) that on average really do benefit people in the ways they are widely believed. In the centre lie the practices (the vast majority) that, whatever we think about them, objectively do no great harm but also do no great good.

What does it mean to be a member of this large and mixed group? After all, it is probably where group analysis has to be placed. Many treatments will remain within this zone because, although there is some

● (red) Treatments that are harmful
(yellow) Treatments with little effect either way
(green) Treatments that are helpful

Figure 1. The usual range of available interventions.

evidence concerning what happens to people who receive this treatment, this is not sufficiently conclusive to put the treatment into either the outer (red) or the inner (green) groups.

"Ah! But I've been taking groups for thirty years," a group analyst may say. "I could name you dozens and dozens of people who have been helped!" But, as in a court of law, there are strict rules about what counts and what does not count as evidence. (For a brief summary as to the details of these methodologies and how evidence for an intervention can be graded, see Mace & Moorey, 2001). These methodologies elaborate how, for a study of an intervention's outcome to be valid, the study has to be planned, systematic, repeatable, meaningful, comparative and viable but relevant.

Against such standards, memory and anecdote do not take us very far. To be objective about the consequences of receiving one intervention compared to another, the procedural rules demand that we not only consider the fate of people who complete it as planned, but everyone who is offered it. Alongside the known successes, the "no-shows" and early drop-outs need to be taken into account—so do those people who stay in the course only to wish they had not, or those who express much gratitude, but underneath carry on exactly as before. In fact, the first major challenge of the evidence-based approach to psychotherapeutic practice is this need to be inclusive, to be mindful of the consequences of what is being done for everyone who is offered a treatment, not only those who stay with it.

So, we return to the aims of evidence-based practice, which can be summarised in Figure 2.

Now we can see two main changes. The (red) harmful interventions are no longer offered, while the proportion of the (green) ones whose usefulness can be demonstrated objectively has increased. There is no judgment here about the actual numbers concerned. This change could be brought about by getting rid of the clearly harmful ones and simply restricting the numbers of those that have not proved their usefulness. This is what many psychotherapists fear. But there is also the potential to swell the actual number of "green" treatments through promotion of orange ones, or the invention of new ones that meet the relevant standards.

That really is the essence of this whole way of thinking. Nothing I shall write in the remainder of this chapter contradicts this principle. So from here onwards, these pictures can be the wheels that carry us forward.

If those are the aims, how are they meant to be realised? We have mentioned the need for studies into the outcome of different

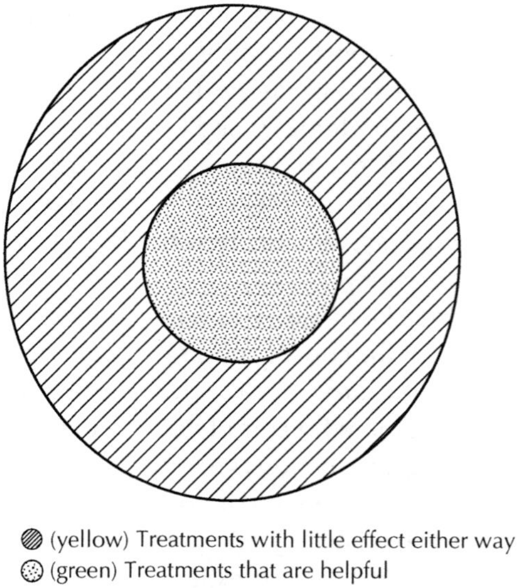

Figure 2. Interventions following introduction of evidence-based practice.

psychotherapeutic interventions and what they are good for. These begin to form a bridge from practice to evidence. However, individual studies count for little, unless their methods have been so rigorous that their results are beyond question. In practice, reliable evidence that a treatment is effective (or harmful) depends upon the pooling of results from several studies. There are well-established methods by which this can be done, which in practice involve the rejection of findings from more studies than those they include. This process leads to "systematic reviews" that, together with research reports, constitute "evidence." Figure 3 summarises this relationship.

The "evidence base" constitutes research reports and systematic reviews, the two items at the bottom of the figure. They are the result of formal research into clinical outcomes. The systematic reviews may be comparative assessments of the usefulness of different treatments for a particular clinical problem, or a critical assessment of the range of uses of a given treatment. There are lots of reviews, produced by different organisations, and they are in the public domain. Even more public, sometimes, is the final link in the loop: the "good practice guidelines". These are recommendations, even prescriptions, for what clinicians should be doing in the light of the current evidence base. The best-known kind of guidelines are clear recommendations of particular treatments for a given condition. Cognitive Behaviour Therapy (CBT) for panic disorder, response prevention for OCD (Obsessive Compulsive Disorder), EMDR (Eye Movement Desensitisation and Reprocessing) for PTSD (Post Traumatic Stress Disorder) and so on. Only treatments

Figure 3. The research–practice cycle.

that have very strong and consistent evidence of their usefulness from research will be recommended in this way, the so-called "empirically supported treatments" (ESTs). Clinical guidelines are the mechanism by which our "green" treatments are given the green light, with the expectation that they will be more widely adopted, so that the overall proportion of helpful treatments increases.

Notice how the very existence of this increasingly public superstructure brings with it an irreversible change. The scrutiny of psychotherapy requires careful classification and description. There is no longer any such thing as "therapy." Instead, every psychological therapy has its own name, a name it will be expected to own and to live up to. And the public are realising this.

Alison comes to her first meeting of the group. She is young, twitchy, and intellectual. Something in her manner reminds the conductor of her assessor's comments about endless battles for control with a pedantic and apparently unfeeling father. In the group, Alison wants to talk to the conductor rather than her fellow members. "What kind of group is this?" she demands. The conductor registers the hostility behind this, but gently reminds her that they already talked a little about the group when they met last month. Perhaps it is feeling different to be here than she had been expecting? Alison is not to be put off. She says now she wants to know exactly what this therapy is called. The therapist senses a hot spot. Does she (always) like things to have clear names? Alison snorts contemptuously. No, she wants to be sure so she can look it up on the Internet.

And as Alison sits glaring at her therapist as if she's from a different planet, all efforts to ground their dialogue in the room, to acknowledge the presence of others and of Alison's personal feelings, are batted back into hyperspace. Whatever the personal meanings here, something has changed in the wider matrix that has passed this therapist by, and made things more difficult than they need have been. Clinicians need to live with the impact of information and the new expectations it feeds.

Evidence-based practice in practice

Practice guidelines are about much more than being precise. They exist to facilitate change through discrimination. It is around this segment of the research/practice cycle that some of the greatest challenges arise. To clarify some of these, I conducted a qualitative research study among practising clinicians (including three group analysts) into their personal experience of "good practice guidelines". Thematic analysis of focus groups is a very different sort of research to clinical outcome studies, but it is very valuable for analysing the deep structures of group discussion.

Simple inspection of a chart depicting the eighty or so themes around which these discussions were organised, and their principal relationships, underlined some surprising findings. Although the participants had been strongly encouraged to examine the direct clinical impacts of good practice guidelines, this received relatively little attention from them in relation to the full scope of the discussions. Instead, the "systemic" aspects of practice, in terms of organisational support and resources available, and the impact which a guideline culture has on individuals and on corporate ways of working and thinking, were dominant. I have reported on these more analytically elsewhere (Mace, 2005) and think the most useful way to convey these perceptions and concerns here is through a form of "presentational knowing" (Reason, 2003) familiar to qualitative researchers. I shall therefore reflect on the respondents' comments about the perceived consequences of evidence-based guidelines in what is, of course, a completely fictitious scenario.

Scenario: a consequence of evidence-based guidelines

Imagine, then, that a dedicated group of researchers have achieved the virtually impossible. They have undertaken, and successfully repeated, randomised controlled trials of group analysis with patients. To do this, they had to define for whom it was a treatment, very likely a group for whom there are few other treatments. Let us suppose that this triumph was achieved with people having dependent personality disorder and a severe (or "major") depressive episode. This is clinically plausible—people fitting this description tend to be under-diagnosed, and could represent as many as 2–3 per cent of the adult population, while accounting for significant use of expensive hospitals. The results of the research trials are therefore taken seriously, and are translated into nationally sanctioned practice guidelines. As an empirically supported treatment, or EST, group analysis becomes group-analytic therapy, or GAT. Health service managers are given due warning that, from the following October, people with this condition should be receiving the recognised evidence-based treatment, GAT. The people who qualify for GAT are defined now in terms of the people who were part of the trial. For instance, because no-one in the trial had been in hospital for longer than one year, this becomes a reason for refusing people the new treatment. However, there are many, many others who qualify and clinicians start actively looking for people who meet the criteria for dependent personality and at least one major depressive episode. The condition is called DIPMAD for short, and gets written into screening protocols. People with it are referred to the GAT team, irrespective of other aspects of their personality, relationships or attitudes to treatment. Crash courses in "GAT for DIPMAD" are provided. Any staff having no clear role with another group of prioritised patients are sent on the courses. For the large numbers of nurses concerned who had not seen themselves as future group psychotherapists, this is a potentially stressful experience. It is mitigated in the short term by a vivifying sense of purpose and potency. The DIPMAD workers may be lucky and receive training and supervision from someone who is steeped in the model, or their questions may be being answered by a well-meaning professional head, who tries to keep a few pages further ahead in the manual.

As the GAT initiative powers forward, patients are classified and groups are held. The managers are praised (and rewarded) for meeting their targets. It matters more that the groups happen than what happens in them. GAT patients, and their relatives, have keen expectations. The modern treatment of choice they have been waiting for has finally arrived. Some, when told they need to wait for a group to be ready to start in their town, make formal complaints about the delay before it has a chance to start. What they finally get is a guided discussion, where they are regularly invited to review relevant events from their past if the dialogue shows signs of flagging. Some are happy, others frustrated. The therapists are rarely at a loss for suggestions. The one fully trained group analyst in the next town winces at the reports that are passed on. Few of these new patients, the group analyst feels, are receiving an experience of true therapy, or even learning what this may be.

Now, evidence-based practice does not have to be this way—indeed those involved in its propagation are usually quick to assert it should not. However, descriptions of the consequences of "dumbing down" (and downright deception) figured strongly in the interviewed therapists' perceptions of what is already happening. It is foolish to deny that evidence-based practice does bring all kinds of unintended consequences into play. And whatever the intentions, these have to be reckoned with. Therapists familiar with researchers' thinking will know the language of "efficacy" and "effectiveness"—and the tension between producing evidence of exactly how well treatments work in pure form under experimental conditions (efficacy) and as they are actually delivered in practice (effectiveness). However, once therapies are being provided as part of a new, guideline-driven initiative, even the results from effectiveness studies seem unlikely to be an accurate guide as to what to expect. And no-one has adequately researched the actual clinical consequences of implementing evidence-based practice of this kind.

Two doyens of the EST model of evidence-based practice are Anthony Roth and Peter Fonagy, authors of *What Works for Whom?* This is what they have to say in the recent second edition of that book:

> ... although there is an increasing requirement for practice to be based on evidence, we are not aware of systematic evidence demonstrating the benefit of this process. At present, implementation is largely based on an appeal to face validity.
>
> (Roth & Fonagy, 2005, p. 502)

In other words, evidence-based practice itself is not, as yet, evidence-based.

This would be unlikely to surprise the clinicians in the focus groups. They felt things weren't working to the overall improvement of clinical care through a mixture of muddle and conspiracy. Indeed, most seemed to feel information was being selectively filtered to drive hidden agendas within a prevailing culture of "spin".

It is a simple fact that evidence-based practice has arisen following the ever-increasing involvement of third parties in the provision of treatment, whether these are arms of government, managed care organisations, or insurers. However strong the rational arguments for a particular reform may be, the motivation bringing it about is likely, in effect, to be over-determined. The impacts of such a complex environment, however, are being felt by everyone providing health services, not only psychotherapists. Psychotherapists have a simple choice between indulging their own paranoia privately, or using their analytic skills to help colleagues to understand and survive in such a deceptive culture. This represents a third clinical challenge for the growing list.

Whatever the motivations—is there something wrong with the way the cycle is being made to work, rather than the underlying

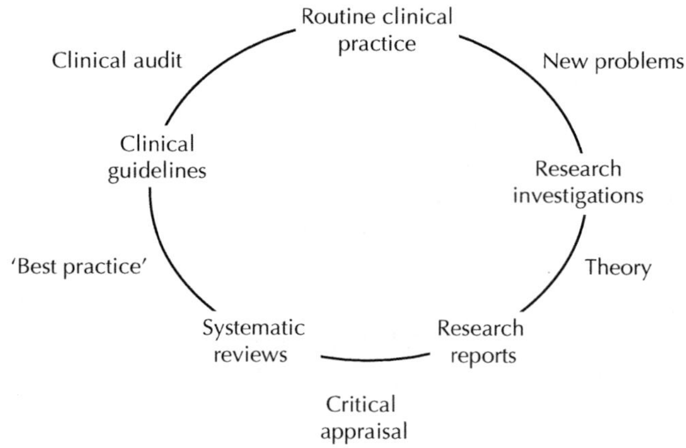

Figure 4. Impact of EBP on the research–practice cycle.

project itself? One symptom of things going awry is that the research practice cycle becomes turned in on itself. Instead of the effort being made to go out from practice, by systematically addressing questions that arise there, the relationships become inverted. (See Figure 4.)

The needs of the so-called "evidence base" determine research needs, and clinical practice is cut out of the loop. This subtle but significant shift is apparent even in overtly benign strategic documents as they talk of changing research priorities exclusively in favour of outcome studies (e.g. American Psychological Association, 2005). Let us go back to research for a moment, and another quotation from a psychiatrist who is a very successful and respected psychotherapy researcher:

> Most psychological treatment studies target patients who in clinical practice would be treated with drugs, and exclude patients who, in clinical practice, would be offered psychological treatment.
>
> (Guthrie, 2000, p.132)

The evidence base that so much effort is being expended on, even if it can be perfected, is of limited value in the justification of psychotherapy. Moreover, it is probably harmful because it is likely to help arguments for pharmacological alternatives seem more rather than less compelling. On this view, the essential problem with practice to date has been the insistence on organising research around diagnostic categories. There is little to justify this except convention. The design of our diagnostic system, in so far as it has any rationale, has been strongly influenced by the therapeutic profile of drug treatments (Healy, 1997). But as long as psychotherapists who do research go on colluding with this, a situation in which real clinical needs fail to be addressed directly is perpetuated. If, in practice, psychotherapy is needed because people do not want or do not benefit from drugs, should not one question be: "what are the most helpful treatments for such people, irrespective of their diagnosis?" Again, if people who are unable to establish or to maintain satisfying relationships with others are disproportionately represented among psychotherapy clients, should not their needs be a starting point for outcome studies? To do otherwise becomes a questionable and even dangerous distraction. Of course, if researchers do start working within a more relevant framework, there is no guarantee that the practical consequences will be better once the resulting evidence base is translated into practice. But the fact that this implementation is likely to happen now mean clinicians need not only know what sorts of research are being done and are not being done. They should seek to influence this choice—our fourth challenge.

Taking action: practice-based evidence

Officially, the evidence base is, as yet, too incomplete to stand as a basis for recommending or choosing treatments except in very circumscribed situations. At the same time, clinicians do have to face demands to demonstrate the value of what they do in a way that is inclusive and objective and goes beyond testimonials. This brings a further challenge, the expectation to collect evidence of one's own. It's an important subject which involves the systematic recording of actual outcomes, together with critical analysis of variations and benchmarking with comparable services elsewhere, but is relatively straightforward. Lucock et al. (2003) provide a good description of its implementation in a UK Service. The usefulness of practice-based evidence in satisfying commissioners, despite the administrative burdens it brings, is difficult to overestimate in most contexts.

Taking the gathering of evidence back into local control brings other opportunities, having far-reaching implications for practice. We can look at one example, based on defining an algorithm for what is likely to happen to a typical patient of a service. It is derived from a combination of local experience and statistical rules established from many psychotherapy outcome data sets. In effect, at any stage in their treatment, a patient could be in one of four categories: "not on track" and

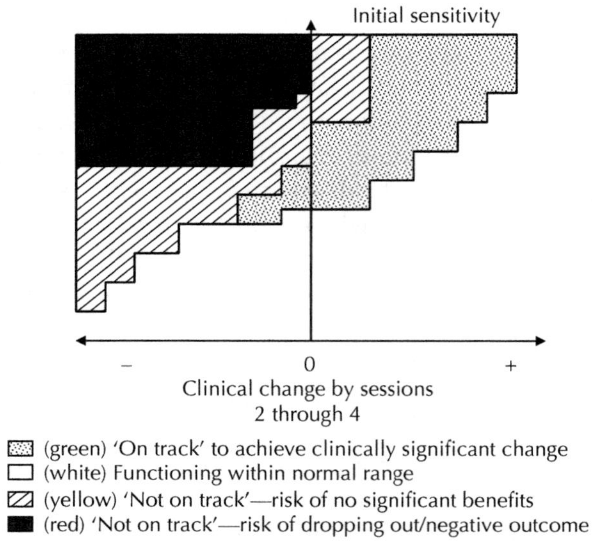

Figure 5. Identification of 'On track' and 'Not on track' cases between sessions 2 and 4 of individual therapy (after Figure 1 of Lambert et al. [2001] by kind permission of Michael Lambert for the Society of Psychotherapy Research and Taylor & Francis).

in danger of ending up worse off than when they began; in danger of failing to improve; "on track" to make gains that will represent a significant improvement; and typical of people who are functioning well rather than people in treatment. They can all be represented in Figure 5.

Take a moment to see that this is really not as complicated as it may appear. The central axis corresponds to initial severity, and the clinical change since the outset of treatment will be either positive (to the right) or negative (to the left). The white area therefore represents people who have made enough change since they started to have stopped being a clinical case: the finishing tape that effectively separates the area off is bound to be a sloping line. The "green" area representing significant positive progress is a function of the degree of positive change relative to the starting point. Negative change is necessary to enter the "red" zone (real danger of negative outcome) while the "yellow" zone of no potential change is a hinterland between these two. This chart sets out their relations between sessions 2 and 4: as therapy progresses, different charts apply as these relationships inevitably change.

Why should it matter that such mapping is possible? During research, it has been shown that sharing the information with a therapist that a patient has strayed into the yellow or red zone as soon as they do so leads to a significant subsequent improvement in outcome, relative to people whose scores also went up, but whose therapists were not given this feedback (Lambert et al., 2001).

Lambert's team went on to suggest the feedback was optimal when given in the form of a colour coded chart (Lambert et al., 2002). See Figure 6.

This work represents a paradigm shift in evidence-based practice. Instead of classifying every instance of a named treatment as red, yellow, or green and trying to shift the balance by increasing the availability of green treatments (the classical strategy), the early classification of individual treatment episodes early in their course is being used to change the overall balance of treatment outcomes within a service. Whereas the ultimate value of the first strategy remains to be proven, Lambert's approach appears to bring an immediate improvement in effectiveness.

Replication studies suggest a major factor accounting for the positive impact on outcomes is that the informed therapists take action that increases the chances of the patient remaining in therapy, rather than dropping out. The average duration of therapy therefore increases, providing more time for recovery (Whipple et al., 2003).

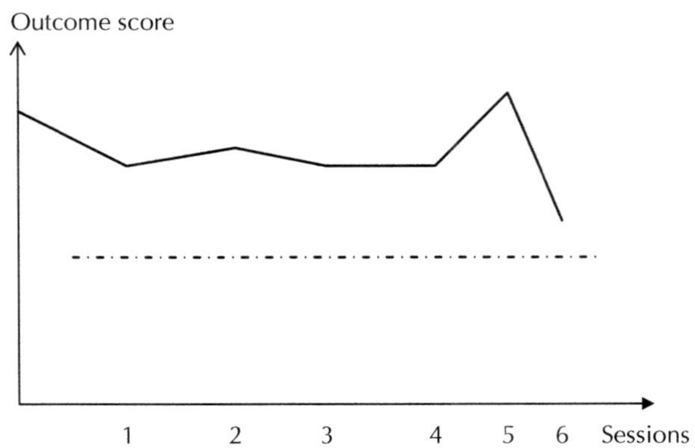

Figure 6. Chart to feedback on patient progress (key as for Figure 5; after Figure 2 of Lambert et al. [2001] by kind permission of Michael Lambert for the society of psychotherapy research and Taylor & Francis).

Like much good research, this chimes with clinical experience. A group conductor recently experimented with giving each member a short outcome questionnaire at every session they attended. It covered much the same ground as Lambert's (Lambert et al., 2001; Lambert et al., 2002).

> After the third session, Albert had used the questionnaire to indicate he was not only functioning very poorly but was feeling severely suicidal. The conductor responded by telephoning Albert and arranging a meeting before the next session. Albert admitted that he had kept his intentions from the assessing therapist as well as his own psychiatrist. He also admitted he had been very unsure about ever returning to the group. Albert was a deeply alienated individual who did not allow his family to feature on his personal horizon. Once it was clear he was unlikely to kill himself immediately, he returned to the group where he survived for several more turbulent months. After he had left, it was possible in a review meeting to confirm how significant acting on that questionnaire information had been for him subsequently.

But what else could this sort of targeted feedback mean in a group context? Earlier in this chapter, we skirted around how small a place group psychotherapies occupy within the established evidence base. This reflects severe limitations on how far you can do good efficacy studies (complicated by the non-comparability of one group with the next) or effectiveness ones (where local factors such as the age of ongoing groups compromise generalisability more than for other interventions). However, a valid local algorithm for the trajectory of individual patients who enter groups within a service is relatively immune to such variations. What is more, in group psychotherapy there is no clear reason why session by session feedback should be given only to the group conductor. Therapy by the group is likely to be supported by feedback for the group. The real (and broadest) clinical challenge here becomes how a group integrates objective feedback about members' progress that is direct, repeated and normative, right there in the room.

Summary

Six distinct clinical challenges from evidence-based practice have been identified in the course of this survey. They apply to every psychotherapist working in a public setting, and many others as well, even if they do not feel their clinical freedom is restricted by some third party's interpretation of what evidence-based practice should be. As all six lean heavily on I-words, this may help in remembering them.

First was the need to include all consequences of clinical practice, the welcome and the unwelcome, in assessments of its impact, even informal ones. Second is an obligation to identify more consistently with a particular brand of therapy, and by implication to work with others to ensure its strengths and weaknesses are properly represented. Third is the challenge of bringing analytic thinking to bear on the complex motivations and institutional processes that accompany evidence-based practice, interpreting these for other health professionals as well as ourselves, to help everyone keep their heads amid many contradictions. Fourth is a duty to influence research objectives within our field, to counter the estrangement of research from practical clinical needs and its over-reliance on a diagnostic system of dubious relevance to psychotherapists' work. Fifth is the need to initiate collection of in-house evidence, to compensate for the partiality and limitations of evidence-based practice as it is currently understood. Finally, as more and more information is inevitably collected about patients receiving treatment, there is the challenge of integrating this information within each patient's treatment, if this can render it more helpful to them and help to prevent calamity. I do not believe that we can shirk any of these challenges any longer.

References

American Psychological Association. (2005). Draft Policy Statement on Evidence-Based Practice in Psychology. Retrieved August 2005, from: http://forms.apa.org/members/ebp/ebp.pdf

Guthrie, E. (2000). Psychotherapy for patients with complex disorders and chronic symptoms: The need for a new research paradigm. *British Journal of Psychiatry, 177*: 131–137.

Healy, D. (1997). *The Antidepressant Era*. Cambridge, MA: Harvard University Press.

Lambert, M., Whipple, J. L., Smart, D. W., Versmeersch, D. A., Nielsen, S. L., & Hawkins, E. J. (2001). The effects of providing therapists with feedback on patient progress during psychotherapy: Are outcomes enhanced? *Psychotherapy Research, 11*(1): 49–68.

Lambert, M., Whipple, J. L., Vermeersch, D. A., Smart, D. W., Hawkins, E. J., Nielsen, S. I., & Goates, M. (2002). Enhancing psychotherapy outcomes via providing feedback on client progress: A replication. *Clinical Psychology and Psychotherapy, 9*: 91–103.

Lucock, M., Leach, C., Iveson, S., Lynch, K., Horsefield, C., & Hall, P. (2003). A systematic approach to practice-based evidence in a psychological therapies service. *Clinical Psychology and Psychotherapy, 10*: 389–399.

Mace, C. (2005). Will good practice guidelines promote good practice? A preliminary study of UK psychotherapists' experience. Unpublished paper presented to 36th Annual Meeting of Society for Psychotherapy Research, Montreal.

Mace, C., & Moorey, S. (2001). Evidence in psychotherapy. In: C. Mace, S. Moorey, & B. Roberts (Eds.), *Evidence in the Psychological Therapies: A Critical Guide for Practitioners* (pp. 1–11). Hove: Brunner-Routledge.

Reason, P. (2003). Cooperative inquiry. In: J. A. Smith (Ed.), *Qualitative Psychology* (pp. 205–231). London: Sage.

Roth, A., & Fonagy, P. (2005). *What Works for Whom? A Critical Review of Psychotherapy Research* (2nd edn). New York: The Guilford Press.

Whipple, J. L., Lambert, M. J., Versmeerch, D. A., Smart, D. W., Nielsen, S. L., & Hawkins, E. J. (2003). Improving the effects of psychotherapy: The use of early identification of treatment failure and problem-solving strategies in routine practice. *Journal of Counselling Psychology, 50*(1): 59–68.

PART IX

ADDICTIONS

CHAPTER THIRTEEN

Beyond the shadow of drugs: groups with substance misusers*

Martin Weegmann and Christine English

Introduction

At the heart of addiction lays a paradox, for, on the one hand drugs provide relief from the difficulties of life, but on the other hand produce unwanted, cumulative suffering.[1] As attachment to and reliance on drugs increases, its very salience reduces the importance of everything, and everyone, else. Orford's (2001) integrative model of "excessive appetites" refers to the inordinate nature of such "strong attachments" to substances which, whilst indicative of a possibly hopeful capacity to attach or invest, carry an enormous cost. Khantzian (1993, 2008) uses a contemporary psychodynamic perspective, based on his seminal idea of self-medication, and postulate a "play off" in which the drug user trades different orders of suffering and, "substitutes a kind of pain and distress which they do understand and control for a distress they do not understand and do not control. Both the pain-relieving and pain-perpetuating aspects of addiction are attempts to regulate human psychological suffering" (Khantzian & Albanese, 2008, p. 80).

---

*This is a revised and expanded version of a paper that was originally published, under the same title, in (2010) *Group Analysis*, *43*(1): 1–21.

Addictions bind the individual because of the illusion of what they promise and in this regard, those with substance misuse can be likened to the mythical figure Sisyphus, endlessly climbing the same futile path in a human-all-too-human struggle to "get somewhere else"(Weegmann, 2009). Addictive desires are desperate and dangerous desires. But addictions are also common, affecting individuals, their families and even entire communities.

This chapter addresses the process of recovery in which individuals move from away from drug use and their related lifestyles, as witnessed and enabled in group therapy. Several models of "modified, dynamic group psychotherapy" with this population group are referenced and although there is no particular group analytic tradition in this area, we hope to show the value of applying some group analytic concepts. To achieve recovery, those with substance misuse have to overcome a whole range of difficulties and entrenchments and, where successful, develop new identities and lifestyles, marking the transition from "active user" to "recovering person." This remains provisional as there are no guarantees in recovery, but neither does having an addiction condemn a person to permanent hopelessness.

Models of group therapy

Those with substance misuse can benefit from a wide range of group therapies that need to be adapted to their stage of change, from immersion in drug use, to emergence from drug use and through into medium-term and long-term recovery. The groups at an earlier stage will include interventions such as psycho-educational groups, preparatory and motivational groups (e.g., preparing a person for detoxification), relapse prevention groups and many others (for further discussion of the range and role of such groups, see Weegmann, 2011). Since this chapter largely addresses the process of recovery we shall concentrate on more exploratory-supportive groups which help to (re-)build confidence, cohesion and psychosocial growth. As for the latter point, it is no exaggeration to compare the process of recovery from substance misuse as a form of "post-traumatic growth."

There are several useful models of group therapy available, drawing variously on (1) attachment-oriented psychotherapy (hereafter "AOT") (Flores, 2003, 2006) (2) interpersonal group therapy as influenced by Yalom (Leighton, 2004), (3) modified dynamic group therapy (hereafter "MDGT"), influenced by self-psychology as well as attachment theory (Khantzian, Halliday, & McAuliffe, 1990) and (4) applied group analysis (Sandhahl, Busch, Skarbrandt, & Wennberg, 2004; Weegmann, 2004a, 2006). All these models emphasise the provision of safety within clear boundaries and adaption to differing patient needs at different stages of recovery, rather than encouraging uncontained disclosure or emotional expression for the sake of it. The group conductor plays a relatively active role, promoting links, offering clarifications and is unafraid to draw upon the wisdom of other traditions, such as relapse prevention or fellowship groups (AA, NA, etc.), at all times seeking to build the reflective capacities of group members. The issue of co-membership, of say a therapy group and a fellowship group, such as AA, is discussed below. One analogy for thinking about the role of more psychodynamic groups in recovery is that of building moral and psychic "muscle," so that the depletion and demoralisation associated with addiction can be addressed (Elliot, 2003). Developmental difficulties, from both early and adult life, and attendant deficits, can be faced and addressed, hence improving capacities for self-regulation. Substance misusers might be treated in homogenous groups, within say a specialised addiction service, or join heterogeneous groups within, say, a psychotherapy department. Our experience is with both settings.

Drug users in group: memory, desire, others

The following diagram illustrates how psychodynamic groups might figure in the lives of individuals struggling with recovery from addictions.

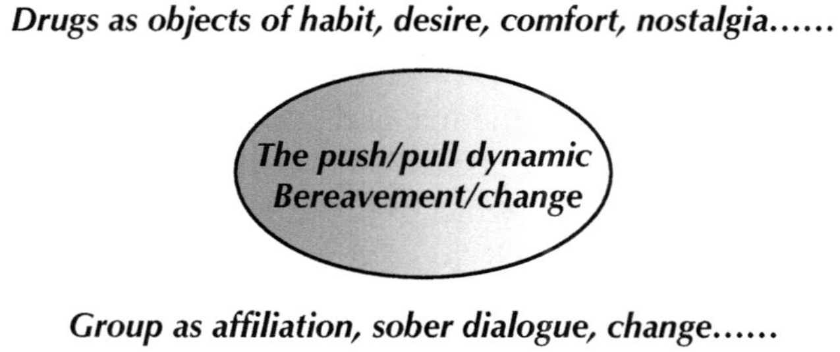

Diagram 1.

The centre of the diagram represents a push/pull, change/threat dynamic central to addictive disorders, and captures how group members are torn between different aims (e.g. the wish to be sober versus the desire to be a social drinker, to change versus not to change) and different parts of the personality, (e.g., parts of the personality seeking relief, and which anti-development, versus parts of the personality seeking growth). "Staying with" these core ambivalences of change is central to psychodynamic group work, even for those whose abstinence is better established, at least in terms of time. The top of the diagram points to the presence of drugs as powerful objects of desire, comfort and nostalgia which symbolically hover over each group session; in the words of one group member, "it's like they never leave me be, they're still there, inside, somewhere, even though I haven't used." Sometimes, whole groups enact a "talking high" through recollections of past using, references to drug effects and so on. We propose the term "memorabilia" to refer to the evocative lifestyle aspects associated to previous drug use, a counterpart to the term "paraphernalia," which refers to the equipment, ritual and so on that surround actual drug use. Nostalgia can be explicit, as in reports of strong desires to use or euphoric recall, but on other occasions, the psychic and group 'pull' towards drugs is subtle, 'underground' if one wills, with memories encoded in feelings, jokes and other indirect, split-off idealisations of drug use. Such evocations and drug resonances are crucial to identify lest the group becomes a substitute for the drug rather than a more positive, hopeful object; "war stories" are not helpful in and of themselves. In self-medication terms (Khantzian, 1999, 2008), particular drugs are compelling for the very reason that they seemingly meet or once met important psychological needs, addressing gaps as it were in the structure. Drug references in groups can feel like "music to the ears," as using fantasies are re-evoked and group energies seduced. "Psychological relapse" can precede actual relapse, even if the link between the two is not a necessary one, provided the process can be located and contained in time, through the efforts of the individual and group. The lure of an "immediate effect," a short-cut way of changing how a person feels, competes with the ethos of the group, which represents wholly different values: gradual re-building of the self, painful working-through of problems and slow progress towards psychic integration.

It is difficult to convey how powerful the operation of desire (to use) and memory (of the various effects of using) are in the lives of drug users. Some in the neuropsychological field talk about drug misuse as a "disease of learning and memory", and for good reasons (e.g., Hyman, 2005). In her literary, psychoanalytic account of melancholia, Kristeva (1989, p. 60) uses the imagery of a "Black Sun", in which individuals are caught, nailed down, as it were in a kind of "exitless personal vault." Addiction too can be likened to a Black Sun, absorbed into its negative energy, with recovering individuals negotiating a process akin to bereavement. Giving up drugs is a tremendous loss, and the shadow of addiction, to use another image, is a long one. If, to use Freud's (1917, p. 249) original model of bereavement, "the shadow of the [lost] object fell upon the ego," in the case of addiction, this is equally so. Indeed, the long "shadow of the drugs" significantly affects the amount of "available light" (i.e., hope, viable alternatives to using) in any given person's life. Rather than negotiate bereavement, the drug user is tempted to short-circuit loss by lapse, or to maintain closeness to the substance through some form of vicarious identification with a lost world. A group member commented that, although clean for a time, she found herself forever reading crime books and sensational crime reports in the newspapers, because, she came to realise, they reminded her of past, drug-linked criminality, with its associated excitement and violence. There is an interesting contest of possibility, expressed in two, seemingly contradictory adages, on the one hand, "absence makes the heart grow fonder" and on the other, "time heals."

Bollas (2009, p. 79), addressing the realm of the "evocative," says, "a mental object, by virtue of the power of absence, crystallises memory so that the mere mental recollection is redolent with meaning" (p. 79). In the context of addiction, one could think in terms of an "evocative substance," which encodes certain expectancies and desired effects- "what the drug does for me," in effect. This is also why neuropsychology suggests. English (unpublished, 2006), using the language of object relations theory, refers to how an "internal substance" can replace a helpful "internal object." Clearly there is a thin and judicious line to be managed between containing, and hence allowing safe acknowledgement of such evocations and recollections, and unwittingly encouraging drug nostalgia, unhelpful ruminating or "war stories." Confidence in the ability to see the past, without wishing to return to it, comes slowly in recovery, but can still come. In the words of poet Seamus Heaney (1991, p. 36),

> "Unless they've been trained out-like memories
> You've trained so long now they can show their face
> And keep their distance"

Or, in the words of person quoting AA wisdom about the past, "Remember: it is OK to look but don't stare".

If giving up drugs feels like losing a part of oneself, and relinquishing a "core function" of self-regulation, *unlike* the loss occasioned by death or unbridgeable separation, an ex-user can return to and be re-united with drugs. Funerals need not happen. Using a Bowlbian formulation, Reading (2002, p. 28) makes the important point that under conditions of stress, the attachment behavioural system is activated; correspondingly, such systems "geared to the maintenance of proximity to the drug will also become activated when the addictional bond is threatened." Locating and discussing this missing, pining and nostalgic pattern is a central component of psychodynamic groups, which encourage concerted discussion focused on what it is like to give something up and thereby to move into new territories. The seduction of drugs is a truly remarkable phenomena; de Quincey (1985 [1856], p. 39), in his famous literary confession, paid tribute to the "mighty opium" as panacea and "portable ecstasy." More grimly, in his 1950s confessional of drug misuse, Burroughs (1977, p. 19) says, "Life telescopes down to junk, one fox and looking forward to the next ....) It is essential for recovery that new structures and inner resources are built or mobilised, to assist and replace those skills and capacities which are not there, or which were there but have fallen into disuse. Indeed, Khantzian (1999) refers to a "disuse atrophy" of normal functions that occurs as a result of years of drug misuse.

The struggle, and determination to move forward is signalled at the bottom of the diagram, with groups promoting "sober dialogue," standing for improved contact and toleration of different parts of the self and others (Weegmann, 2005, 2006). By way of contrast, group "anti-dialogue" is refusal to learn, a ruthless non-openness to experience and hence the reinforcement of known prejudices and patterns. Others in the group are either seen as allies in recovery or represent former, even potential drug peers. They may indeed move between these two positions. Relationships are easily devalued or rendered instrumental, with a central part of recovery consisting of relational reparation. In a child group therapy context, Canham (2002) draws a contrast between "group states of mind," in which individuals can tolerate, explore and value differences and alternative viewpoints, and "gang states of mind," in which thinking and creativity is undermined, with the individual/group locked into a primitive identity or outlook. This gang state is akin to "anti-group" process (Nitsun, 1996). The following example illustrates just how powerful and deadly this can be.

"Tony and the precipice": a clinical example

One of us (Weegmann, 2004) has previously written about the individual psychotherapy which preceded Tony's group therapy, detailing his need to keep the upper hand by various postures of aggression and self-sufficiency—e.g., beating up his therapist in an imaginary fight. His therapy was animated by this and many other direct challenges to the value of "just talking and listening" as he put it. He once envisaged my other patients dying, a fantasy based consciously on the idea of ruining my professional, if not my personal life, which, I pointed out, would also kill his own prospects of care. This background has relevance to the following scenario.

> After several week of gloom in the group, despair that any one of them could sustain recovery, Tony elaborated a thought that at first sounded like a sick joke. "What if all of us in this group went up that tower block (pointing outside the room) and jumped off ... ... at least it would be over". He smiled at the thought of 'no more Thursdays' (the day of the group), to which someone added, "no more any other days". After a shocked lull, there he elaborated, including the idea that it would be in full view of the clinic. I commented that in the fantasy, the group is killed off and all pain comes to a halt, but that there is an aftermath, a morally destroyed, but still alive therapist whose errors are visible to the whole world. Tony laughed, as if high on the thought. Two other reactions were interesting. One person observed that Tony was acting like a cult leader, "just like 'Jones' town'". Peter, who often struggled with suicidal issues, confronted Tony by retorting, "You jump if you want to, but don't fucking include me!" The mood of the group shifted, became more reflective, if sad; Tony, taken aback by Peter's retort, was calmer.

Discussion

When does destructiveness destroy communication and all good possibilities, and when is it really a reaching out, to be heard, relieved and understood? These are tough questions of psychotherapy and in the group we see the expression of an ultimate destructive fantasy: the death of the group. Can life be survived, or does living become so tormenting that it has to cease? Is there a total obliteration of states of mind and reflective space in this example, or the glimmer of communication? (Hinshlewood, 1997, explores the concept "reflective space" and attacks upon it; English, 2009, explores the idea from an object relations perspective). Is this an example of dialogue or of anti-dialogue, a thought-provoking or thought-stopping moment? Perhaps there was hope in the bleak scenario, not least because it was a "safe fantasy" that could not be actualised. Tony may be articulating ultimate despair and the wish to bring down the whole edifice of recovery, his and that of others. In a forceful projection, a still suffering therapist is ruined in spirit but not in body and paradoxically it is here, in this final conflagration, that hope exists. Can the group conductor bear, bear him, bear with them, imagine their depths of despair, and still carry on?

The group response was of great interest, ranging from grim amusement to insightful observations and challenges. The idea of Tony becoming an alternative leader, with a superior solution is present, compared to a "cult leader". In a moment of group differentiation, however, Peter, a man with a serious history of despair of his own, protested, along the lines of, "don't include me in your solution." Tony seemed to appreciate a rare act of counter assertion by Peter. The group carried on and dialogue was resumed, with more thoughts, more links and different passions.

"The Son's Room": clinical example

The next scenario occurred approximately one month after the group suicide fantasy.

> Tony had seen an Italian film, "The Son's Room",[2] which affected him, partly because it was so "ordinary" and illustrative of "chance tragedy". Almost without realising the connection, Peter said, "but isn't Martin a psychoanalyst?" Tony, convinced that I had not experienced true suffering in my life, wondered how I would respond to such a tragedy. Others spoke to how unpredictable life is and how difficult it was to know if their recoveries could be sustained. I ventured two ideas:- one that there was real interest in my life and those 'others' (people and values) which sustain me, and a theme of tragedy. How would I deal with suffering of this kind? "Maybe",

> I said, "this brings us back to the recent idea of the group suicide. What if this group, 'Martin's Group', my son or family, as it were, met with tragedy? Could I survive even the bleakest times and be able to carry on?"

Discussion

If the reader is surprised at the depth and range of group communication, it is important to note that this group was a seven-year venture, with several core members staying for more than three years. It is testimony to the group culture that so much could be expressed, including, in this case, an interesting and evocative link to the cultural-personal realm. Depressive feelings were aired, different in nature to the destructive group suicide idea. There was greater curiosity and intimacy, which can also be seen as a form of "into-me-see". This is not to underestimate "anti-group forces" and how individuals might well flirt with disaster. However, this is quite different from enactments in the real-world that carry serious risk and danger.

If the course of true recovery never ran smooth, this is echoed at the level of the group as a whole. Groups demonstrate constant forward/backward, destructive/constructive patterns and necessitate the working-through of many crises, and actual or threatened relapses. Thus there are progressive struggles and reactionary retreats, and, as argued, the risk of anti-dialogue or anti-group process that challenge the principles of sober, tolerant dialogue.

A useful metaphor from the world of political theory is Gramsci's (1971) "war of position" (*position terurgo*). The notion conjures up trench warfare and protracted struggle involving different "camps" and "forces," which can be likened to different parts of the personality aiming for different outcomes, e.g., the desire to live without drugs, indeed the terror of relapse, versus the desire to use again, evading all negative consequences (Weegmann, 2002, 2004). Often drug users operate with an implicit hierarchy of drugs in mind, like the patient who entertained himself with the thought of re-using cocaine, as, unlike his primary drug of choice, opiates, it had "no payback." His memory had done a considerable amount of editing ('forgetting') to reach such a conclusion. By the same token, patients are often equally clear and convincing about recovery goals and ideals, such as "living normally, without chemicals," "complete abstinence," "sobriety" and the like. In group there are wide possibilities, with confluences, contradictions and tensions between positions and forces. Recovery is a protracted struggle, a struggle of positions, if one wills, as illustrated by the diagram:

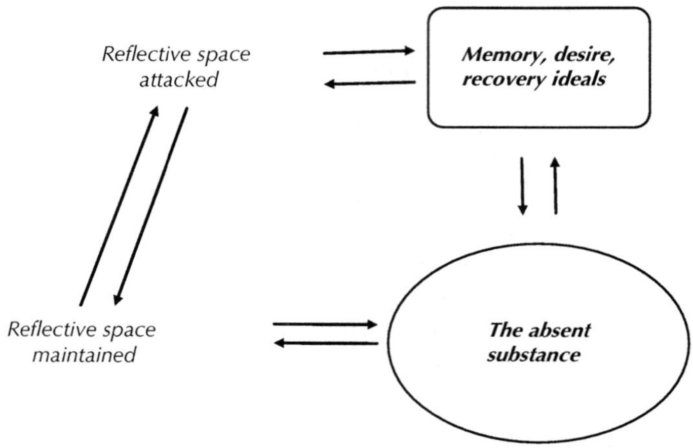

Diagram 2. Theatre of group.

Cohesion and conflict in recovery groups

Addicted individuals present complex needs and distorted motivational systems, in which the drug stages a psychic "takeover" of the personality (indeed brain patterns), with other interests demoted, commitments extinguished and relationships rendered secondary (West, 1996). Consider the impact on how other are treated, dramatically encapsulated in the NA saying, "We don't make relationships, we take hostages." Complex defensive structures, built over the years, serve to reduce dissonance and justify continuation of drug use. In psychodynamic terms, the individual is caught in a web, trapped by their own attempts at self-treatment and omnipotence (English, 2009; Weegmann, 2002). Groups may, in time, provide a much needed alternative (re-)source of affiliation and attachment, the (becoming) "safe-base" in which healthy exploration of life can resume. It is in the harnessing of the potential of groups, with all their destructive and constructive possibilities, that the group's real labour consists. Reflection is feared and avoided, but is at other times is sought and demonstrated, by the conductor but more often than not between peers.

Some approaches, like MDGT (Khantzian, Halliday, & McAuliffe, 1990) are non-confrontational, emphasising the cultivation of cohesion, an ethos of "we are all in it together." But this is not a denial of differences, simply a way of focusing one's attention. Achieving cohesion is the equivalent in group terms to the "positive therapeutic alliance" of individual therapy. The group conductor directs the group's attention to four therapeutic areas: (1) affect tolerance, (2) building of self-esteem, (3) working upon and improving interpersonal relationships and (4) the development of better capacities of self-care and self-comfort. Thus, in the scenarios presented, the group eventually rendered demoralised states manageable and provided perspectives that made black and white, life and death thinking redundant. A degree of calmness and acceptance was restored. In their assessment, Khantzian, Halliday, and McAuliffe (1990, p. 157) suggest that, "it is reasonable to assume that there are at least as many forces at work in a group to assure cohesion and growth as there are forces that threaten fragmentation and regression."

By way of contrast, but not contradiction, AOT (Flores, 2006, p. 22) predicts that dyssynchrony, conflict and its successful resolution are integral to healthy relationships: "Because group therapy is inherently more frustrating than individual therapy, its increased potential for dyssynchrony provides more opportunities for individuals to learn that conflict and resolution can deepen the affective bonds of a relationship". When difficult affective states, adverse interpersonal styles and conflicts are manifest and worked-upon in the group, this becomes an aid to better self-regulation in the future. There are plentiful signs of conflict and struggle in the above examples, but many were faced and rendered less toxic. In conflictual situations, of dissonance rather than resonance, it is important to approach groups with due confidence, acceptance and support, aided by a good working knowledge of the nature of addiction and group process. Group therapists in this field, as in any other, need to feel sufficient affinity with the client group and an appreciation of the nature of their suffering. Clients often need many resources to support recovery, simultaneously or at different stages, and this includes encouragement that clients commit to a programme of personal recovery that AA, for example, enable.

AA: group therapy without the group therapist

All groups, from the psycho-educational to the analytic, from the structured and time-limited to the unstructured and "slow-open", have their own norms of interaction, leadership- or its absence- and what can be called "speech-acts", i.e. discursive norms (forms of speech, if one wills) as to what constitutes a contribution and act of sharing. AA meetings are no exception to this. In fact there are particular discursive norms and structures in a standard AA meeting (clearly analysed by O'Halloran, 2008), beginning with a reading of the AA preamble (which begins, "AA is a fellowship of men and women who share their experience, strength and hope with each other ....", and ends, "Our primary purpose is to stay sober and help other alcoholics to achieve sobriety"). Following a "main share" by a nominated speaker (agreed in advance), for up to 15 minutes, the meeting is opened up by the chair (all posts rotate in AA) for others to share "experience, strength and hope", as indicated by hand-raising. Sharing in AA means identification with the main share and revelation about one's struggles, achievements, week's progress, life events and so on. There is no debate or "cross-talk", with each person addressing their situation only. There may be other conventions, such as an invitation to "shy sharers" to talk if they wish, with the 12 Steps and 12 Traditions, and sometimes other AA sayings, displayed on wall posters. The "serenity saying" ends the meeting.

At first sight, this is all very different from the professional group. But of course there are powerful group therapeutic factors in *all* groups (as an aside, 19th century Temperance and fraternal societies were a stunning and popular example of this), such as identification, modelling ("social learning"), inspiration, instillation of hope and others. Indeed, sometimes the content of groups is secondary to the process. In the group analytic language, there is a process of resonance, exchange and reciprocity, richly expressed in AA's emphasis on "look for similarities not differences" and in the process of identification; the particular speech act, "Hello, my name is ... and I'm alcoholic" is a ritualised expression of this. One could think about such identifications in terms of a process of "twin-ship", hence relating to what one has in common with one's "fellows" (Flores, 1988). In attending many "open" AA meetings (anyone can attend, including non-alcoholics), I saw an ordered rhythm which, in following a set practice allows the individual to find a unique voice, which is an interesting example of a predictable- (i.e. structure) unpredictable (i.e. the shares) dynamic (Weegmann, 2004b). There is "self-soothing" in this innovative familiarity, tapping into, as it does, human needs for affiliation and acceptance (Robinson, 1996). There are many other aspects to group process in AA meetings and it is important to acknowledge the wider milieu in which meetings take place, including their regularity, association with other meetings, the "pre-meeting" welcome and in-gathering and "post-meeting" socialisation, coffees and so on. The discursive exchanges between members, in formal and non-formal time, help create a sense of solidarity which, when internalised, can sustain individuals through the many challenges which they face. Learning toleration of self (inner toleration, toleration of affect, etc.) and others (listening, connecting with, learning) is a vital constituent of developing the art of "sober dialogue". Group analysts can learn a great deal from the appeal and functioning of such mutual-help group traditions.

Anti-dialogue and sober dialogue

In the following scenarios, from a slow-open, mixed group-analytic group conducted by author MW, a recovering drug user (Natalie) and recovering alcoholic (Barbara) talk about their experiences of growing up with addiction in the family, in their parent(s). Both were in the group for at least one year before the following scenarios and had, predominantly, family-like transferences to group:- e.g. seeking safety as a key concern, regarding me as guardian of order and permission (e.g. was I a safe parent who could allow closer feelings to arise and be validated or an unprincipled figure who might violate vulnerability if they opened up?), seeing group members as siblings to be protected and so on.

Reflective space under pressure: clinical scenario

Natalie originally joined group therapy, concerned about a tendency to "fly into rages".

> "I've a thousand thoughts and no fucking thread," exclaimed Natalie, half-way into the group, others stunned by her aggressive tone. She continued, "It's like everyone can say what they want, in some kind of order, and get help-well I don't work that way, I'm a mess up, a total mess up!" she insisted, red-faced. As others tried to reach her, she spurned their efforts, dismissing their problems as minor compared to hers, whilst apologising for "rudeness" in the same breath. She vaguely linked her state to recent contact with her father, who was in his "usual, half-pissed state". "He always makes me feel this way-imagine what it was like when I was a kid!"

> Barbara said she had a 'pretty good idea' of what it is and was like, to which Natalie responded, "You've no fucking idea what it's like for me … and neither has that guy (glancing at me)". She left the group early, tearful, muttering an embarrassed apology en route.

Discussion

Natalie's rage demonstrated her core problem and poor self-regulation; emotions soon reached danger point. Was she, however, in disturbing the peace of the group, attacking reflective space? Was she, showing a version of her father's self-opinionated, bombastic ways, when drunk, giving the group a taste of what he is like to be with? Group members were meant to feel lesser or insignificant, their capacities to imagine her state dismissed and derided. Was this how she felt with an intoxicated father? On the other hand, there was a distressed, suffering Natalie, confused, with little sense of a coherence, illustrating spiralling of "affect dysregulation" *in vivo*. Perhaps there was hope in her distress, hope that the group would not be bowled over by her outbursts and that I/we could hold a stable "family" together, maintain sober dialogue, where no one's needs and requirements would be overlooked. Can an anti-dialogue of attack and accusation be mitigated by the quiet strength of those reflective, still interested and consistent responses from others who have not been demolished in practice?

Addiction in the family, internal and real: clinical scenario

Barbara joined the group with an explicit wish to work on "family issues". Like Natalie, she experienced an acute sense of violation at times, but unlike her, tended to turn aggression inwards rather than outwards.

> At the start of the group, Barbara quietly voiced uncertainty about me, "I'm not sure I can trust you … don't know why … it's like irrational, but feel something bad may happen". Others encouraged Barbara to take courage, except Natalie who looked frozen. Barbara spoke about her 4 years abstinence from alcohol and how little interest her parents showed in the achievement. She recalled "Jekyll and Hyde" behaviour from both parents in the past, "one minute verbal abuse, next affection. You never knew what they wanted-except not to have their drinking interrupted, not to get in their way". Natalie relaxed, congratulating Barbara for her clarity.

When I reminded them of the forthcoming break, Barbara was disappointed, "Just when I get going ....". A group member reminded us that many of Barbara's memories of holidays were coloured by images of her parents in pubs and her having to entertain herself.

Discussion

The group seemed actively engaged in solid, reflective dialogue, Barbara bravely voicing mistrust of me and Natalie, psychosomatically affected, able to identity with and support Barbara in a difficult process. Barbara's recent encounter with her parents, their non-response to her achievement, transports her to earlier times, growing up in a drink-dominated household. It is hard to imagine the confusion that must arise when one's parents are habitually "out of it" or "coming down", but Barbara managed to articulate something of the experience. She was beginning to be better able to thematise confusing experiences and others helped her to make links, such as the reference to booze-filled holidays and the group break; the group were promoting sober dialogue. In this regard, Barbara's new found ability to vocalise fears about me (will I do something unpredictable or keep the situation safe?) was an immensely important breakthrough.

We are all born of desire (and even if we are not wanted, there is the negative parental desire, "I didn't want a kid") and live life within interpersonal networks of interest, desire and attachment. Laplanche (1993) refers to "enigmatic signifiers" to capture something of this entanglement and inherent dependence on "unconsciousness" around us; his emphasis however, like that of Nitsun (2006) in a group context, is on sexual seductiveness or desire. Here, we are interested in non-sexual desire, such as the desire in an alcoholic parent(s), say, to drink uninterrupted as well as the wish to give good things to a child even when in the midst of a hangover. "Seductions"—in the form of inducements, rationalisations, excuse-making, blame and initiation to alcohol use, may all figure in a substance misusing household. However, substance misusing parents are not universally "bad" in all contexts, far from it and their children often grapple with the difficult states and contradictory desires of their parents, whilst simultaneously seeking to express their own needs and wishes. It is important to underline that the family experience of those growing up with addiction differs widely and cannot be reduced to a single category or effect, but worse of all are situations in which children are exposed to serious discord and are treated as mere accomplices to the drinking/using parent (Vellerman & Orford, 1999). Perhaps best of all are situations in which a child has at least a non-using parent and/or an alternative network upon whom to depend and turn. The enigmatic question, "what does the parent want" translates into the treatment setting as, "what does the therapist want" and "what does the group desire?"

In the example at hand, will the group notice Barbara's achievement of abstinence and its foundational significance for recovery? Substance misusers in recovery can easily feel, with some justification, that those without substance misuse histories will not understand the importance to them of total abstinence. Barbara is only able to think about acutely upsetting family experiences, because she is now able to regulate her states without herself requiring alcohol. Natalie, struggling with comparable childhood and contemporary experience, and better connected in this particular group, recognised this and provided Barbara with therapeutic mirroring. In the transference, Barbara may have required me, in particular, to recognise and share pride in her achievement, but was afraid that I would not, and would instead miss an opportunity to help repair disastrously rejecting and confusing messages from her parents throughout life.

"Hopeless hope": group as counter-depressant

With so much self-debasement and depravity associated with addiction, it is easy to be pessimistic about the prospects for change. How is life beyond the "fix" ever possible? The internal pessimism, indeed cynicism, of addicts can be formidable, but there can also be a pernicious professional-based, "treatment pessimism" (not to mention society stigma), an attitude not justified by the evidence that many substance misusers do achieve significant change, although this usually requires considerable time (Miller, 1992). One useful principle is to cultivate a non-naïve openness to "today" and "tomorrow" (including to each episode of care or each group occasion) and a willingness to see, indeed enjoy, surprise, including that of "small steps" taken towards recovery; it is impossible to predict who will escape the circle of addiction and who might remain permanently trapped. The playwright Eugene O'Neil, who knew alcoholism from the inside, used expression, "hopeless hope", implying that something good can come from things that are discouraging or damaged (cited in Gelb & Gelb, 1960). On a not dissimilar note, an AA saying about "the gift of desperation" recognises that major change can be prompted by, or conditional upon, major, accumulated crises. Progress does happen and as individuals establish more secure recovery in group, communication shows greater laterality, psychic reality being less in grip of the substance or its immediate aftermath. This ushers in the possibility of self-forgiveness, compassion as well as a re-building of the resources of self.

Identity voids: clinical example

> A female co-therapist had recently joined the group, whose presence stimulated new explorations. One was how group members—all male at the time—related to women and femininity. One said that he tries to "manipulate" females, including female key-workers; "I can usually get round them" he boasted. Others spoke about the prospect of "ideal relationships"—could they happen or were they just chasing dreams? Ahmed contributed, with some prompting, "I've never thought about relationships with women before, I've kinda always assumed that they are either sexual or else don't really matter". He and others began to think more deeply about their respective styles of masculinity and how they responded to relationships, both sexual and non-sexual. Although there were jokes (transference jokes?) about the pretensions and myths of "new men", there were interesting explorations of how they could develop different ways of being with others as well as being more receptive to female influence or authority. Some weeks later, Ahmed made links to wider issues of identity, growing up as the elder male sibling in an Asian family. "I'm not sure what my role is anymore and my parents cling onto their old ways. Gear (i.e. heroin) made me lose everything, especially status, so it's a question of where do I go from here and win back respect from my family? What do I do with my life, when I'm not the junkie?" At the end, he declared, "It's been good today, it makes me think things I'd never even have realised were going on".

Discussion

Chronic addiction leaves a trail of depletion, including loss of meaning and purpose, as more and more life energy is centred upon an inanimate substance. People and things that might matter increasingly become people and things that do not; roles are lost and a sense of purpose eroded. Sociologist's refer to the formation of a "spoilt identity" (Goffman, 1963). The "addict" does not have to be concerned with his identity in the eyes of a substance, which is inanimate, nor with is use using peers, as he would with another, non-using person. A void forms with the squeezing out of alternative, healthier values and experience.

As clients get used to the freedom of non-using, they face the tasks of how to re-build the self and carve new trajectories of living. Clients grapple with an identity void, and emotional desert, concerning not only how to make use of vast expanses of "clean time", but also, as in the example, how they move from active drug using identities (e.g. "addict" or "junkie") to being someone else. Recovery is a continuum, initially an "empty space" filled by different solutions, some problematic, others advantageous and many of a mixed nature. If a person has had previous periods of recovery, followed by serious relapses, they have to begin all over again, or so it seems.

Ahmed, caught and invited by the spontaneity of group dialogue, was helped to look at issues he had not thought about before, including implicit models of masculinity and ethnic identity.

Growth with and humour: clinical scenario

> Barbara; "I heard this joke in AA last week about a man complaining that he was still having drinking dreams. His sponsor advised, 'Well drink as much as you can before you wake up!'." The group fell apart in laughter, as did Barbara, who observed that it felt "healing" to have "good distance" from her drinking years. "Life is there to be lived," she added, happy that she could better trust experiences of enjoyment. Later in the group, someone wondered whether I was tired and if the couch in the corner of the room was there for me to have rests. People were amused. I commented—"So, we have an exhausted therapist and an exhausting group!"

Discussion

Groups invariably enjoy at least some moments of lightness and humour, particularly as members become acquainted and attached. As group-life is inter-subjectively produced, this is also likely to reflect the qualities and styles of the conductor. Groups with substance misusers are no exception, as the vignette illustrates, although, as with any patient or group, the quality and function of humour still has to be understood. As therapists, it is essential to foster playful capacities and not to pre-judge humour as inherently "avoidant" or "manic". As Khantzian (2004, p. 23) notes, the role of "friendly and supportive" elements in groups should not be underestimated, including "the ability to laugh, as much as to cry, about ourselves". Learning, be it in life, or in therapy, proceeds best when associated with enjoyment, rather than frustration and that therapists can play with the transference as well as "interpreting" it is, we think, an important, humanising and contextualising capacity. Humour improves cohesion. In the group it seemed important to acknowledge that the members could imagine a tired, all-too-human therapist (whether or not this was "true" at that specific moment) and that this can be linked to the realistic burdens and privileges that accompany a group conductor's role:- thinking, mulling-over, waiting, inviting, noticing, remembering, responding, affirming and other things besides. Patients work hard, in different ways and for different reasons, and are also exhausted by the task. In the example, my closing response acknowledged that *both* can be true- an exhausted therapist and an exhausting group. On the other hand, tiredness is another enigmatic signifier, whose significance, once named, can be subject to further inquiry.

Conclusion

> "The reasons that … substance misusers need groups, are often the same reasons that keep them out of groups. Substance misusers are avoidant, counter-dependent and self-absorbed. Groups are powerful antidotes to these characteristics …"
>
> (Khantzian, Halliday, & McAuliffe, 1990, pp. 152–153).

This chapter explores some of the precise challenges of group work, ably encapsulated by Khantzian and colleagues. The journey through freedom from drugs, to freedom to life and its possibilities, is fraught with difficulty, and the notion of "war of position" suggests that its course is seldom linear. Recovery has to be "fought for" and viable, new narratives created, especially because the enslaving cycle of relief and suffering that characterises addiction seems hermetic in nature. Group therapy is one possible means of building and strengthening resources, psychic muscle and nurture, that may finally break the addictive cycle. The overall context of a person's life and relationship to substances is of ultimate importance and substance misuse treatment ignores this at its peril (Elliot, 2003; Moos, Finney, & Cronkite, 1991). We are indeed, "nodal points", to use more Foulksean metaphors. As the examples above show, groups also provide a context in which the long shadow that is cast by drugs can be surpassed. Thus, the vacuum in which hope and possibility are extinguished in the lives of our clients may be broken and recovery started.

Notes

1. I use the generic term "drug" for any potential substance of misuse, including alcohol. Addictions without substances, such as gambling or sex addiction are "process" or "behavioural" addictions. Orford (2001) argues that these problem behaviours have more characteristics in common with substance use disorders than those that separate them. Keane (2004, p. 189), on the other hand, explores some theoretical tensions produced when "different forms of excessive desire" are placed within a singular model substance-based addiction.
2. *La Stanza del Figlio* (2001) is an award-winning film by director Nanni Moretti. It is the story of a psychoanalyst and his family who are faced with the death of his adolescent son, in a scuba-diving accident. Their world is shattered, the film's harrowing, open question, How do we go on ...?

References

Bollas, C. (2009). *The Evocative Object World*. London: Routledge.

Burroughs, W. (1977). *Junky*. London: Penguin Modern Classics.

Canham, H. (2002). Group and gang states of mind. *Journal of Child Psychotherapy, 28*(2): 113–127.

de Quincey, T. (1985 [1856]). *Confession of an English Opium Eater.* Oxford: Oxford University Press.

Elliot, B. (2003) *Containing the Uncontainable.* Chichester: Wiley.

English, C. (2006). Internal landscapes of addiction. Unpublished talk. *Psychotherapy of Addiction Conference* (2nd edn). London.

English, C. (2009). The regulatory function of addiction: Maintaining internal cohesion by the drugging of parts of the personality. *Psychodynamic Practice, 15*: 4, 341–349.

Flores, P. (1988) Group Psychotherapy with Addicted Populations. Binghamton, NY: The Haworth Press.

Flores, P. (2003). *Addiction as an Attachment Disorder.* Northvale, NJ: Jason Aronson.

Flores, P. (2006). Conflict and repair in addiction treatment: An attachment disorder perspective. *Journal of Groups in Addiction and Recovery, 1*(1): 5–26.

Freud, S. (1917). Mourning and melancholia. *Standard Edition of the Complete Psychological Works of Sigmund Freud, 14*: 243–258.

Gelb, A., & Gelb, B. (1960). *O'Neill.* New York: Harper and Brothers.

Goffman, E. (1963). *Stigma: Notes on the Management of Spoiled Identity.* New York: Simon and Schuster.

Gramsci, A. (1971). *Selections from the Prison Notebooks.* Quintin Hoare & Geoffrey Nowell-Smith (Trans.). London: Lawrence and Wishart.

Heaney, S. (1991). Bedside reading. In: *Seeing Things.* London: Faber & Faber, p. 36.

Hinshlewood, R. (1997). Attacks on reflective space. In: M. Pines & V. Schermer (Eds.), *Ring of Fire, Primitive Affects, Object Relations in Group Psychotherapy* (Chapter 4). London. Routledge.

Hyman, S. (2005). Addiction: A disease of learning and memory. *American Journal of Psychiatry, 162*(8): 1414–1422.

Keane, H. (2004). Disorders of desire: Addiction and problems of intimacy. *Journal of Medical Humanities, 25*(3): 189–204.

Khantzian, E., Halliday, K., & McAuliffe, W. (1990). *Addiction and the Vulnerable Self; Modified Dynamic Group Psychotherapy for Substance Misusers.* New York: The Guilford Press.

Khantzian, E. (1993). Substance misuse, repetition and the nature of addictive suffering. In: A. Wilson & J. Gedo (Eds.), *Hierarchical Concepts in Psychoanalysis: Theory, Research and Clinical Practice.* New York: The Guildford Press, 263–283.

Khanztian, E. (1999). *Treating Addiction as a Human Process.* New York: Jason Aronson.

Khantzian, E. (2004). Group psychotherapy as corrective for addictive vulnerability. In B. Reading & M. Weegmann (Eds.), *Group Psychotherapy and Addiction* (Chapter 2). Chichester: J. Wiley, 19–26.

Khantian, E., & Abanese, M. (2008). *Understanding Addiction as Self-Medication: Finding Hope Behind the Pain.* Plymouth, UK: Rowman & Littlefield.

Kristeva, J. (1989). *Black Sun: Depression and Melancholia.* Leon Roudiez (Trans.). New York: Columbia University Press.

Laplanche, J. (1993). *Seduction, Translation and the Drives: A Dossier.* London: ICA documents.

Leighton, T. (2004). Interpersonal group therapy in intensive treatment. In: B. Reading & M. Weegmann (Eds.), *Group Psychotherapy and Addiction* (Chapter 6). Chichester: J. Wiley, 81–93.

Miller, W. (1992). The effectiveness for treatment of substance misuse: Reasons for optimism. *Journal of Substance Misuse Treatment, 9*(2): 147–172.

Moos, R., Finney, J., & Cronkite, R. (1991). *Alcoholism Treatment: Context, Process and Outcome.* New York: Oxford University Press.

Nitsun, M. (1996). *The Anti-Group: Destructive Forces and their Therapeutic Potential.* London: Routledge.

Nitsun, M. (2006). *The Group as an Object of Desire.* Hove: Routledge.

Orford, J. (2001). *Excessive Appetites: A Psychological View of Addicitons.* Chichester: J. Wiley.

Reading, B. (2002). The application of Bowlby's attachment theory to the psychotherapy of addiction. In M. Weegmann & R. Cohen (Eds.), *Psychodynamics of Addiction* (Chapter 2). Chichester: Wiley.

Robinson, C. (1996). Alcoholics anonymous as seen from the perspective of self-psychology. *Smith College Studies in Social Work, 66*(2): 129–145.

Sandhahl, C., Busch, M., Skarbrandt, E., & Wennberg, P. (2004). Matching group therapy to patient's needs. In B. Reading & M. Weegmann (Eds.), *Group Psychotherapy and Addiction* (Chapter 4). Chichester: J. Wiley.

Vellerman, R., & Orford, J. (1999). *Risk or Resilience: Adults who were Children of Problem Drinkers.* The Netherlands: Harwood Academic.

Weegmann, M. (2002). Motivational interviewing: A psychodynamic appreciation. *Psychodynamic Practice, 8*: 179–195.

Weegmann, M. (2004a). Alcoholics anonymous and fellowship: A group-analytic appreciation. *Group Analysis, 37*(2): 243–258.

Weegmann, M. (2004b). If each could be housed in separate personalities .... Therapy as conversation between different parts of the self. *Psychoanalytic Psychotherapy, 19*(4): 279–293.

Weegmann, M. (2005). Dangerous Cocktails: Growing up with addiction. In M. Bower (Ed.), *Psychoanalytic Perspectives on Social Work.* London: Routledge.

Weegmann, M. (2006). Tenuous to tenacious: Psycho-dynamic group therapy with substance misusers. *Journal of Groups in Addiction and Recovery, 1*(1): 51–67.

Weegmann, M. (2009). Is AA a TC? *Therapeutic Communities, 30*(1).

Weegmann, M. (2011). Psychodynamic groups or psychodynamics in groups? In: R. Hill & J. Harris (Eds.), *Principles and Practice of Group Work in Addictions* (Chapter 19). London: Routledge.

INDEX

For Product Safety Concerns and Information please contact our EU representative GPSR@taylorandfrancis.com Taylor & Francis Verlag GmbH, Kaufingerstraße 24, 80331 München, Germany

Batch number: 10725937

Printed by Printforce, the Netherlands